KU-309-351

FACING THE TECHNOLOGICAL CHALLENGE

ILO STUDIES SERIES

The ILO's work in the field of employment aims to encourage and assist member-states to adopt and implement policies and programmes designed to promote full, productive and freely chosen employment and to reduce poverty.

In response to the pressing challenges of the 1990s, including the rapidly growing interdependence of national economies, increasing reliance on market mechanisms, technological innovation and environmental concerns, the ILO has refocused its work on employment. Specific attention is now devoted to assessing the impact of the above challenges on employment, migratory pressures, unemployment and poverty, examining ways of coping with them and understanding the linkages between macro- and micro-economic policies. Greater emphasis is put on policy-oriented research and technical advisory services. This is to ensure a swift response to requests for assistance, further enhanced through the worldwide network of fourteen ILO multidisciplinary advisory teams.

Through these activities the ILO is helping national authorities and social partners to take advantage of the opportunities created by current global changes, so as to achieve more and better employment. They also provide a basis for continuing dialogue with other international organizations on employment and the social dimensions of growth and development in the world economy.

This publication is an outcome of such work, and is intended to disseminate information that will be of relevance to a variety of countries and to a wide audience.

Facing the Technological Challenge

A. S. Bhalla

THE ECONOMICS LIBRARY
WITHDRAWN
UNIVERSITY OF OXFORD

A study prepared for the International Labour Office

First published in Great Britain 1996 by
MACMILLAN PRESS LTD
Houndmills, Basingstoke, Hampshire RG21 6XS
and London
Companies and representatives
throughout the world

A catalogue record for this book is available
from the British Library.

ISBN 0–333–63652–X

First published in the United States of America 1996 by
ST. MARTIN'S PRESS, INC.,
Scholarly and Reference Division,
175 Fifth Avenue,
New York, N.Y. 10010

ISBN 0–312–12901–7

Library of Congress Cataloging-in-Publication Data card number 95–19328

© International Labour Organization 1996

All rights reserved. No reproduction, copy or transmission of
this publication may be made without written permission.

No paragraph of this publication may be reproduced, copied or
transmitted save with written permission or in accordance with
the provisions of the Copyright, Designs and Patents Act 1988,
or under the terms of any licence permitting limited copying
issued by the Copyright Licensing Agency, 90 Tottenham Court
Road, London W1P 9HE.

Any person who does any unauthorised act in relation to this
publication may be liable to criminal prosecution and civil
claims for damages.

10   9   8   7   6   5   4   3   2   1
05   04   03   02   01   00   99   98   97   96

Printed and bound in Great Britain by
Antony Rowe Ltd, Chippenham, Wiltshire

The designations employed in ILO publications, which are in conformity with
United Nations practice, and the presentation of material therein do not imply the
expression of any opinion whatsoever on the part of the International Labour Office
concerning the legal status of any country, area or territory or of its authorities, or
concerning the delimitation of its frontiers.

The responsibility for opinions expressed in studies and other contributions rests
soley with their authors, and publication does not constitute an endorsement by the
International Labour Office of the opinions expressed in them.

Reference to names of firms and commercial products and processes does not imply
their endorsement by the International Labour Office, and any failure to mention a
particular firm, commercial product or process is not a sign of disapproval.

To my sons, **Ranjan** and **Arman**,
who will have to face the technological challenge
no matter what they choose to do in later life

Also by A.S. Bhalla

BLENDING OF NEW AND TRADITIONAL TECHNOLOGIES (*co-editor*)
ECONOMIC TRANSITION IN HUNAN AND SOUTHERN CHINA
ENVIRONMENT, EMPLOYMENT AND DEVELOPMENT (*editor*)
NEW TECHNOLOGIES AND DEVELOPMENT (*co-editor*)
SMALL AND MEDIUM ENTERPRISES: Technology Policies and Options
TECHNOLOGICAL TRANSFORMATION OF RURAL INDIA *(co-editor)*
TECHNOLOGY AND EMPLOYMENT IN INDUSTRY *(editor)*
TOWARDS GLOBAL ACTION FOR APPROPRIATE TECHNOLOGY
(*editor*)
UNEVEN DEVELOPMENT IN THE THIRD WORLD

Contents

List of Figures

List of Tables

Preface

This collection of essays would not have been written but for a request by the Macmillan Press UK for me to write one, based on my several articles on technology published in different economic and technological journals during the past thirty years. I welcomed the idea since the issue of technological innovation is back on the agenda, with increasing globalization of production and trade and pressures on individual countries and enterprises (multinational or national) to compete in the international market place. Technology is clearly a key to this process of the emerging global economy (although this is generally not appreciated) and the capacity of producers and trading partners to improve cost and quality of their products *vis-à-vis* their competitors.

This book attempts to provide a Third World perspective on this new technological challenge. I have drawn on a number of my articles which were published in the following journals: *Greek Economic Review, Economic and Political Weekly, Journal of Developing Areas, Economic Journal, Oxford Economic Papers, Futures, Revue Tiers-Monde, International Labour Review, Labour and Society, Science, Technology and Development* and *World Development*. A number of these articles were written jointly with friends and former colleagues, notably Jeffrey James of the University of Tilburg, The Netherlands; Dilmus James of the University of Texas at El Paso, USA; and Fred Fluitman of the ILO. Their thoughts are therefore also reflected in Chapters 2, 3, 5 and 9. I owe them a debt of gratitude for allowing me to use the material for this book.

I have also drawn on the material contained in the following two books co-edited by me: *Blending of New and Traditional Technologies* (Dublin, Tycooly, 1984), and *New Technologies and Development* (Boulder, Lynne Rienner Publishers, 1988).

Most of the articles and book chapters included in this volume have been updated, revised or substantially rewritten. In an attempt to produce a coherent volume, some sections of articles had to be rearranged or shifted around between chapters. Chapter 8 on technological dependence, originally published in an ILO/JASPA volume, has been substantially rewritten. Chapter 7 on some aspects of cleaner production and technologies is a condensed version of a paper, presented at the Commonwealth Scientific and Industrial Research Organization (CSIRO/Australia) and UNIDO Conference, on *Economic Growth with Clean Production* (Melbourne, 7 to 9 April 1994). Chapter 1 is an updated version of a contribution to the UNU Volume, *The Uncertain Quest: Science, Technology and Development* (1994). Finally, the Introduction to the book puts the essays in the context of the current debate on globalization and international competition.

I am grateful to a number of friends and colleagues, notably Regina Galhardi, Rizwanul Islam and Armand Pereira of the ILO and Dr Massoud Karshenas of the School of Oriental and African Studies, University of London, for reading earlier draft chapters and for their valuable comments. None of them is however responsible for the views expressed. Lynda Pond and Cheryl Wright did typing and word processing skillfully.

A.S. BHALLA

Acknowledgements

The author and publishers gratefully acknowledge the following for permission to reproduce copyright material:

1. Butterworth Scientific Limited, Westbury House, Bury Street, Guildford, GU2 5BH UK for reprinting part of my article (with Jeffrey James) on 'Flexible specialisation, new technologies and industrialisation' (*Futures*, 1993) as Chapter 5.

2. Western Illinois University, 900 West Adams Street, Macomb, Illinois, 61455, USA, for using parts of my article (with Dilmus D. James), 'Integrating New Technologies with Traditional Economic Activities in Developing Countries: An Evaluative Look at "Technology" Blending' (*Journal of Developing Areas*, July, 1991) as Chapter 7.

3. Pergamon Press, Oxford, for using my article (with G.A. Fluitman) on 'Science and Technology Indicators and Socioeconomic Development' (*World Development*, February 1985) as Chapter 9.

4. Papazisis Press, Athens, and Greek Society for Economic Research, Athens, for using my article (with J. James), 'New Technology Revolution: Myth or Reality for Developing Countries?' (*Greek Economic Review*, December 1984).

5. Frank Cass & Co. Ltd, London, for using my article on 'Clean Technologies with Special Reference to Small Enterprises', (*Science, Technology and Development*, April 1995) as Chapter 7.

6. United Nations University (UNU), Tokyo, for using my chapter on 'Technology Choice and Development' in Jean-Jacques Salomon et al., *The Uncertain Quest – Science, Technology and Development* (Tokyo, United Nations University, 1994).

Introduction

The technology debate in the Third World has assumed new dimensions ever since the emergence of new technologies like microelectronics, biotechnologies and new materials. The process of globalization to which they have contributed (see below) poses a new challenge to policy makers and businessmen in developing countries. They need to achieve an appropriate balance between the importation of the most advanced and up-to-date technologies, and the use of indigenous and small-scale technologies. The problem is to ensure a mix of new, conventional and traditional technologies so that the developing countries do not remain as 'hewers of wood and drawers of water'. This technology debate is reminiscent of the earlier controversy on whether 'appropriate' technologies were not promoted by the North to keep the South perpetually technologically dependent on it.

Developing countries cannot afford to remain indifferent to the new technological developments that are taking place in the industrialized countries. They must examine the implications of these new developments for their socioeconomic structures. Indeed, as latecomers, the developing countries may enjoy an actual comparative advantage in utilizing the new technologies to leap-frog and achieve international competitiveness in terms of price and quality. However, mere reproduction or use of borrowed technology is unlikely to strengthen the technological capabilities which are essential for becoming competitive. The process of leap-frogging and 'catching-up' will often require a capacity to improve and adapt imported technologies and develop new ones.

Some developing countries are believed to enjoy a potential advantage in the development of software even though they may not enjoy any comparative advantage in the development of hardware which requires domestic R&D capabilities. It is argued that software development is a labour-intensive activity, the promotion of which should generate employment and even earn foreign exchange (as indeed is the case for India, the Philippines and many other Asian countries with a good stock of educated and skilled manpower) (UNCTC, 1988). Since software costs are a substantial portion of total production costs the development of software capabilities should in principle enable some developing countries to participate in the microelectronics revolution. However, Gaio (1992), writing on the Brazilian software industry, argues that 'neither LDCs nor NICs have shown evidence of reaping significant benefits from their comparative advantage of cheap skilled labour' (p. 106). It remains

1

unclear whether the software capability can be effectively developed without basic capability in the hardware technology itself. Without local technological capacity, the developing countries are likely to find it difficult to 'unpackage' technology to develop the software locally (Watanabe, 1989).

The world market for software and computing services has been growing rapidly during the eighties, and will continue to do so with a more rapid diffusion of new microelectronics-based technologies. As a result, employment in the software and computer services industry has grown substantially in the industrialized countries. For example, in the United States such employment is estimated to have increased from 0.8 million in 1972 to 1.4 million in 1980 and 2.2 million in 1987 – an annual rate of increase of nearly 8 per cent over the 15-year period (UNCTC, 1988; Watanabe, 1989). In the case of Japan employment in software and information services grew from 75 000 in 1980 to over 350 000 in 1990 (Baba et al., 1990). In the developing world, the countries whose exports of software have been rising (though still rather limited) are the ASEAN countries, India, Brazil and more recently, Mexico and Venezuela. In the case of India, almost all the software exports are in the form of contracts with specific end-users. Tata Consultancy Services and Tata UNISYS (formerly Tata Burroughs) accounted for the bulk of these exports.

Whether the software industry in the developing countries will grow during the nineties as a foreign exchange earner and as an employer depends on the pace of new technology diffusion, which depends in turn on the rates and patterns of economic growth and the process of globalization. It is generally assumed that technology diffusion, economic growth and job creation will accelerate with greater North–South trade, increasing international competition and internationalization of production. These issues are discussed below.

GLOBALIZATION, TECHNOLOGY AND COMPETITION

The concept of globalization

The term globalization to describe the shape of the world economy today is fashionable but its meaning and implications, particularly for developing countries, with respect to technological innovations, employment and global distribution of jobs, etc. remain diverse and controversial.

First, globalization is often described in terms of multilateral trade liberalization. It is true that barriers to trade have been progressively lifted.

Between the late forties and early eighties 'average OECD tariff levels were reduced from 40 per cent to 5 per cent ...' (Oman, 1994, p. 31). But during the eighties the OECD area witnessed an increase in non-tariff barriers in agriculture, steel, electronics, footwear and textiles and clothing. The increasing application by the industrialized countries of anti-dumping and countervailing measures against developing-country exports (known in current jargon as 'social clauses' in trade) is a clear trend in this direction. The threat of invoking a clause on the use of child labour by the garment-exporting firms of Bangladesh has already hit the industry badly (Muqtada and Basu, 1994). Does this mean then that the OECD area is less globalized today than it was a decade or two ago? It seems clear that the explanation for the specific nature of today's globalization has to be sought elsewhere.

Significantly, the volume of world trade in the 1980s increased at a slower rate than in the sixties and seventies. It is noted that 'between 1965–80 and 1980–91 the annual rate of growth in world merchandise exports declined from 6.6 per cent to 4.1 per cent ... '(Khan and Muqtada, 1994, p. 2). But despite this slower growth of world exports, the world economy has been globalized in terms of increased international flows of capital and foreign direct investment and greater integration of national markets resulting in global competition. Most developing countries, which hitherto followed import-substitution industrialization, supported by protection, tariff barriers and quantitative restrictions, have switched to industrialization based on production and export of tradeables. There has also been freer trade within regional blocs, particularly in the European Union and North America.

The renewed interest in and emergence of regional groupings (e.g. the European Union, NAFTA, MERCOSUR) raises the question whether such groupings are 'building blocks or stumbling blocks' towards a unified global market and the development of a multilateral system (see UNCTC, 1992). One view is that these regional schemes are a first step towards a more global economy. By harmonizing the regulatory foreign investment regimes, and policies and practices of multinational enterprises (MNEs), these schemes can act as building blocks towards a global multilateral system. Such harmonization may initially be easier when dealing with a small number of countries. The other view is that regionalization might pose a threat to a global trading system especially if the regional blocks create tariff walls around them. Such protectionism would be inconsistent with the free movement of capital and goods and services which a global and interdependent economy presupposes.

The second meaning of globalization is presented in the form of 'increasing internationalization of the production, distribution and marketing of goods and services' (Harris, 1993). Oman (1994) defines globalization in somewhat similar terms, that is, '... as the growth of economic activity spanning politically defined national and regional boundaries ... increased movement across those boundaries of goods and services, via trade and investment, and often of people via migration'. He further notes that globalization 'is driven by the action of individual economic actors – firms, banks, people – usually in the pursuit of profit, and often spurred by the pressures of competition' (p. 33).

The emergence of this new world economy has been triggered by the globalization of financial and monetary markets, the use of new communications technologies, and the new organizational forms of production by multinational enterprises and their new corporate strategies to reduce the influence of entrenched oligopolies. Large multinational enterprises are a major driving force behind flows of foreign direct investment (FDI) in manufacturing and services.

Thus, at a more microeconomic level globalization is often defined in terms of the corporate activities of multinational enterprises, 'strategic alliances' as well as inter-firm competition, and the evolution of global firms and industries. The second half of the eighties witnessed a number of mergers and acquisitions among MNEs. In the nineties this phenomenon has been extended to strategic alliances and partnerships to create global competitive advantage, reap greater economies of scale in R&D particularly in new technology development, and reduce risks and uncertainty about market shares. This new trend of cooperation among competitors is but one response to emerging global competition. Regional economic integration and closer interdependence between national economies may have further reinforced this trend (see Hamill, 1993).

Globalization: a technology-driven process

Defined in terms of world corporate strategies of the multinational enterprises, globalization is based on the premise of integrated regional markets and an increasingly homogeneous world market. The so-called 'new technology revolution' has partly facilitated the emergence of such markets. And greater interdependence of the North and the South, and of national economies in general, has occurred as a result of breakthroughs in telecommunications systems and networks. The new information technologies and telecommunications systems have reduced the distance between national economies and have made the evolution of global production possible. At the same time, relocation of some economic activity from the developed to developing countries continues to take place, in order to take advantage of lower labour costs, investment incentives, proximity to bulky raw materials and access to local and regional markets.

Relocation of productive activity from the North to the South in the eighties has mainly involved unskilled labour-intensive production. This phenomenon (which is by no means fully empirically tested) has occurred more recently within the South when labour-intensive production has shifted from growing labour-short economies such as the Republic of Korea and Taiwan (China) to other developing countries (Thailand, China, India, Pakistan and the Philippines) offering relatively cheaper labour. The economies of these latter developing countries have gained as a result even though unevenness between regions may have occurred in the distribution of these gains (see ILO, 1994, p. 61).

In the past, several authors (Rada, 1980; Kaplinsky, 1984; Hoffman and Rush, 1988) have suggested that with the spread of new technologies labour-intensive off-shore operations may be relocated back to the North. However, empirical evidence to support this argument remains limited so far. While new technology reduces the demand for unskilled labour, it does not necessarily follow that this should lead to relocation of production. Labour cost is one of many factors, and not always the most important, which induces firms in the North to set up off-shore operations in the South. For example, in metal engineering industries labour costs account for no more than 10 to 20 per cent of total production costs. The ILO industry studies included in Watanabe (1993) do not provide any empirical support for relocation.

It is often not sufficiently appreciated that globalization and international competition are largely technology driven (Ernst and O'Connor, 1989; Harris, 1993). The spread of new technologies which influence economic organization, work, consumption and production has led to a new shift in the techno-economic paradigm (Lipsey, 1992). Oman (1994) cites three ways in which new technologies have contributed to globalization. First, by enabling the transmission of large amounts of data cheaply over long distances, the diffusion of new technologies has facilitated the creation of global financial markets. Secondly, the new information technology contributes to globalization of demand in many sectors by making information available worldwide to buyers and sellers of goods and services. Thirdly, these technologies also promote globalization of competition among suppliers. New technologies enable manufacturers to shorten product life cycles which puts pressures on firms to expand their share of markets worldwide in order to amortize fixed production costs in a shorter period of time. Many firms' response to that pressure has been one of investment in global advertising, global marketing and the establishment of global brand name – which of course reinforces the globalization of demand as well. (Oman, 1994, pp. 84–5)

However, all technical change does not necessarily contribute to globalization. It is mainly the new communications technologies, which reduce distance and transaction costs, that play a role in flexible production and globalization. In fact, technical change in the form of robotisation may actually militate against internationalization of production by reducing the demand for unskilled labour and thus the importance of outsourcing to low-wage countries.

While recognizing the role of the technological factor, Oman (1994) argues that globalization has more to do with new forms of organization which may be independent of information technology. Although this may be true, and in some cases organizational innovations may even precede technological ones, in Chapter 5 we take the position that flexible specialization has been made possible by the new information technologies which facilitate globalization and fragmentation of production. It is difficult to imagine new forms of organizational innovations without the advent of information technologies and their pervasive influence on production and its location (see below).

Implications of globalization

1. Impact on growth and employment

Increasing global interdependence between developed and developing countries in respect of trade, finance, foreign investment and technology, discussed above, is assumed to provide a fillip to economic growth (see World Bank, 1991). The globalization process, particularly through flexible production systems, has led to a phenomenal growth of (labour-intensive) manufactured exports and the economic growth of many developing countries particularly in the East Asian region. The East Asian experience also shows that apart from exports, economic growth has been accelerated by information and communications technology and the quality of human resources (Freeman, 1993; World Bank, 1993).

Although the economic performances of countries in the East Asian region vary, most of them have benefited from high rates of investment including FDI and high productivity growth. The World Bank (1993) attributes this superior productivity performance of the East Asian economies to the 'combination of unusual success at allocating capital to high-yielding investments and at catching up technologically to the industrial economies' (p. 8).

Globalization and international competition are changing the nature of industrialization (UNCTAD, 1993). The earlier strategy of import-substitution-led industrialization was based on policies of protection at the national level. Globalization and corporate strategies of MNEs are now leading to the emergence of *global* industries which sell their products worldwide and integrate their activities across national markets. The nature, characteristics and global strategies of these industries are likely to vary according to the nature and structure of markets facing them. For this reason, *inter alia*, some industries such as automobiles and metal trades are more likely to be globalized than food and leather and footwear, where local tastes and consumer preferences tend to militate against product standardization and cross-border organization (see Campbell, 1993).

While the NICs enjoy good prospects of gaining from the globalization process through growth, expanding markets and integration into the global economy, many developing countries, particularly the least developed ones, may suffer, being unable to fulfil the conditions necessary for participating in this process. Globalization may intensify existing uneven development between countries and regions, particularly between low-wage assemblers in developing countries and high-skill producers in industrialized countries. One cannot exclude the possibility of polarization of production activity attributed to differences across regions in skill availability and market size (ILO, 1993, pp. 298–9). Least developed countries, mostly in Africa, may be particularly adversely affected. Their possibilities of forming regional blocs in response to globalization are slim due to their lack of complementarity and simplicity of production structures as well as the small size of their markets.

As a result of recent economic reforms and liberalization, particularly in the economies of Eastern Europe and more generally in most developing countries, freer trade and economic interdependence are bound to grow. Replacement of protective import-substitution policies by outward-looking policies of export orientation and incentives to foreign investment are likely to lead in future not only to competition but also to greater international technology transfers (see below).

It is true that foreign direct investment (FDI) grew very rapidly in the second half of the eighties. However, its growth has been highly concentrated among the industrialized countries and a limited number of NICs in East Asia and Latin America. Africa's share is quite small and may remain so for years to come in view of the continuing political instability, lack of creditworthiness and well-functioning capital and financial markets, low human resources base and adverse balance of payments position. The group of least developed countries (many of which are in Africa) taken as a whole accounted for only 0.1 per cent of total world investment inflows and 0.7 per cent of inflows to all developing countries in 1989 (see OECD, 1992).

The role of multinational enterprises in generating substantial employment in developing countries through FDI is therefore not entirely certain. Griffin and Khan (1992) conclude that 'foreign direct investment is of little significance in terms of employment or the provision of capital for development' (p. 26). Parisotto (1993) notes that employment by multinationals in developing countries constitutes no more than 2 per cent of their economically active population. However, such employment is noted to have increased in Hong Kong, Singapore and the Republic of Korea, thanks to the successful off-shore operations of MNEs.

To the extent that outsourcing to developing countries is reduced in the future due to the technological factor, employment losses of unskilled workers will occur. However, the protagonists of globalization argue that global firms will create more and better jobs in developing countries on the assumption that these firms will enjoy a comparative advantage in locating less capital-intensive new plants in these countries. Although the theory of comparative advantage à la Heckscher–Ohlin assumes that technology is the same everywhere, in practice production processes are likely to vary in their degree of capital and labour intensity.

ILO (1994) notes that while current semi-conductor waffle manufacturing plants will tend to have roughly the same capital intensity regardless of location, this will not in principle hold true for the assembly of cars or consumer electronics. Developing country gains in employment will therefore depend on whether the production of consumer goods (which are generally more labour intensive) or producer/intermediate goods is relocated. Better jobs may be created 'because new industrial jobs will tend to upgrade general skill levels, wages and conditions of work ...' (see ILO, 1994, p. 60).

2.   Impact on technological innovations

In principle, FDI will continue to be a main channel for international technology transfers and the adoption of new technologies. This is clearly demonstrated by the recent experience of the East Asian economies whose rapid and consistently high growth is explained by FDI and high technology absorption. But many other developing countries, especially in the Latin American and African regions, have suffered from serious indebtedness which limits the scope of new investments into new technologies. Yet such new investments are an important prerequisite for successfully facing the challenge of increasing global competition.

Foreign direct investment and international technology transfer through MNEs are leading to a shift from 'mature' low-tech industries to more 'high-tech' industries. This implies more and more that the old emphasis on *national* technological capabilities may become less important than capabilities at the *firm-level* to compete internationally. Initiatives and incentives to strengthen national technological capabilities will, therefore, have to give far greater importance to technology innovation and diffusion at the firm level than has been done in the past. Mytelka (1994) notes that several factors, among them increasing knowledge-intensity of production which raises production costs and greater uncertainty under intensified global competition, make planning by firms more difficult. Greater flexibility is therefore required to respond to changing market demands (see the following section).

Increasing competition in international markets seems to be inducing firms to pay a much higher premium on quality than on profitability, *price* and *cost* considerations. This is revealed for example by ILO research on microelectronics (results of which are discussed in Chapters 3 to 5) and other industries. Considerations of quality may include product characteristics and variety of models for which innovative research is required at the firm level. Acquisition of technological knowledge varies between firms, depending on their initial capability, marketing strategy, and the degree of intra-firm innovation which offers learning and experience. Innovative firms are more likely to succeed in facing the global competition than non-innovative firms.

How and to what extent competitive market forces spur innovation will, *inter alia*, depend on the nature of the industry and the market structure. As we noted above some industries are more globalized than others and may thus suffer from greater global competition. In this context, James (1993) raises the pertinent question of whether the new forms of global competition will erode the competitive advantage of those firms 'that cater primarily to markets in which demand changes relatively slowly and in which price rather than product differentiation is dominant' (p. 419). Here it is useful to make a distinction between specialized niche markets and the standardized product markets. It is mainly in the former that quality is more important than price (see Perez, 1994). In the high-volume standard products delivery and price are likely to continue to be important factors.

The nature of innovations is also changing. The pattern of technology development is also likely to shape its diffusion. The traditional distinction between innovation, imitation and diffusion is becoming more arbitrary in view of cooperative networks and alliances among firms to reap collective benefits from R&D (see below). Product quality, design, maintenance and organization of production are becoming more important. This enhances the need for producers to establish closer contacts with suppliers, clients and financial institutions. Close proximity and interaction between suppliers and users facilitates the design of new technologies and products.

The systemic nature of new technologies and the scope for synergy between them further reinforces the need for closer linkages between users and suppliers. Combining different sets of new technologies is a costly affair in terms of both R&D and production. Partly for these reasons, some cooperation among competitor firms is taking place through the creation of international computer-based networks. These networks are designed to spread costs of R&D over a larger number of firms in order to ensure a more rapid access to new technologies and markets as well as sources of know-how external to the firm (see OECD, 1992; Ernst, 1994). Developing countries may be able to improve market access and acquire technology more easily if they could obtain access to such networks. These technology-driven networks are claimed to be superior to trade-driven or investment-driven forms of South–South cooperation (Mytelka, 1994). By transferring production and management technology to local firms in developing countries, new forms of international sub-contracting may in future also strengthen those firms' ability to innovate.

However, it is not certain that many developing countries will be able to enjoy access to the above networks which are at present concentrated mainly in the industrialized countries. Only advanced developing countries such as the Republic of Korea, with well-developed communications infrastructure, local technological capabilities and a successful record of past innovations, are likely to enjoy such access. One cannot rule out the possibility that firms may cooperate (within networks) in a collusive manner to protect a key technology – a phenomenon which will tend to hinder rather than facilitate access to such technology.

Are technological innovations more likely to occur under integrated competitive markets resulting from the process of globalization? According to the neo-liberal view a competitive environment in national and international markets should induce innovations. Government interventions lead to inefficiencies which are more serious than those resulting from market imperfections. While this may be true, historical experience of import-substituting industrialization in many developing countries shows that innovations also took place under protective environments. In contrasting the neo-liberal and neo-Schumpeterian approaches to a high-tech policy to industrial development, Schmitz and Cassiolato (1992) note that far less attention has been paid to market failures than to government failures. Recent experience of industrialized countries shows that markets continue to remain ineffective in compensating for technology-induced unemployment.

It is difficult to imagine that developing countries can develop high technology without at least some 'infant industry protection' by the government. The historical experience of Japan, Brazil and the Republic of Korea shows the importance of strategic government intervention and public-funded R&D. In a study of automation in the Brazilian banking industry, Cassiolato (1992) notes that many locally-developed technology systems were internationally competitive thanks to the government's protective policy on informatics.

In Japan, which does not have anything more than an indicative planning framework, the Ministry of International Trade and Industry (MITI) plays an important role in making strategic decisions and in bringing together the economic planning and other involved agencies from each government ministry or department, banks and enterprises. High technology development involves long gestation periods which calls for long-term strategic decisions (regarding, *inter alia*, investment allocation) which are best undertaken by the government.

Within the Third World, Brazil and the Republic of Korea took such long-term decisions to develop high technology. Thanks to a clearcut strategy the Republic of Korea managed to build a strong technological base by developing modern metal engineering industries and by implementing an investment strategy for such new technologies as microelectronics. In the case of Brazil, the rapid growth of the computer industry resulted from the creation of a reserved market (Schmitz and Hewitt, 1992). In the case of India, it is perhaps a lack of a clear policy and investment strategy in the sixties and seventies that inhibited the development of high technology.

We believe that despite globalization some role for strategic government intervention and public policy will continue to be necessary for the adaptation, development and diffusion of new technologies. No doubt the market criterion of commercial profitability will govern the decisions of private firms to adopt new technologies. But public policy is likely to play a crucial role in creating a suitable environment for the effective utilization and diffusion of these technologies. Government support can facilitate technological innovations by preparing a realistic assessment of existing technological capabilities and their strengthening, by providing the infrastructure, by allocating adequate resources for R&D to develop and adapt new technologies, and by coordinating the efforts of different investors involved. To take a specific example, an initial assessment of a country's existing technological capabilities at different levels is essential to determine the scope for leap-frogging. This assessment cannot be done by a large number of private firms. While micro decisions are made by these firms on the basis of some notion of choice and feasibility, it is up to the central system to examine how these micro decisions fit into a macroeconomic framework which would provide a basis for investment and consumption planning (Enos, 1991).

In future technology policies will be increasingly determined by the new external environment and the globalization of R&D by the multinationals, thanks to information technologies which enable worldwide control of R&D and sourcing of scientific and technological knowledge. Decentralization of R&D to subsidiaries and new partnerships with research institutions may have positive spill-over effects and 'new windows of opportunity' for innovation in developing countries. Added to this, Mytelka (1994) notes that multinational enterprises have 'been turning their subsidiaries into independent profit centres' which may further induce them to innovate to reduce cost, improve quality and expand exports. However, it is unclear how global R&D activities for high technology development spill over to local firms in the form of increased technological capabilities. So far internationalization of R&D has taken place mainly between the United States and Europe and not between the industrialized and developing countries. Even in the former there is a lack of adequate and systematic information on the implications of globalization for the location of innovations (OECD, 1992).

FLEXIBLE SPECIALIZATION AND SMALL-SCALE PRODUCTION

Although we argue above that globalization is technology driven, organizational innovations also play a role. Post-war patterns of industrialization through import substitution have, by and large, been abandoned and replaced by market liberalization and export-led industrialization. Market liberalization, and resulting competition in domestic and foreign markets, reinforces the need for improving the productivity of the technologies used in the modern and informal sectors. From this point of view, the emergence of microelectronics and complementary organizational innovations (that form part of the so-called new Industrial Revolution) seems attractive, because they are considered by some to be capable of facilitating a pattern of industrialization based on flexible, small-scale production, rather than on the large-scale, capital-intensive technology of mass production. The 'descaling' properties of the new technologies, 'flexible specialization', and the ability to tap into rapidly changing niche markets should facilitate efficient production at small scales.

The historical experience of today's industrialized countries shows that continuous waves of rapid technical change led to what Schumpeter called a 'process of creative destruction' of traditional crafts and artisan skills. Will a similar process be repeated in the developing countries as a result of the application of new technologies? While this question has been empirically neglected, this book explores some options for minimizing this destruction.

One option is the integration of new technologies with traditional technologies and production systems. This concept of technology blending implies that improvements will take place in traditional technologies and products in terms of unit costs and quantity and quality of output.

The problem of low-productivity traditional technologies still being used in several parts of the Third World can be mitigated if new technologies can be geared especially for the improvement of traditional technologies rather than their displacement. Despite the hundreds of years of scientific and technical progress manifested first in the Agricultural Revolution, then the Industrial Revolution and now the Information Revolution à la Toffler, the bulk of the world's population located mostly in the Third World continues to suffer from hunger and starvation, malnutrition, illiteracy and low incomes.

A proper integration of new technologies into traditional modes of production offers much better prospects of learning-by-doing, of local experiments in adaptation and capacity development, than an indiscriminate use of new technologies in the advanced sectors of economic activity. The latter are linked more directly to the international world economy rather than to their domestic economies. Further, considering the severe resource constraints facing the developing countries, technology blending may offer an avenue for spreading the benefits of new technologies in a more egalitarian and participatory fashion than does the introduction of a necessarily limited number of enclave-like, large-scale capital-intensive facilities.

However, the process of blending is far from easy. It presupposes that the traditional technologies and productive activities have a capacity to use and assimilate new technologies. This may or may not be true given the low purchasing power of the traditional producers in the Third World and the rather high cost of producing and using new technologies. However, practical examples of blending (Chapter 3), though small in number, show that the concept is already being operationalized.

CLEANER OR ENVIRONMENTALLY-SOUND TECHNOLOGIES

The development of new technologies discussed above has to take into account the need to preserve and protect the environment. The goals of sustainable development and environmental protection, enshrined in Agenda 21 and adopted at the Earth Summit in Rio in 1992, give a prominent place to the development, transfer and application of environmentally sound technologies throughout the world.

There is no consensus on what cleaner or environmentally sound technologies are, but they are generally characterized by lower pollution, lower energy and resource intensity, greater use of renewable resources, and recycling of waste products (see Chapter 7 and Bhalla, 1992). Some existing technologies may already pass these tests, and may simply need to be improved and modified. Others may have to be created *de novo*. In the latter case, the design and development of new technologies will need to reduce energy input per unit of output and improve conservation.

It is somewhat ironical that the spectacular technical progress which led to rapid productivity and output growth in the past is also blamed for the costs in terms of resource depletion and environmental degradation. Technological change has been lavish in the use of natural capital and resources partly because for far too long these resources have been treated as a free good. Furthermore, by allowing free disposal of waste and subsidizing the use of energy and raw materials, the policies in developing countries may inhibit the demand for environment-friendly technical change (Panayotou, 1994). But technical progress also has positive environmental attributes in the shape of, for example, technologies that reduce waste and enhance recycling opportunities.

The pace of development and diffusion of cleaner technologies has been slow even in the industrialized countries, not to speak of developing countries. The United States Office of Technology Assessment (OTA) states that '50 per cent of all environmentally harmful industrial waste could be eliminated with the technology that was available in 1986 and another 25 per cent with additional R&D' (cited in UNIDO, 1992a). To quote OECD (1992a), 'in most countries only a small share of total expenditures goes directly to the development of environmental technologies, particularly those relating to industrial pollution control and clean-up'.

A number of factors account for this situation: prolonged economic recession which may have discouraged new investments; insufficient economic incentives; inadequate R&D resources; and lack of enforcement of environmental regulations and standards. Notwithstanding these limitations, many industries and firms in the industrialized countries have been induced to promote cleaner processes through mounting public pressure, increased competition, rising costs of waste processing and disposal, and government regulatory measures.

It is necessary to examine the status of cleaner technologies in industrialized countries which are at present the main source of these technologies. The dilemma facing many developing countries is that they have only small industrial sectors; this limits the demand for such technologies. As they are net importers of these technologies, cost considerations may weigh heavily particularly in the case of small and medium firms. Such firms tend to be more polluting but they are also more constrained by the lack of resources than the larger firms (see Chapter 7).

Two questions are particularly important, namely (i) are cleaner technologies more costly than the ones they replace? and (ii) do countries which do not produce these technologies have access to them on reasonable terms and conditions?

Information on comparative costs of cleaner and existing technologies is rarely available but there is some indication that the capital costs of the newer and cleaner technologies are generally higher, particularly for small enterprises in developing countries (Chapter 7). To the extent that the new technologies are protected by patents, their price includes monopoly rents which makes them very costly. There would be a disincentive to use cleaner technologies if the existing (generally polluting) technologies were cheaper.

Relatively lower environmental standards in developing countries, and a lack of their enforcement, continues to limit demand for cleaner or environmentally-sound technologies. It remains to be seen to what extent the recent call by the Clinton Administration to link environmental (and labour) standards with trade will be acceptable to US trade partners in the developing world. A move in this direction may in the long run lead to pressure on the developing countries to introduce environmental regulations which could induce greater and more efficient use of environment-friendly technologies.

The second issue of access to cleaner technology is part of a more general problem of access to any technology that is not produced by the developing countries. Even when environmentally-sound technologies exist, access to them may be restricted by their proprietary nature, by the fact that they are no longer used in the industrialized countries, by the reluctance of multinational enterprises to make them available, especially if they expect to make low profits on their sales owing to the small size of the market, or by the lack of physical infrastructure.

The developing countries may also face the problem of a limited capacity to absorb cleaner technologies. To some extent, constant technological challenge and obsolescence should raise environmental assimilation capacity. It should also induce at least the more industrialized of the developing countries, such as the NICs, to develop cleaner technologies. Whether developing countries in general can do so will depend on the current stock of their technological capabilities, R&D resources and scientific manpower and infrastructure, etc. This is the subject to which we now turn.

TECHNOLOGICAL CAPABILITIES VERSUS TECHNOLOGY IMPORTS

We noted above that a minimum level of technological capabilities is an essential prerequisite for leap-frogging and successfully meeting the new technological challenge. Although some work on building technological capabilities has already been accomplished, our understanding of the nature and magnitude of the task is still far from adequate. Enos (1991) states 'the economists' efforts to promote appropriate technology took for granted the environment in the developing countries and imagined techniques to be variable: the current efforts to stimulate technological capability take technology for granted and imagine the environment to be variable'. A change in this environment would be necessary to develop better the latent human potential to raise the level of capabilities in the developing countries. Also, to what extent is the technological capability of a country an intermediate input to the achievement of objectives, and to what extent is it an output? Do liberal technology imports facilitate or hinder a country's efforts to develop indigenous technological capabilities? These questions remain unanswered despite some empirical research in recent years. A more critical analysis of developing-country experiences is needed. It may be useful to compare and contrast open and closed economies to examine their experience in building indigenous technological capabilities over time.

As the development of technological capabilities is a slow and long-term process, the developing countries in particular have to resort to the import of technology. The experience of the Republic of Korea shows that all technology imports need not necessarily increase dependence and hinder capacity building. A clever adaptation, innovation and improvement of imported technology (which would, of course, depend on the achievement of a minimum level of technological capability) can in the long run facilitate technological self-reliance (Watanabe, 1985). The experiences of Japan and the Republic of Korea suggest that a judicious use of imported technology helped industrial firms build up their technological capability and improve their international competitiveness. It remains uncertain whether their experiences are replicable in other developing countries, or whether other combinations of factors can lead to comparable experiences. In Africa some analyses suggest that the import of foreign technology did not lead to domestic learning, which seems to have been given lower priority than the achievement of output targets (see Chapter 8 and Wangwe, 1992).

While different experiences can be expected, increasing international competition is continuing to induce firms in developing countries to import modern technologies which may have positive learning effects. Whether such imports hinder domestic innovation will depend very much on the initial level of capabilities and the adequacy and relevance of R&D resources. One thing is however clear. The process of internationalization of production and global competition discussed above will in future make the firm-level capability and mastery of technology far more important.

The concept of capacity building is steadily being reoriented towards the attainment of the goals of sustainable development and environmental protection. It is being viewed as a much more holistic and intersectoral concept which, in a dynamic perspective, involves an ability to anticipate technological, market and related changes that are likely to occur in the future. The environment for indigenous capacity building is also changing with the increasing pace of internationalization of production and freer flows of capital and investment at the international level and economic liberalization at the national level. From the point of view of developing countries, this issue increasingly boils down to access to markets for goods and services, and to technology. The present global environment is such that the developing countries face 'restrictions on access to technology and to major OECD markets' (OECD, 1992; Ernst and O'Connor, 1989).

In discussing the relationship between technological capability and imports of technology, Stewart (1979) classifies capability into a three-stage process: the first stage refers to capacity for independent search and selection; the second, to local generation of minor technical changes; and the third, to the generation of new technology. The nature and impact of foreign technology inflows would vary according to the stage at which a developing country is, the industry in question, and the level of local capacity. Thus, depending on these factors the relationship between technology imports and local technology capacity can encompass 'both conflicts and complementarities' (Stewart, 1979).

SCOPE AND OBJECTIVES OF THE VOLUME

Having outlined the main themes covered in this volume, it is now time to introduce the individual chapters. The volume contains nine chapters which can be divided into two broad categories: Chapters 2 to 6 deal mainly with the new technological challenge and the ways and means by which this challenge can be effectively faced by the Third World; Chapters 1 and 7 to 9 are concerned with broader issues involving both new and conventional technologies. They relate respectively to the technology debate during the past thirty years or so which is placed in the context of changing perceptions of development (Chapter 1); the growing concern with cleaner technologies and products needed for environmental conservation and sustainable development (Chapter 7); technological dependence (Chapter 8); and national technological capability (Chapter 9), which is a precondition for overcoming dependence and for the successful absorption and assimilation of new and conventional technologies.

One of the major concerns of this volume is to assess mechanisms through which the advent of new technol⁄ gies may be capable of bringing about an alternative and more egalitarian pattern of development in the Third World. Can the developing countries exploit the potential of rapid technical change? Can new technologies become a reality for developing countries? Our objective, therefore, is to explore not *whether* but *how* these countries can exploit the new technological revolution to their advantage, to remove poverty, to generate incomes and to acquire competitiveness in world markets.

We argue that no developing country can escape the challenge posed by the new technologies. Yet countries at different stages of development enjoy different levels of capacity to take full advantage of these technologies. For most developing countries technology blending would initially be more feasible and egalitarian.

To fulfil our objective, we have adopted a pragmatic and an empirical approach rather than a purely theoretical one. We attempt to describe in various chapters the potential for using microelectronics-based information technologies and biotechnologies in specific economic activities in the agricultural and industrial sectors. Nevertheless, we are also interested in a conceptual framework for analysis and application of new technologies to traditional small-scale activities designed to improve their productivity. Attempts at such conceptualization are made in Chapters 3 to 5.

Our conceptual analysis shows that technological innovations need to go hand in hand with institutional innovations. For example, we argue that for technology blending to come of age, it is essential to explore what we call institutional blending – an appropriate mix of inputs by different actors, be they private sector, governments and NGOs.

We now describe the scope and content of individual chapters.

Chapter 1 is essentially a historical account of the debate on technology, investment and employment generation in the context of the changing development paradigms. It underlines the importance of macro policy issues as well as of the technological capability essential to meeting the challenge presented by new technologies. It also speculates on the prospective role of technology and its development and utilization in the nineties and beyond, during periods of structural reforms and curbs on public expenditures.

Chapters 2 to 5 discuss different aspects of the challenge posed by new technologies. Can the developing countries leap-frog and catch up through a selective and judicious use of new technologies? What are the potentials and limitations of leap-frogging? What is the present extent of diffusion of new technologies in the Third World? Within the Third World, great heterogeneity prevails; will technological gaps widen among developing countries?

Chapter 3, which should be read in conjunction with Chapter 2, introduces the concept of technology blending. It is focused on the technological improvements of low-productivity economic activities through the use of high technology. The concept of technology blending is distinguished from that of appropriate technology, which dominated much of development thinking during the seventies and early eighties. Examples are provided of practical experiments of technology blending in Asia and Latin America. A special section is devoted to the experience of the Green Revolution as a case of blending in agriculture.

What are the prerequisites for the developing countries to adopt a policy of blending? Under labour-surplus conditions, would it be economically feasible and socially desirable to apply new technologies in place of traditional or conventional technologies? These issues are discussed in Chapters 3 to 5.

Chapter 4 on microelectronics for small-scale production examines the extent to which the technology is attractive for small-scale manufacture and the relevance and importance of scale economies. Experiences of high-tech use by small and medium enterprises, in both developing and industrialized countries, are examined.

The concept of flexibility or flexible specialization is seen as an institutional alternative to the choice of technology framework. These two, together with decentralization, are examined in Chapter 5 in the context of emerging industrialization strategies in developing countries. So far adoption of the new technologies and organizational innovations have been confined largely to the more advanced of the developing countries and to certain types of firms within those countries, most notably firms that possess well-developed technological capabilities and a strong orientation to international competition. Diffusion of the complex of new technologies to the majority of firms in the industrial sector of most developing countries is likely to be a long-term phenomenon; after all, most previous waves of innovation have taken numerous decades to spread widely,' even in the countries for which the changes were originally designed.

The structural adjustment measures introduced in the eighties are continuing into the nineties. As a result of these measures, in many developing countries large numbers of people are being pushed into small and micro-enterprises to make a living. Can new technologies, through greater flexibility in production (so-called 'flexible specialization'), enable a more successful small-scale industrialization than has been possible in the Third World in the past? Are flexible specialization and small-batch production universally applicable, or are they likely to be confined, at least in the nineties, to only the industrialized countries? These questions require further investigations and are discussed in Chapter 5.

The socioeconomic impacts – on cost effectiveness, on employment and on income distribution – of new technologies such as microelectronics and biotechnologies are examined in Chapter 6. The issues examined include: trade-offs between the direct and indirect employment effects of new technologies; under what circumstances can new technologies and blending raise overall employment; do new technologies have a capacity to enhance skills and resources.

The remaining three chapters in the book, viz. Chapters 7 to 9, discuss respectively: the emerging preoccupation with the development and use of cleaner technologies (with particular reference to small and medium enterprises); technological dependence; and how to reduce such dependence through building up of national capacities within the framework of overall development objectives. Chapter 7 on cleaner technologies examines whether enterprises in developing countries, particularly small and medium enterprises, enjoy access to these technologies, whether these technologies are more or less costly than conventional technologies, and their impact on employment, skill requirements and worker safety. Chapter 8 on technological dependence examines the nature and characteristics of the concept and explores suitable indicators of its measurement, for example, skilled manpower, patent grants and applications, capital goods imports, foreign investment, ownership and control and R&D expenditures. The final chapter on technological capabilities sets out a framework for capability building which considers objectives, elements and determinants at different levels of aggregation side by side. An illustration of such a framework is also provided.

1 Technology and Development: An Overview*

The debate on the role of technology continues unabated, and its new dimensions are emerging constantly. In the fifties the debate concentrated largely on technological determinism, that is, there were few technological alternatives for producing a given well-defined product. Product differentiation was simply regarded as a new product. The paradigm of determinism was followed by that of technological pluralism, thanks to the growing empirical evidence (that emerged in the late seventies) to support the existence of a fairly wide technology choice – particularly in manufacturing – not only in peripheral and material handling but also in manufacturing proper. The concept of technology blending discussed in Chapter 3 is but one new aspect of the issue of technology choice. Studies done at the ILO World Employment Programme, at the Yale Economic Growth Center and at the David Livingstone Institute of Overseas Development Studies at the University of Strathclyde – among others – all pointed towards considerable technical choice in consumer goods industries and, to a lesser extent, in intermediate goods. It is true that empirical evidence in support of the existence of technology choice in capital goods industries requiring greater precision is less clear-cut. Yet even in these industries, examples of technological adaptations have been reported, although definite alternative choices may not exist (Teitel, 1978; Katz, 1987).

A new dimension to the technology choice issue has been added by the advent of new technologies like microelectronics-based innovations, new materials, telecommunications and new biotechnologies, etc. In many ways, these technologies provide a superior alternative to existing conventional and automated technologies. In other cases, they provide a complement to the conventional, and perhaps to a lesser extent, traditional technologies. When the new technologies are superior to the existing ones, they will dominate and supersede the latter – a case of Schumpeter's 'creative destruction' in the capitalist growth process. But Strassmann

*An earlier version of this chapter was originally published in Francisco Sagasti, Jean Jacques Solomon, Céline Sachs-Jeantet (eds) *The Uncertain Quest-Science, Technology and Development*, Tokyo, United Nations University Press, 1994. I am grateful to Frances Stewart for useful comments.

21

(1959) has shown that historical experience during 1850 to 1914 is one of a coexistence of old and new technologies, without necessarily involving a replacement of the old by the new for several decades. In fact, it is this coexistence, and to some extent, combination – e.g. retrofitting – which has partly inspired the emergence of the concept of technology blending, which is discussed in Chapters 3 and 4.

Thus, the recent technology debate has brought out into the open a dilemma facing the developing countries. What mix of new, conventional and traditional technologies should they use? Another aspect of the challenge is to strike an appropriate balance between the import of new technologies (which most developing countries do not yet have the capacity to produce) and the use of conventional and indigenous technologies.

The developing countries will no doubt continue to be influenced by the technological advances being made in the industrialized countries. There is a controversy as to whether developing countries (particularly those with labour surplus) should use 'high' technology, with its negative social and economic consequences like labour displacement and possible worsening of income inequalities. Some argue that their utilization will involve further technological dependence of the developing countries on the industrialized ones, thus hindering the process of indigenous capacity building (see Chapter 8). Others argue that the developing countries cannot remain indifferent to the selection and utilization of high technology. For improved competitiveness in the international markets, it is imperative that these countries examine the feasibility of using these technologies on a selective basis. Few developing countries today are both producers as well as consumers of high technology. This means that at least a limited number of developing countries will need to possess a capacity to develop new technologies in order to reduce their dependence on the industrialized countries. The fact that only a few industrialized countries are the major sources of supply of these technologies creates a sellers' market in which the buyers (the developing countries) have a very weak bargaining position. Yet the international economic environment, and the structural adjustment programmes that are underway in most developing countries, lead to austerity in government spending. The first programmes to receive the cuts are likely to be R & D expenditures and scientific projects whose benefits are perceived to be essentially long-term.

We review the technology literature in an evolutionary perspective and group it into three periods: the sixties (including the fifties), the seventies and the eighties. In the sixties, emphasis on technology issues related mainly to investment allocation and the growth-inducing influence of capital-intensive technologies through reinvestible surpluses (Sen, 1957, 1960; Dobb, 1956; Galenson and Leibenstein, 1955; Bhalla, 1964, 1965); to international technology transfer and to the cost of transfer and choice of transfer modes (Stewart, 1977; 1981; UNCTAD, 1975; Patel, 1974; Germidis, 1977; Hawthorne, 1971; Kojima, 1977; Mason, 1970, 1971). The sixties also noticed the beginnings of the appropriate technology concept as a reaction against the failure of heavy industrialization strategies to remove social ills like unemployment and poverty.

In the seventies attention therefore shifted to technology choice as an instrument of employment policy. A major emphasis was placed on technology choice and change in the context of employment generation, poverty alleviation and the satisfaction of basic needs. The issue of appropriate technology, which led to a long and rather sterile debate, really belongs to the class of technology choice and change issues. The protagonists of AT (Schumacher, 1973) simply brought to the fore the need to widen the set of alternatives through labour-intensive technical change. This need to widen the choice also embraced such issues as choice of appropriate products and issues of consumer demand and income distribution.

In the eighties it was realized that too much emphasis on micro issues alone was misplaced. The issues of technology choice and transformation of developing countries needed to be placed in a macro perspective. This underlined the importance of appropriate government policies to promote employment-generating technologies. The issues of the application of these technologies could not be left purely to the economists. The non-economic forces also influenced decision making. This decade could therefore be associated with the macroeconomic and political economy of technology decisions, intersectoral linkages to promote technology improvements and reduce technology gaps between modern and informal sectors, and the emergence of new technologies (See James and Watanabe, 1985; Stewart, 1987; Stewart, Thomas and de Wilde 1990).

In the final analysis, rational technology selection could not be made without the existence of national or indigenous technological capability on the part of the producers and policymakers in developing countries. The subject of capability building is therefore a major long-term goal in Third World development (see Chapters 8 and 9).

We discuss below different facets of technology choice and development in the above context. The first section, covering the fifties and the sixties, is concerned mainly with the issues of growth, investment allocation, technology transfer and technology choice. The second section then is devoted to the seventies, when technology choice debate shifted emphasis from growth and investment *per se* to employment, poverty and the satisfaction of basic needs. The eighties were devoted more to the sectoral and macroeconomic and political economy issues of technology choice as well as change, which are discussed in the third section.

THE FIFTIES AND SIXTIES: GROWTH, INVESTMENT ALLOCATION AND TECHNOLOGY CHOICE AND TRANSFER

In the fifties and sixties the issue of technology choice was secondary to that of maximization of growth. Therefore, technology choice was to be geared to the achievement of this objective. A choice was invariably recommended in favour of the most capital-intensive and advanced technology because it contributed to maximizing of savings rates and investment. The reinvestible surpluses, it was assumed, would be higher with capital-intensive technology than with a labour-intensive one because all profits (accruing from capital-intensive techniques) are saved, whereas most of the wages earned by labour are consumed. If labour-intensive technology was chosen, additional employment would lead to an additional wage bill and higher consumption, thus reducing reinvestible surplus.

The above thinking of Dobb (1956), Sen (1957, 1960) and Galenson and Leibenstein (1955) dominated the development literature throughout the fifties and the sixties. The issue of technology choice was directly linked to the planning objectives. If growth was the major objective and capital the major constraint to development, then choosing the most advanced technology was clearly the best option. If, on the other hand, the objective was to maximize employment or immediate output, the choice in favour of labour-intensive technology might be rational.

During this period, empirical testing of the above hypotheses was not very fashionable. One notices only a few studies of a micro nature which attempted to verify the validity of the assumptions that all profits are saved and all wages are consumed, and that capital-intensive techniques necessarily maximized reinvestible surplus. One such study on the textile spinning technology in India (Bhalla, 1964) estimated the orders of magnitude of total reinvestment and total additional output and employment that could be obtained from a given initial investment made into alternative techniques. It came to the conclusion that while the factory technique (or the capital-intensive technique) maximized reinvestment, it did not maximize either output or employment. The traditional labour-intensive technique did not maximize reinvestment but it maximized output and employment. These trade-offs between growth, output and employment were to preoccupy scholars until much later, well into the 1980s.

THE SEVENTIES: TECHNOLOGY, EMPLOYMENT AND BASIC NEEDS

In the fifties and sixties it was generally believed that rapid economic growth and industrialization in developing countries would automatically remove poverty through a 'trickle down' effect on the poor and the underprivileged. Despite the tremendous influence of development thinkers, in actual practice the growth maximization strategies did not lead to any substantial trickle down affecting the unemployment and poverty problem. Empirical evidence generated during the seventies also showed that in many cases, at least in Africa, even the absolute standard of living of the poor had declined. The relatively new international programmes, like the ILO World Employment Programme, and the World Bank's anti-poverty programme during the McNamara years, therefore advocated a dethronement of GNP and the fetish of growth *per se*. The emphasis was placed instead on the broader-based development strategies which gave a pride of place to employment generation, human capital formation, a more egalitarian income distribution and the satisfaction of basic human needs. In other words, what became important during the seventies was not simply *what* was to be produced but *how* it was to be produced and *for whom*. This new orientation towards development also meant a reorientation of the analysis of technology choice, development and transfer. The criteria for choosing technology was no longer to be the reinvestible surplus of growth, but instead employment, output and income generation and the reduction of inequalities.

The early seventies saw a major shift towards research on socioeconomic and employment implications of technology choice in developing countries. It also witnessed the emergence of the concept of appropriate technology.

Appropriate technology (AT)

Appropriate technology was defined differently by different people. It is not our purpose here to enter into a long discussion on the controversy and debate on the subject. Suffice it to say that the concept emerged mainly as a reaction to the failure of growth-maximizing strategies of development to alleviate the unemployment and poverty problems. AT has been defined in terms of criteria and *objectives*: employment, basic needs and environment, etc.; and in terms of *characteristics*: simplicity, small scale of operation, labour intensity, low skill requirements, etc. (see Stewart, 1977). The underlying premise of the AT concept is the limited relevance of the advanced-country technologies to the different factor endowments of developing countries. There are different ways in which existing technology can be adapted and made more appropriate to the developing country conditions. Three such ways have been discussed in the literature, namely (1) downscaling of large-scale technology; (2) upgrading of traditional technology; and (3) adaptation of imported technology.

As conditions vary between developing countries, no single technology can be considered appropriate for all countries at all times. Endowments change over time which would make some technologies in future less appropriate than others. Thus AT does not represent a particular tool-kit of technologies, even though the modes of production considered appropriate are usually related to small-scale consumer goods production. Instead, it is more useful to consider some priority areas and sectors in which the need for gradual technological transformation is greater than others. The development of appropriate and adapted technologies needs to be concentrated on these priority areas (Bhalla, 1979; Kaplinsky, 1990).

Appropriate products

The question of technology choice is closely linked with that of product choice and consumer demand. The argument for linking technology choice with product choice runs as follows. The basic goods and services consumed by low-income groups in a society (e.g. food, footwear and clothing) tend to be more labour intensive than those consumed by the rich (e.g. consumer durables). As goods for the masses are generally produced with simple labour-intensive techniques, a redistribution of income in favour of the poor should raise demand for these goods and thereby employment. This view, presented in the ILO Comprehensive Employment Mission Report to Colombia (1970), was further elaborated by James (1976), Stewart (1977) and Stewart and James (1982). To test empirically the validity of the assumption that (a) the poor necessarily consume labour-intensive goods,and (b) production of these goods will promote appropriate technology applications generating employment, the ILO World Employment Programme undertook empirical research on specific products and countries, namely the soap market in Barbados and Bangladesh, bicycles in Malaysia, metal household utensils in India, footwear in Ghana, furniture making in Kenya, and passenger transport in Pakistan (van Ginneken and Baron, 1984). These studies generally confirmed the above hypothesis of an increase in demand for labour-intensive goods resulting from redistribution. However, the evidence from the above ILO studies and others (James, 1976; Morawetz, 1974; Tokman, 1974) is mixed: although a higher consumption of basic goods does take place, it does not necessarily raise employment substantially. This limited employment impact may be due to the fact that some basic products may use capital-intensive but cheap inputs like synthetic fibres, which are not environment-friendly. Secondly, the employment effects may be small because the macroeconomic studies are too aggregative. Taking the Indian sugar industry as an example, James (1976) shows that aggregating crystal sugar (capital intensive) and *gur* (labour intensive) underestimates the effects of changes in income distribution. If they were taken separately, the positive employment effects would increase by 50 per cent. Furthermore, in some cases, even capital-intensive goods (e.g. Bata shoes produced with modern technology) may be more appropriate for the poor than the labour-intensive goods because the former are cheaper and more durable.

Technology and employment

Far more studies have been undertaken on the effects of alternative technologies on employment than on the effects of appropriate products. One of the early objectives of research on technology under the ILO World Employment Programme, and at Yale and Strathclyde Universities, was to examine empirically the technological determinism which influenced much of development thinking in the fifties and the sixties.

The notion of technological fixity and rigid production functions dates back to the classic article by Eckaus (1955) in which he shows how substitution possibilities between capital and labour were limited in the industrial sector. According to him, in general there was only one efficient technique for producing a well-defined industrial product. This technique would be mostly capital intensive and would be imported from industrially advanced countries. At the time of that writing, little empirical evidence existed to challenge this assertion. However, during the seventies and eighties a substantial number of empirical micro-industrial case studies (dealing mainly with consumer goods, but also to a lesser extent with intermediate and capital goods sectors) (White, 1978; Pickett, 1977; Timmer et al. 1975; Bhalla, 1975 and 1985; Stewart, 1977) clearly pointed towards wide technological choice. The range of choice is broader for crude products and for simple consumer goods industries than for those requiring high degrees of precision and quality product specifications. Nevertheless, in these latter cases, as is noted above, there is evidence to suggest that the technological determinist view is exaggerated.

One attractive approach to technology and employment during the 1970s was offered by Sen (1975). Policy implications of technology choice are linked to the production and employment modes, namely family employment, extended family, wage employment and cooperatives. The technological sophistication increases with the mode of production/employment. For example, technologies that can be economical for wage-based firms are unlikely to be available to small household production units. With an increasing emphasis on private sector development, and growth of small enterprises, a comparative analysis of technology choice by employment modes (e.g. wage employment and self-employment) seems to represent a fruitful inquiry.

One has to be careful about making hasty generalizations on the basis of a very small and heterogeneous sample of industrial and agricultural case studies. There is clearly a dilemma here. Aggregative studies tend to blur the issue of technology choice made essentially at the micro level of firms and farms; they also tend to underestimate the employment effects. But at the same time very micro studies do not lend themselves to easy generalizations.

Notwithstanding the above caveat, some general conclusions can be drawn from the wealth of empirical case studies which are listed in Table 1.1. First, the studies show that factor price distortions (of only two factors, capital and labour), while relevant to technology decision making, are not as important as many other factors. Furthermore, two-factor models which consider the role of factor pricing are somewhat oversimplified. In cases such as processing industries like sugar, the prices of raw material inputs may be more important in the choice of technology.

Second, even when factor pricing policies play a role as incentives or disincentives for appropriate-technology decisions, they may not be sufficient. They would be more effective if they were combined with such measures as the establishment of appropriate institutions for technological information collection and dissemination, appropriate infrastructure and adequate planning, organization and implementation machinery, etc.

Third, the choice of technology is significantly influenced by the existing market structures and the associated risk and uncertainty which may arise due to imperfect knowledge about alternative technologies. The monopolistic advantages of a firm or industry are more likely to encourage the choice of capital-intensive technology than the more competitive structures.

Table 1.1 Coverage of empirical studies on technology choice in manufacturing

Product or industry	Author	Country or region[1]	Scale	Prod-uct	Skills	Raw mat-erial	Ma-terial hand-ling trans-port	Factor ef-ficiency	Lo-cation	Energy	Em-ploy-ment	En-viron-ment	Used machin-ery
Consumer goods													
Beer brewing	ILO and Strathclyde	–		x	x	x	x	x			x		x
Bread	ILO and Strathclyde	–						x			x		x
Bread	ILO	Kenya	x				x	x					
Can-making	ILO	Kenya, Tanzania, Thailand		x	x	x	x	x	x				x
Cane sugar production	ILO	–	x					x					
Clothing	Michigan State	Sierra Leone	x	x	x	x		x	x				
Coconut oil production	ILO	–	x		x	x	x	x			x		
Cotton spinning	Yale	Brazil				x	x	x			x		x
Fish preservation	ILO	–		x		x		x			x		
Fruit, vegetable preservation	ILO	–	x	x	x	x		x		x	x		

Table 1.1 Continued

Product or industry	Author	Country or region[1]	Scale	Product	Skills	Raw material	Material handling transport	Factor efficiency	Location	Energy	Employment	Environment	Used machinery
Gari production from cassava	ILO	–	x	x	x	x	x	x					
Jute processing	ILO	Kenya	x	x	x	x	x	x			x		
Leather shoes	ILO	Malaysia		x	x	x	x	x	x				
Leather shoes	Yale	Brazil	x	x	x	x	x	x		x			
Maize milling	ILO and Strathclyde	–						x					
Milk processing	ILO		x	x	x	x		x		x			
Rice milling	ILO and Strathclyde	–	x	x	x	x		x		x			
Salt production[2]	Enos	Tanzania	x	x	x	x		x		x	x		
Sugar processing	ILO	South-east Asia	x	x	x	x		x		x	x	x	
Sugar processing	Strathclyde	India	x	x	x	x		x		x	x		
		Ghana		x	x	x	x	x		x	x		
		Ethiopia											
Textiles	ILO	United Kingdom	x		x			x					
Textiles	Strathclyde	Africa	x	x	x		x	x					
Intermediate goods													
Bricks	ILO	Malaysia	x	x	x	x	x	x	x	x	x		
Cement blocks	ILO	Kenya	x	x	x	x	x	x	x	x			

Table 1.1 Continued

Product or industry	Author	Country or region[1]	Technology characteristics covered										
			Scale	Prod-uct	Skills	Raw mat-erial	Ma-terial hand-ling trans-port	Factor ef-ficiency	Lo-cation	Energy	Em-ploy-ment	En-viron-ment	Used machin-ery
Copper and aluminium	ILO	–		x		x		x			x		
Fertilisers	Strathclyde	India							x	x			
Iron foundries	Strathclyde	–	x	x	x		x		x	x			
Nuts and bolts	Strathclyde	–	x	x	x	x		x			x		
Capital goods													
Agric. machinery[3]	Mitra	–	x	x	x			x	x	x	x		
Engineering	ILO	Colombia	x	x		x	x	x	x	x			
Metal working	ILO	Mexico	x	x		x				x			x

1. A dash (–) in this column indicates that the study is based on international cross-section data.
2. J.L. Enos: 'More (or less) on the choice of technique, with a contemporary example', in *Seoul National University Economic Review*, Dec. 1977, pp. 177–199.
3. A.K. Mitra: 'Interlinkage in agricultural machinery industry for rural industrialization in developing countries', in United Nations Industrial Development Organization (UNIDO): *Appropriate industrial technology for agricultural machinery and implements* (International forum on appropriate industrial technology, 20–24 November 1978, New Delhi, and 28–30 November 1978, Anand, India, selected documents), Monographs on Appropriate Industrial Technology, No. 4 (New York, United Nations, 1979), Part Two: 'Selected background papers', pp. 25–123.

Source: Bhalla (1985).

Fourthly, substitution between skilled and unskilled labour, and supervisory and management costs hinder the use of labour-intensive technologies. Substitutions take place not only between capital and labour but also between semi-skilled labour and skilled supervisory plus unskilled labour. Our stock of empirical knowledge about the skill implications of alternative technologies remains quite limited.

Finally, socio-cultural and political forces, the vested interests of decision makers and government intervention may facilitate or hinder the use of more appropriate technologies.

The issues of energy-saving and environmental conservation have no doubt come to the forefront in recent years (see Chapter 7). This has raised the number of criteria against which technology decisions need to be judged. As noted in Table 1.1, few of the existing studies consider environmental effects and energy consumption as important variables in technology choice (Bhalla, 1985). Far more emphasis in the early studies was placed on the issues of employment and income distribution which can be regarded as a legitimate concern of most developing countries.

The analysis of a relationship between technology, environment and employment is of recent origin (Pereira, 1991; Bhalla, 1992). It is therefore not surprising that even in the industrialized countries it is difficult to find many good industrial studies which attempt to analyse quantitatively (or even qualitatively) possible trade-offs between the energy intensity, labour intensity and pollution intensity of alternative industrial technologies. One of the major difficulties in undertaking such analyses is not so much the vagueness of definitions of environmental considerations, as the lack of adequate data about polluting and non-polluting technologies and industries. As we discuss in Chapter 7, Japan is one of the few countries where such data are available for small and large enterprises and industries.

Technology transfer

In the seventies the issue of international technology transfers was in the fore only partly for their unsuitability to the factor endowments of developing countries. Interest in the subject arose also from the high cost of technology acquisition by the developing countries. Generally, the costs of transfer were higher the less developed the country and the smaller the amounts it devoted to technology acquisition and assimilation (Enos, 1989). UNCTAD (1975) spent considerable effort in analysing the costs of technology transfer to developing countries, and the weak bargaining position of the latter which partly explained these high costs. Also it negotiated the formulation and implementation of a code of conduct for technology transfer which has still not been accepted and adopted by all the negotiating parties. Despite the availability of impressive literature on the cost of technology transfer, there seem to be no comparative-cost studies of transferring advanced (or new) technologies, second-hand technologies and appropriate technologies (Enos, 1989).

Modes of technology transfer, for example, foreign investment, licensing, joint ventures, small and medium enterprises and multinational enterprises, involve more than just a transfer of technology. Equipment and materials, skilled manpower and know-how and organizational innovations are also transferred. In the seventies it was common for many developing countries (e.g. India and Brazil) to control foreign investment and licensing in order to make sure that the technology was actually transferred and that it did not inhibit the creation of national technology capability. With a move towards rapid economic liberalization in most countries and globalization of production, these controls have been replaced by more liberal policies on foreign investment and technology transfer which make the developing countries increasingly dependent on the advanced-country corporations for technology and investment.

Dynamic considerations

The bulk of the literature on technology choice in the seventies was of a *static* nature, examining issues of technology choice at a point in time, rather than the *dynamic* effects – social as well as economic – of technical change over a period of time. While some studies have been undertaken to examine how technology changes take place and what effect they have on the modification of known techniques (Atkinson and Stiglitz, 1969; Stewart, 1977; Stewart and James, 1982), the stock of empirical knowledge on the subject still remains relatively limited. Yet historical studies of technical change are essential to guide the planners and policy makers in making intertemporal choices regarding the growth of output and employment.

There is another context in which the dynamic issues of technology development are relevant. As we will discuss in Chapters 8 and 9 one of the major objectives of developing countries is to develop indigenous technological capability, not only to select from existing alternatives but to widen the technology choice set. A pre-requisite for this is that at least some technological development activity is located within developing countries to ensure positive effects of domestic learning. These issues became important in the eighties and are examined in the following section.

THE EIGHTIES: MACRO AND SECTORAL ISSUES

In the eighties, the evolution of development thinking shifted to more macroeconomic and sectoral aspects of technology policy and its implementation. These issues have been somewhat complicated by the emergence during this period of new technological innovations like microelectronics, telecommunications and biotechnologies, whose potential influences on production, income distribution and employment are not easily foreseen (see Chapter 6). We first examine issues of the macroeconomic effects of technology choice and their policy implications before examining the potential effects of new technologies and technology blending.

Macroeconomic aspects of technology

Three sets of analyses have been undertaken to trace the macroeconomic effects of technology choice. The first has to do with the political-economy considerations as a rebuttal to the neoclassical paradigm (James, 1985; Stewart, 1987; Stewart, Thomas and de Wilde, 1990). The second deals with quantitative modelling based on social accounting matrices (Khan and Thorbecke, 1988; Khan, 1985). The third is concerned with inter-sectoral linkages (Haggblade and Hazell, 1989; Ranis and Stewart, 1993). These are discussed below.

(a) Macroeconomic policies and political-economy considerations

A word on the definition of the term 'political economy' (which is not without ambiguity) is in order. The political-economy aspects refer to the influences of interest groups and their power on macro decisions, and the external environment in which micro units operate. The government exercises an *indirect* influence on technology decision-making through its factor and product price policy; through control or encouragement of monopolistic structures, and through distribution, credit, fiscal and import policies, and so on. Macroeconomic policies provide a broad framework and environment within which technology decisions are made. These policies affect the technological decisions made largely at a micro level in firms, and farms, of different ownership and organization.

Different socioeconomic groups and technology decision-makers have conflicting interests and motivations. They are also likely to be affected differently by different technology choices. For example, liberalization of tractor imports is likely to benefit large farmers (who can afford them) more than small farmers. Some groups are likely to gain and others likely to lose from a given technology decision, as is shown by Ranis (1990) and

Stewart (1993) through an illustration of the promotion of rural linkages in the Philippines and Taiwan (China).

Some writers (Galtung, 1980) have argued that governments mainly represent the views of one set of interests, namely, that of 'researchers, bureaucrats and capitalists' rather than the social welfare of the whole nation. A given technology is closely associated with a particular economic, social and political structure which it is in the interest of the government to protect.

A variant of the political-economy considerations of technology choice is to consider its impact/implications under alternative development strategies. Implicit in this view (James, 1985) is the assumption that a particular development strategy is shaped by the politico-economic interests of the government which has formulated it. For example, a redistributive strategy, favouring an increase in incomes of the poor and fulfilment of their basic needs, is more likely to be based on support from small farmers and rural masses than a purely growth-oriented strategy. The former strategy is much more likely to use technology choice as an instrument of income redistribution than the latter.

(b) Macro-modelling

Although no one would dispute a common assertion that technology affects the entire economy and society, few macroeconomic studies have ventured to trace these effects on an economy-wide basis. Most of the empirical studies, as noted above, are of a micro nature which trace only the *direct* effects of micro decisions. Also there are very few studies which aggregate these effects and the *indirect* ones at a sectoral level, much less for the economy as a whole. Yet indirect effects – through backward and forward linkages – may be far more important for output and employment generation. These indirect effects could only be traced through input–output analysis of sectoral interdependence in an economy. An improvement on this analysis is the SAM framework which enables tracing the effects of alternative technologies on macroeconomic variables and policy objectives. Khan and Thorbecke (1988) use the SAM technique to examine the technology-production interactions in the energy sector of Indonesia. The production activities are classified along dualistic technological categories, that is, products which could be produced either with traditional labour-intensive technology or with modern capital-intensive technology. The effects of changes in output of selected dualistic production activities on the aggregate output of agriculture and mining, energy and other sectors, and the whole economy, are then estimated. Further, assessing the effects on factor income and employment and household income distribution is also attempted. The Indonesian case study (Khan and Thorbecke, 1988) concludes that 'the traditional technology generates greater aggregate output effects on the whole economic system than the corresponding modern technology' and 'the effect of the increased production of traditional technology has a greater impact on total employment and a much greater impact on the incomes of lower skilled workers than the corresponding modern alternatives' (p. 5).

These results cannot be used as definitive; further refinements of the methodology and many more empirical studies of this kind are needed before we can be certain of their policy/practical relevance. At present, the analysis is arbitrarily based on only two techniques for producing each of the selected products; yet there may in practice be several technological alternatives. Further micro analyses are essential to provide an improved understanding of their macroeconomic effects.

A pioneering aspect of the Khan–Thorbecke study (1988) is the use of R & D as a separate productive activity in the SAM framework. Notwithstanding the conceptual problem of reconciling the *static* nature of SAM with the *dynamic* effects of R & D, the authors have made a bold attempt to study the contribution of R & D expenditures to the development and adaptation of technology as a tool for better technology planning and policy making. For lack of data, it was not possible to test the methodology for the Indonesian economy. It is ironical that despite the clear recognition of the economy-wide effects of technology choice and change, the macro modelling has remained hampered partly by the limitations of methodology and partly by the absence of required disaggregated data.

Another macroeconomic study which also attempts to measure the contribution of technological advance to economic growth relates to the Republic of Korea (see Kim and Park, 1985). In the tradition of Denison (1962), the authors investigate the sources of economic growth and measure Korea's overall success in technological advance through the growth of total factor productivity.

(c) Intersectoral linkages

Macroeconomic studies also enable an investigation of intersectoral linkages. Much of the technology literature is concerned with the supply-side issues – technology development and utilization – assuming that demand for technology exists. In practice, experience has shown that very few of the small-scale but improved technologies, considered appropriate for many developing countries, have been commercialized by the private sector on any significant scale (Bhalla and Reddy, 1994). The problem is not simply one of engineering and the development of prototypes. Instead, one of the major constraints to the commercialization of alternative technologies is the low effective demand for AT from a large number of small-scale producers. The poor engaged in small-scale activities, for whom the AT devices are intended, cannot afford to purchase them even if they perceived the merit of using them for raising their productivity and incomes.

The promotion of rural and urban, and farm and non-farm linkages can help relax the demand constraint. A strong and positive relationship is known to exist between agricultural growth and changes in the rural non-farm sector (Fei, Ranis and Stewart, 1985; Haggblade and Hazell, 1989; Ranis, 1990; Ranis and Stewart, 1993). Three types of linkages between agriculture and non-agriculture are relevant. These are: (i) backward production linkages (e.g. equipment inputs to agriculture); (ii) forward production linkages (e.g. food processing); and (iii) forward consumption linkages (e.g. an increase in demand for industrial products induced by increased purchasing power in the agricultural sector). The third type of linkages are noted to be the most important. They depend on a number of factors like the growth of agricultural output and income distribution, the state of agricultural technology, the crop mix, and so on. An increase in agricultural incomes should also provide an impetus to the demand for agricultural technologies, both biological and mechanical, assuming that they exist and that the factor price distortions do not keep them beyond the reach of those who need them most.

The linkages need not move from agriculture to non-agriculture. They are also induced from the urban to the rural sector through such mechanisms as sub-contracting between large and small enterprises. Watanabe (1983) noted three types of linkages, viz. (i) technological linkages: transfer of technology and skills; (ii) input linkages: supplies of raw materials and equipment; and (iii) market linkages between a large-scale parent firm and its small-scale sub-contractors. The flow of technology and skills from the large- to the small-scale rural sector is essential to bring about a narrowing of technology gaps between the modern and informal sectors of developing countries. Invariably, the rural sector does not have any internal source of technology generation and equipment supply, most of the R & D being concentrated in the urban sector. Therefore, any strategy of gradual modernization of traditional technologies in rural areas calls for external inputs, as was clearly evidenced by the experience of the Green Revolution in the sixties.

The above issues of intersectoral linkages can be handled at a macro level mainly through the input–output and SAM techniques mentioned above. But the data requirements, as noted above, are serious constraints to undertaking empirical studies in developing countries.

New technologies

The issue of intersectoral linkages becomes even more important with the advent of new technologies, which are likely to exercise an increasingly pervading influence in different economic sectors, for example, agriculture, manufacturing, banking and financial services. The new technologies have been heralded almost as a revolution on a par with the previous ones brought about by the steam engine, steel and electricity (Freeman, 1984, 1993; Perez, 1985).

The emergence of new technologies in the early eighties first produced doomsday scenarios predicting unprecedented negative employment effects and social evils pervading the entire economies and societies of industrialized countries. Very soon however it was realized that the pace at which new technological breakthroughs were expected did not really materialize, due partly to economic recession and the resulting sluggishness of demand, in part to a shortage of the new types of polyvalent skills required, and perhaps also due to the inertia of conventional types of managements and the ignorance of policy makers about the potential benefits of new technologies (see Chapters 2 to 5).

Some stock of empirical knowledge on the impact of new technologies has now been accumulated, although by no means adequate enough to make any definitive generalizations. Three sets of studies, namely global or 'synthetic' studies, sectoral investigations and micro analyses, may be noted. Much of the work (like that on technology choice and appropriate technology reviewed earlier) is of a micro nature. A study by Kaplinsky (1987) considers microelectronics-based technologies in a socioeconomic framework and a global economic context of economic recession. It notes that available studies on the quantitative impact of microelectronics on employment are undertaken at different levels of aggregation – process, plant, firm, branch, regional, sectoral, macroeconomic and meta level – which explains why they are non-comparable and often conflicting in their conclusions. Furthermore, conflicts also arise because their results are highly sensitive to the assumptions made about growth of output and productivity, qualitative and organizational changes, and the indirect and multiplier effects, which are rarely considered.

With the possible exception of some NICs, knowledge about the impact of microelectronics technologies is limited in most developing countries (see Chapter 6). Also limited is the stock of knowledge concerning other new technologies such as biotechnologies and new materials whose frontiers in many areas yet remain to be explored even in the industrialized countries, not to speak of the developing countries. One of the major requirements for successfully facing the new technological challenge is therefore the extension of the existing knowledge base.

A PERSPECTIVE FOR THE NINETIES AND BEYOND

Perspective for technology work in the nineties will depend on the scenarios regarding the strategies and prospects of development in the Third World. The Fourth Development Decade of the United Nations gives a prominent place to human resources development and employment generation. Similarly, the UNDP has adopted human development as a major goal for its development efforts (UNDP, 1990) and the World Summit for Social Development (Copenhagen, March 1995) focused on employment generation, poverty alleviation and social integration as three pillars of people-centred development.

If the development of human capabilities and potential is the goal of the current decade, technology policies and programmes would need to be considered in the context of an achievement of this goal. Human resources are essential inputs to embodied and disembodied technical change. They are equally important for the strengthening or building of technological capability (see Chapter 8).

In the 1990s, the new technological challenge will continue with increasing innovations and new breakthroughs in such new technologies as biotechnologies, new materials and telecommunications. An analysis of these technologies and their contributions to human as well as material development (through greater food security made possible by new biotechnologies) would merit further attention. This challenge is particularly formidable for Africa, where achievement of food security would depend on a breakthrough in agricultural productivity. The use of new biotechnologies may give a helping hand here (see Chapter 3 for the potential of these technologies).

In the short run the benefits of new technologies are likely to be exploited more by the NICs which have already entered the international markets with exports of capital goods and new technology. There may also be scope for accelerating the technological transformation of least developed countries, through a selective application of new micro-electronics-based technologies, on a sub-regional or regional basis (e.g. distance learning), to take advantage of scale economies. The new biotechnologies, as we discuss in Chapter 3, can have a potential beneficial effect in the least developed countries for their agricultural and rural development. They promise greater food production and food security by raising agricultural productivity, by allowing an extension of cultivation into marginal areas and by making new and improved crop varieties possible (Bhalla, 1993).

The new technologies are likely to exercise significant influence on the developing countries, both directly and indirectly. Directly, with increasing globalization of production and international competition (see Introduction), the export-oriented countries would be compelled to adopt new technologies to compete with the industrialized countries as is already being done by many East Asian countries. The fear of being left behind industrialized countries is likely to put pressures on many more developing countries to make a start with new technologies in an effort to catch up and leap-frog. As we note in Chapter 2, as latecomers, developing countries may be able to take advantage of new technologies to leap-frog by jumping from manual methods directly to flexible manufacturing systems without having to adopt fixed automation. However, leap-frogging presupposes the existence in these countries of organizational and innovation capabilities to produce new products through the use of high technology. It also assumes that the developing countries possess a minimum of technological capability to master the use of high technology.

Indirectly, the use of new materials and new biotechnologies in the industrialized countries is already hurting the exports of primary materials and commodities from the developing countries. The developing countries have little control or influence on the 'dematerialization of production' and the substitution of new for old commodities taking place in the industrialized countries.

Under the influence of new industrial technologies, new macro-economic policies (including structural adjustment programmes and new methods of industrial organization) and the internationalization of production, the labour markets in both industrialized and developing countries are going to become more flexible. Informalization of the labour market and of production is already being witnessed in the form of an increase in casual employment, part-time and self-employment, flexible hours of work, etc. The possible impact of new technologies on the 'informalization' of work remains to be explored. Our knowledge about the impact of new technological developments on skill formation and substitution is also quite limited.

The nineties may also witness a decline in the national R & D resources allocated to technology development in the Third World. This is likely to happen under the stringent application of structural adjustment programmes, being pursued by most developing countries, since the results of R & D are essentially long-term and often uncertain. This turn of events will have adverse implications for the diffusion of new technologies within the developing countries, unless the shortfall in national resources can be made up by external grants.

2 New Technologies: Myth or Reality?*

In this chapter we examine the implications of the so-called new technology revolution for developing countries. The protagonists of new technologies argue that these technologies can enable the developing countries to leap-frog and to catch up with the industrialized countries. But there are clear preconditions for such take off which many developing countries may not fulfil. Recent empirical studies (Watanabe, 1993) show that these technologies are at present concentrated largely in the newly industrializing countries (NICs), with very limited applications in the industrial sectors of other low-income developing countries. This is confirmed by the specific examples of the adoption of microelectronics-based technologies (see Chapters 3 and 4).

The purpose of this chapter is to examine the potential and limitations of new technologies for developing countries. The first section discusses technological leap-frogging. The concept is defined and the scope for its application in developing countries at different stages of development is examined. The second section discusses the potential benefits of new technologies for developing countries, with special reference to advanced biotechnologies. The third section outlines bottlenecks in the adoption of new technologies in these countries.

TECHNOLOGICAL LEAP-FROGGING

The existence of technological and economic gaps between the South and the North is a powerful motivation for the former to look for ways and

---

*This chapter is largely though not exclusively based on 'New Technology Revolution: Myth or Reality in Developing Countries?' (with J. James), *Greek Economic Review,* Vol. 6, No. 3, December 1984; 'Third World's Technological Dilemma', *Labour and Society,* Vol. 9, No. 4, October–December, 1984; 'Towards New Technological Frontiers' (with D. James), *Productivity,* October–December 1984; 'Can High Technology Help Third World Take Off?', *Economic and Political Weekly,* 4 July 1987; 'Assessment of the Social Impacts of New Technology', *ATAS Bulletin,* UN, New York, No.5, 1987; and 'Conclusions and Lessons' in A.S. Bhalla and Dilmus James (eds), *New Technologies and Development,* Boulder, Lynne Rienner Publishers, 1988.

means of catching up or leap-frogging. Whether aspirations can be transformed into reality is, however, another matter.

The concept

Three interpretations can be given to the concept of leap-frogging. First, it implies the narrowing of gaps between countries at different stages of development. Secondly, and related to the above, it would involve the adoption of advanced technology in the leap-frogging countries ahead of the other more industrialized countries. For example, Bessant and Cole (1985) define leap-frogging as the use of 'advanced generations of IT-based capital goods ahead of developed country competitors which may still be tied to existing generations of investment'. Thirdly, leap-frogging may mean that developing countries can jump some steps and avoid having to go through stages experienced by the present industrialized countries.

The experience of some industrialized countries such as Japan (whose economy was in complete ruin after the Second World War) suggests that technological progress can act as a powerful engine of growth. The rapid growth of the Japanese electronics industry and the growing importance of information-intensive products and services bear testimony to the significance of high technology. Table 2.1 shows how the growth of investment in high technology has contributed to the overall growth of investment in the Japanese economy. It also shows that the growth of 'high tech' outlays was fairly high in almost all the manufacturing sectors. Only in the category 'non-manufacturing industry' was this share rather low. However, some caution is needed in interpreting the data. The growth rate of high technology outlays (viz. 31.3 per cent for all industries) relates to the fiscal years 1983–84 and 1984–85 – a period too short to be very meaningful.

Yet this is the type of information that is needed to assess the contribution of 'high tech' R&D to the overall investment and growth of developing economies. Data similar to those in Table 2.1 are difficult to find for most developing countries. The Republic of Korea is perhaps one of the few developing countries in which the capital outlay on imported technology, as well as on R&D, has increased substantially over the seventies and eighties. High R&D expenditures and a major investment drive for growth in the Republic of Korea has led to the emergence of several major producers and exporters of memory chips. In other developing countries, even when R&D in new technologies has grown, its positive contribution to productivity growth and local technological development is not clearly established. This is a fertile area for further research.

Table 2.1 Trends in high technology capital outlays (Japan 1984) (percentages)

Industry	Growth rate of overall capital investment	Growth rate of high technology outlays	Share of high technology capital outlays in total investment	Contribution of high technology growth to overall capital investment
All industries	10.5	31.3	22.4	56.2
Materials industries[a]	8.2	35.5	28.2	63.2
Materials industries (excluding steel)	23.5	34.7	25.1	34.0
Processing and assembly industries[b]	25.1	50.6	39.9	66.8
Non-manufacturing industry	10.9	13.5	16.5	37.3

(a) Textiles, paper and pulp, chemicals, non-metallic mineral products, steel and non-ferrous metals.
(b) Food, non-electrical machinery, electrical machinery, transport-equipment and precision instruments.

Source: Questionnaire survey by the Japan Development Bank (August 1984); taken from UNIDO *Industry and Development – Global Report* (Vienna, 1986), p. 15.

Scope and potential

The scope for leap-frogging by the developing countries would depend, at a given point in time, on the current levels of domestic technological capability in general and the capacity to absorb high technology in particular. For example, production, design and engineering capabilities may be needed to improve on imported technologies and to develop new ones (Perez and Soete, 1988; Soete, 1990). Such capabilities are at present to be found in a handful of NICs such as the Republic of Korea, Hong Kong, Singapore, Taiwan (China), Brazil and Mexico. The NICs possess the capacity to develop some of the new technologies, which is essential to benefit from learning-by-doing and for reducing technological dependence, which can be costly. Large and increasing investments in high technology sectors in the North are rapidly redefining international competition and comparative advantage. Unless the Third-World countries introduce high technology in their export-oriented industries in order to raise product quality, ensure quality control, reduce costs and raise productivity, they are unlikely to retain or capture export markets even in traditional industries (e.g. textiles, footwear and leather goods), which are being revived in the North thanks to the adoption of new technologies like CAD/CAM and laser cutting. The East-Asian experience noted in the Introduction shows how exports and the adoption of new technologies led to the rapid growth of several countries in the region.

Several arguments can be presented in support of leap-frogging. First, competition in the international technology market for microelectronics is so keen that prices are falling rapidly. This decline in prices should in principle make the developing countries' access to the technology much easier. Secondly, in view of the rapidly changing character of the technology it is difficult to appropriate its benefits through patents – this factor should facilitate technology diffusion. Thirdly, one of the unique characteristics of the electronics technology may be that it is both capital-saving and labour-saving – in other words, it may be technologically superior. To the extent that it is capital- and skill-saving it should be attractive for developing countries suffering from shortages of capital, skills and foreign exchange. Fourthly, new technologies are mainly science-based and require less learning-by-doing and experience (scarce inputs in many developing countries) and more scientific and technical education, which many developing countries (particularly NICs) already possess (Soete, 1985).

The case for technological leap-frogging is based on a number of assumptions which may not be valid for many developing countries, particularly the least-developed ones at very low levels of industrialization. First, it presupposes an organizational capacity for manufacturing new products using new technology. Secondly, it assumes that the indigenous technology capability in production, design engineering and so on, is at a stage at which the new technology can be assimilated and efficiently utilized, and that at least some of its components can be domestically produced. As a corollary to this, it further implies that the use of new technology will raise productivity significantly and thus contribute to overall economic growth and social welfare. As technological progress and leap-frogging are not wanted for their own sake (they are essential inputs to the process of economic growth), it is important that the technological innovations in developing countries make a positive and significant contribution to economic growth. Leap-frogging or 'catching up' by the developing countries will also depend on opportunities of collaboration with industrialized countries and the speed and extent of technology diffusion. Such opportunities are likely to improve in future with the increasing globalization of 'strategic alliances' between the leading multinational firms. While these alliances may promote efficiency through greater information diffusion (see Mody, 1990, for this argument) this collusive behaviour can also lead to inefficiencies (see James, 1993, p. 407).

The development and diffusion of new technology requires an interface between mechanical and chemical skills on the one hand and electrical skills on the other. Such an interface is generally weak in most developing countries; this may make leap-frogging there rather difficult in the foreseeable future. Even in the case of some NICs (e.g. Singapore) Hobday (1994) argues, by using evidence from the electronics industry, that technology accumulation occurred through a gradual process of learning (in pre-electronic areas such as mechanical, electro-mechanical and precision engineering) rather than by leap-frogging. This was true of both the subsidiaries of MNEs and local firms. Watanabe (1993) concludes that in the ASEAN–4 (Indonesia, Malaysia, the Philippines and Thailand) and Mexico, 'the driving force in industrial development (including applications of microelectronics-based product technologies) still rests with foreign direct investment and international sub-contracting, while FA (flexible automation) technology works as a sort of lubricant or facilitating factor' (p. 158).

In the light of the above discussion one can argue that leap-frogging is likely to be more feasible and prevalent among countries of the North than among the countries of the South. This is to be expected since the economic and industrial structures of countries within the North are very similar, and preconditions – skills, infrastructure and indigenous technological capability – exist although the degree to which they do may vary from country to country. This is no longer true when one considers developing countries, which are structurally different with the exception of a few NICs. Watanabe (1993) notes that 'so far ... only the Republic of Korea and Taiwan (China) appear to have been really exploiting the new technology for the purpose of "catching up" ' (p. 11).

Within the North, the gap between the technological leaders and followers is much narrower than the gap between the North and the South. Thus, 'catching up' becomes feasible. The existence of technological gaps between the North and the South can be illustrated in a schema presented in Table 2.2, showing technological leaders, followers and borrowers.

Since the Second World War Japan is perhaps the only country of the North which has moved from the category of technology borrower to that of a leader. This rapid leap of Japan seems to be explained by massive R&D expenditures which rose from US$129 million in 1953 to US$1060 million in 1964 and US$14 200 million in 1977–78. According to Soete (1981), 'it is the gradual shift of its endogenous technological effort from an auxiliary role to the import of technology, to autonomous technological development,

Table 2.2   Technology leaders, followers and borrowers

Leaders	Followers	Borrowers
North	**North**	**South**
United States	Western Europe	NICs
Japan		Other developing and least developed countries

which seems to be the crucial characteristic of Japan's emergence as a technological leader'. With the exception of Japan, most countries, including Western Europe, have often fallen further behind at some stage because they failed to perceive correctly the direction of technical change in microelectronics technology. The leadership of Japan and the United States is stated to be due mainly to high R&D expenditures on information and communications technology. But even in the case of Japan, her technological position varies depending on the type of technology considered. For basic science and technology Japan continues to remain a follower or a borrower. The Ministry of International Trade and Industry (MITI) in Japan has therefore decided to choose biotechnology as one of the 'next generation basic technologies' (Fransman, 1991, p. 47).

Expenditures on R&D by Japan, Germany and the United States continue to be much higher than those in the Third World, including the NICs. The United States' position as a technological leader has weakened partly as a result of falling levels of R&D expenditure, especially in the private sector. Thurow (1992) argues that 'today's spending levels will eventually lead to a secondary position for American science and engineering and lower rates of growth in productivity' (p. 157).

Since the technology gaps between the North and the South are quite vast – the gaps may in fact have widened at least in some cases since the development of new technologies – it is unlikely that any of the borrowers in the South can emulate the example of Japan in the near future. As Bagchi (1986) notes, countries which respond to technical change with a fixed lag to changes taking place abroad can never really catch up with new frontier technologies. Quoting the example of India, Bagchi states that there was no possibility of the spread of technologies through interpersonal communication and transfer of personnel between different companies as in the case of the famous Silicon Valley of California.

For the South then, is there an alternative to leap-frogging and catching up? We believe that a different technology path – a blending of new and traditional technologies – offers a far more realistic option to the South. As we show in Chapter 3, this alternative strategy may indeed be seen as another interpretation of technological leap-frogging and intermediate technologies in the sense that the blending is somewhere between traditional and high technology.

Technology gaps also exist between the NICs and the non-NICs. A recognition of the fact that developing countries vary enormously depending on the stage of development of the country concerned and its resources, both natural and human, is essential for studying the implications of new technologies. Very rarely has the existing literature paid much attention to the needs and problems of least developed countries, for example: most studies on new technologies (e.g. information technology) are concerned almost exclusively with the industrialized countries and the 'newly industrializing countries' (NICs). A study by Bessant and Cole (1985) is an exception since it examines explicitly the impact of microelectronics by distinct groups of countries: technologically progressive, technologically declining, centrally planned, newly industrializing (NICs), resource exporting, less industrialized developing, and others.

While an improvement on many studies, the Bessant–Cole classification of countries mixes up several criteria, namely, stage of development, technological maturity and mastery, and the nature of economic systems. To avoid confusion, we prefer to simplify the classification of developing countries into three categories – least developed, intermediate and newly industrializing (NICs) – based largely on the criterion of stage of development characterized by such economic features as the role of subsistence or commercial agriculture, industrial development, R&D infrastructure, the system of education, rate of literacy and so on (Watanabe, 1987).

As an illustration Table 2.3 speculates on the potential of microcomputers and advanced/new biotechnologies for rural development by three groups of countries. The diffusion of new technologies is likely to be very limited in the least-developed countries, in which the requisite skills and a physical and research infrastructure are quite scarce. The international and regional centres on tropical agriculture and cassava can play an important role in technology diffusion in these countries. While the diffusion may be a little more widespread in the case of the 'intermediate' group of countries, in general a scarcity of skilled manpower may make the use, particularly of advanced biotechnology, rather limited. Only the newly

Table 2.3   Differential impact of new technology in agriculture/rural development

	Least developed	Intermediate	Newly industrializing (NICs)
I. MICROCOMPUTERS*	Lack of skills, capital and infrastructure; use of microcomputers unlikely except in agricultural planning and administration.	Some scope for adoption as part of agricultural mechanization policy.	Increasing labour shortage and increase in wage costs will induce greater use of new technologies especially in commercial agriculture and rural non-farm activities.
II. ADVANCED/NEW BIOTECHNOLOGIES**	Lack of skill in advanced biotechnology (recombinant DNA) potentialities in cloning of plants. Unlikely use of new biotechnology on animal husbandry. Adoption for environmental protection; simple fermentation processes to increase efficiency in food production.	Adoption of new plant biotechnology in micro-propagation and cloning/fertilization. Fermentation processes to increase efficiency in traditional food processes. Some possibilities to adopt animal biotechnology. In general scarcity of skilled manpower for more advanced biotechnology. Single Cell protein production is possible in countries with abundant feed stock. Potentialities for environmental protection and sanitation.	Adoption of new biotechnology in practically all areas including animal husbandry and food processing. Adoption also for environmental protection and control. Combined applications of microcomputers and biotechnology in animal husbandry and food production.

*   Adapted from Bessant and Cole (1985).
** Provided by Pablo Bifani.

industrializing countries (NICs), with a growing labour shortage and a minimum of requisite skills and research infrastructure, are at present ready for the effective adoption of new technologies as has been evidenced by the experience of East-Asian countries.

So far we have discussed the above issues in a static framework. In a dynamic context, as least-developed countries reach a higher stage of development, they should in principle be able to take advantage of new technologies. Already countries such as India, Brazil and China, and smaller countries such as Cuba and Singapore, are entering the field of biotechnology. In general, at present the access of developing countries to microelectronics-based technology and biotechnology is rather easy thanks to the fairly loose nature of the intellectual property system. In support of this argument regarding biotechnology, Fransman (1991) notes the proliferation of small firms in this field in the United States and the United Kingdom. In future, the situation of developing countries may become more difficult once the existing intellectual property system is modified. For example, the privatization of biotechnological knowledge, which is already taking place, may further limit developing-country access to these technologies.

POTENTIAL BENEFITS OF NEW TECHNOLOGIES

The concept of leap-frogging discussed above has been applied mainly to information technology which has already made substantial headway. But other types of new technologies also hold promise for developing countries. Advanced biotechnologies (discussed in detail below) and new energy technologies, as well as remote sensing and telecommunications, seem to be particularly promising for agriculture and rural development (see Table 2.4). In the cases of microelectronics, telecommunications and remote sensing, the applications relate more to planning and management, and data processing and research, than to direct production processes. However, the potential benefits from new technology applications in production (e.g. in feed and disease control in animal husbandry and in pest control and management in plant agriculture) can also be significant. As we discuss below, the new biotechnology applications are more likely to transform the agricultural production process and the genetically-engineered plants (like the traditional varieties) are most easily accessible to the farmers, both small and large.

Microelectronics-based technologies can perform a number of functions in production and in management, accounting and marketing. In direct productive processes the use of these technologies is mainly of the following types: control of movement of new materials, component parts, finished

Table 2.4 New technology applications in agriculture and rural development

Technology/ sector and applications	*Examples*
MICROELECTRONICS	
A. *Agriculture*	
project planning	Project planning control, data
farm management and data collection	collection, research in
crop planning	Portugal
cultivation and harvesting	use of microcomputers for
	fiscal management and
	budgeting in Kenya
livestock monitoring and management	computer-aided agricultural
evaluation of soil moisture conditions,	planning for rubber
plant temperature and moisture stress	smallholders in Malaysia
irrigation and water control	
agricultural statistics and modelling in	
research laboratories	
B. *Rural development*	
electronic load controllers for micro-	community-owned saw mill in
hydroelectric power generation	Colombia
processing of data from rural surveys	drying of tea leaves in
family planning and rural health care	Sri Lanka
rural education	power irrigation in Thailand
NEW BIOTECHNOLOGIES	
food production	use of rhizobial inoculant in Brazil
improved strains for biological	symbiotic nitrogen fixation in
nitrogen fixing	China, Egypt and India
food preservation	
single cell protein (SCP)	SCP production in Cuba and
as supplement	Mexico based on cane
to animal feed	molasses
pest and disease resistance	production and use of bio-
production of fertilizer from improved	pesticides in Brazil and the
biomass processes	Philippines
genetically engineered microbes	
improvements in quantity and quality of	experimental project on BHG
livestock through bovine hormone	in Mexican dairy industry
growth (BHG)	

Table 2.4   *Continued*

Technology/ sector and applications	Examples

TELECOMMUNICATIONS

meteorological data provision
weather forecasting
warnings about disasters like floods
provision of information on food prices,
   cropping patterns and agricultural
   innovations
distance learning through
   satellites computer-based conference
   systems, quality and diversity of rural
   education can be improved by
   offering courses previously available
   only in urban areas
monitoring delivery of drugs and medical
   diagnostics

use of telephone in Sri Lanka
   by small farmers to obtain
   crop prices

use of ATS-1 satellite for tele-
   conferencing by University
   of South Pacific (Fiji)
use of PEACESAT satellite net
   to summon medical teams
   (South Pacific)

REMOTE SENSING

land and water resources and soil surveys
forestry and wildlife
fisheries (coastal, inland and marine fisheries)
pasture and rangeland development
natural disasters
monitoring and anticipation
weather forecasting
forecasting of crop production
pest control
geological resource exploration
determination of areas of urban and rural
   settlements

hydro-geological investigation
   in Niger

rice production forecasting in
   Mali and Guinea
locust control in Africa

NEW ENERGY TECHNOLOGIES (PHOTOVOLTAICS)

water pumping for irrigation
village water supply (for human beings
   and cattle)

street lighting
household lighting

powering refrigerators for rural health care
radio telephones for rural telecommunications,
TV receivers for rural educational programmes

water pumping for agriculture
   in Bangladesh, India, China,
   Philippines, Kenya, Egypt
Water pumping for village water
   supply in Zaire, Burkina Faso,
   Uganda, Sudan, Zimbabwe
rural lighting in India, Fiji,
   Thailand, Zaire, Republic of
   Korea

product, etc.; shaping, designing, cutting, mixing and moulding of materials; assembly of components into sub-assemblies and finished products; product quality control through inspection, testing and analysis; design, manufacture and maintenance operations (see Bessant et al., 1981, p. 199). In the case of management functions a number of computer applications have been noted in: stock-keeping, inventory control; allocation of tasks and ordering and handling of materials; cost accounting and invoicing and other financial data collection; and job control and personnel data collection (see Bhalla et al., 1984; Bhalla and D. James, 1988).

In general, there seems to be greater immediate scope for the application of microelectronics and other devices in management, materials-handling and marketing functions, than in manufacturing proper. Examples of the Prato textile industry in Italy described in Chapter 4 show that the use of computers is much more noticeable in marketing, banking, information exchange, etc. than in the fabrication of textiles or shop-floor monitoring and work-scheduling. This may be explained by a number of factors. First, small firms based partly on the use of household labour are likely to have only a limited demand for computer use for shop-floor monitoring which would be much more economical at larger scales of centralized production. Secondly, tighter and more detailed control at the shop-floor level requires the adaptation of broad management systems and software packages to the specific requirements of firms. Higher development and utilization costs are likely to result from such adaptations. The experience of developing countries such as China is somewhat similar. Computer applications have been reported in the management of finished products in the Shanghai (No.1) Printing and Dyeing Mill. Prior to these applications, manual methods resulted in an unnecessarily high stock-piling, and a high wastage rate (Bhalla, 1990). This is partly because manufacturing requires greater skills in the handling of microelectronic technology than non-manufacturing activities. The management applications are less likely to displace jobs and more likely to raise efficiency through waste reduction, faster deliveries, and so on.

Advanced biotechnologies*

The new biotechnologies offer good potential for poverty alleviation in developing countries. First, these technologies can reduce farmers' production costs by eliminating their dependence on agro-chemical inputs

---

*This section was written with the very valuable assistance of my colleague, Regina Galhardi.

which were associated with the Green Revolution. Thus, besides being pro-poor, they are also environment-friendly. Secondly the potential of the technologies for raising agricultural production should help reduce food prices and thus offer significant benefits to the poor landless workers and urban consumers. Thirdly, the new biotechnologies can increase food availability, especially in sub-Saharan Africa, but also elsewhere (Ahmed, 1992). Increased food availability should reduce malnutrition which is so widely prevalent in developing countries. Finally, the fact that new biotechnologies facilitate decentralized production should in principle help reduce income and social inequalities. Whether this happens in practice will depend on the existing pattern of income and asset distribution as well as social and political relations.

The vast majority of traditional technologies are located in the rural sector of developing countries. Because several of the new bio-technologies have applications in this sector, they offer considerable scope for the integration of HYV technologies with the new innovations which can accelerate the development of renewable agricultural resources available within the developing countries. For example, the benefits of the Green Revolution in many parts of the Third World could not be fully tapped for lack of adequate fertilizers and irrigation inputs.

Recombinant DNA techniques such as gene splicing could offer new ways to provide varieties of plants and crops that can make their own fertilizers or fix their own nitrogen. Moreover, genetically-engineered plants and crop varieties, that are adapted to low levels of fertility and to saline conditions, may be suitable for areas of marginal land for which the conventional HYVs are not appropriate.

Besides these potential revolutionary achievements, natural nitrogen-fixing bacteria would minimize the need for costly petroleum-based chemical fertilizers. The poor farmers who at present have no access to the expensive fertilizers could hope to realize crop yield increases. Biological control of pests, weeds and diseases can also benefit small producers in developing countries by reducing production costs through the replacement of agro-chemicals by biopesticides.

Evidence from China reveals that gains in yield and incomes through the use of biofertilizers in a wide range of crops have been remarkable. Increases were reported in yield of 10 to 30 per cent in the production of rice, wheat and corn. In the specific case of wheat, an increase in yield of 76.2 million kg resulted in revenue increasing by 15.7 yuan per 1 yuan investment in biofertilizers (Yuanliang, 1989).

In the case of beans production, the Brazilian experience shows that doubling the average yield requires 40 kg of chemical nitrogen and 80 kg of phosphorus per hectare. This level of productivity, however, can be attained by the adoption of new varieties inoculated with biological fertilizers. According to the Brazilian Agricultural Research Enterprise (EMBRAPA) the replacement of chemical fertilizers by biological ones in only 10 per cent of the area cultivated with beans (about 4 million hectares) will result in savings of 60US$/ha, which corresponds to about 24 million dollars annually. As far as soybeans are concerned, the nitrogen biological fixation by selected inoculant has enabled the total substitution of chemical nitrogen fertilizers in Brazil. The saving from this substitution was estimated at about US$500 million per year.

Besides the reduction of costs, an increased demand for labour should occur due to enhanced soil fertility through the surplus of nitrogen that remains in the ground after harvest and, by implication, an increase in production yields. Small farmers may improve their incomes in Thailand by about 17 to 42 per cent through the adoption of this biotechnological process (Galhardi, 1993). Remarkable savings were also achieved through the use of biological control. A major Brazilian problem on soybean plantation has been a caterpillar responsible for as much as 40 per cent of losses due to insects. In 1972, a virus was isolated by one of the EMBRAPA regional laboratories. In 1983–4 the virus was successfully applied in more than 11 000 hectares (this area was increased to 300 000 in 1984–5) of the states of Parana and Rio Grande do Sul, and the cost of protection in soybean cultures of these states was reduced by 75 per cent in relation to the traditional chemical control. By 1985, 12 cooperative schemes had been created for the commercial production and diffusion of the virus (Bifani, 1992).

The prospects of single cell protein (SCP) production are bright for developing-country suppliers of alternative raw materials, especially considering that the SCP has a higher protein content than soybean meal and is rich in vitamins. Cuba has already established 13 plants for the SCP production based on a by-product of the sugar industry (molasses).

Advanced biotechnologies such as genetic engineering and cell fusion are also promising for developing countries. They are expected to improve the existing techniques as well as to make other techniques available. But, as the above evidence suggests, it is the blending of new and old biotechnologies that will allow the accomplishment of this potential. It is the new ways of tackling old problems, through the application of biotechnologies ranging from the long-established commercial use of microbes and other living organisms to advances in genetic engineering of plants and animals, that may affect the current stage of rural development in the Third World.

Yet this potential is unlikely to be exploited fully in the near future. For one thing, much of the biotechnological research in the industrialized countries is confined to the pharmaceutical and other industrial sectors. It is understandable that these countries devote little R&D on biotechnology for agriculture and rural development. The problem there is not of food shortage, but generally of surpluses. Thanks to support by public action (e.g. agricultural subsidies) the agricultural sectors of the industrialized countries produce foods in quantities which are in excess of domestic consumption. In contrast, most developing countries continue to suffer from food shortages. Even some advanced developing countries are facing severe production constraints due to inadequate support given to cash and food crops. In Mexico, for instance, incentives to produce cash crops and price control on food crops transformed the country from an exporter of basic grains to a net importer in the mid-seventies.

The prospect of biotechnology applications to cash crops is especially relevant for those countries which are excessively dependent on export earnings from one or two commodities. The biotechnological improvement of oil palm production is an example of how biotechnology research addressed to the cash crops of developing countries can also help rural development. In the case of Malaysia, for instance, a new biotechnological method, for cloning high-yielding palms developed by Unilever, may increase yields by 30 per cent. On the one hand, this could help the country to maintain its position as the principal exporter of palm oil. On the other hand, the resulting over-production may not benefit Malaysian producers because the surpluses will depress international prices. It seems, however, that biotechnology still offers an alternative for the farmers who might be affected by mass-production of clonal palm oil. With advancement in biotechnology (new enzymatic methods of oil extracting), low-cost oils such as palm oil can be transformed into high-quality oils, similar to cocoa butter, for instance. Several private companies in the industrialized countries are pursuing this objective. If a process to synthesize high-value oils using biotechnology is commercially successful, the worldwide suppliers of palm oil would undoubtedly supply a large share of the expensive real cocoa butter market. This of course would have a negative impact on the developing countries such as Ghana and the Philippines which export cocoa and coconut oils.

In animal husbandry also, new biotechnologies like genetic engineering hold out much promise. The development of animal vaccines and antibiotics permit some control over animal disease, and the supply of bovine growth hormones (BHG) helps raise the yield of milk. In most developing countries the demand for milk generally exceeds the supply.

Therefore, an increase in the yield of milk can be an important factor in raising the nutritional levels of the population. In Mexico, it was estimated that the BST technology could reduce the daily deficit of 12.5 million litres of milk and make it more accessible to the whole population (37 per cent of the population currently consumes only 14.5 per cent of the available milk supply). On average, it may increase milk production by 25 per cent. This is like having extra milk without extra feed. It is estimated that the Mexican dairy industry might be able substantially to increase milk supply locally and, therefore, to reduce the drainage of foreign exchange through imports of dairy products (Otero, 1992).

Furthermore, single cell protein (SCP) production makes possible the improvement of animal feed. Through applications of new biotechnologies, the so-called 'fermentation industry' has been able to utilize agricultural waste materials to produce alcohols, organic acids, vitamins, vaccines and fodder SCP. By using the SCP instead of grain in animal feed vast amounts of grains and legumes, hitherto consumed by animals, can be released. Production of animal protein can be raised and demand for expensive proteins like soybeans and fish meal for livestock can be reduced. It is estimated that 'one SCP plant making 100 000 tons per year can produce about as much protein as that which could be extracted from 120 000 hectares (300 000 acres) of soybeans, or as much beef (cattle) as could be grown on 2 million hectares (5 million acres) of grazing land' (Héden, 1979). Many SCP plants are in operation in the former Soviet Union and Cuba which suffered from a shortage of animal feed.

So far we have considered new technologies in isolation. Comparing biotechnology with microelectronics, one finds that its characteristics may be quite different. For example, the biotechnologies for agricultural crops and plants are likely to be crop and location specific – they would be conditioned by the climatic, ecological, biological and genetic diversity of each region or location. Although the basic biotechnology characteristics are the same, local adaptations may be required. This imposes constraints on the transfer of ready-made biotechnology packages. Local adaptations should be conducive to building local technological capacity. In contrast, the development of microchips is not constrained by such diversity. The microelectronics-based technology is much more universally applicable, its applications being conditioned mainly by the availability of regular supplies of power/electricity, skills, and repair and maintenance facilities. The two sets of new technologies are also divergent in terms of their impact. The direct employment impact of microelectronics technology (unskilled labour-saving bias) may not necessarily be similar to that of the advanced biotechnologies (see Chapter 6). Further, even though the new information technology is at present more advanced in its development and diffusion than the new biotechnologies, the latter is likely to be far more important in its impact on agriculture and rural development.

THE ADOPTION OF NEW TECHNOLOGIES: DIFFUSION AND CONSTRAINTS

Diffusion

A whole constellation of reasons explains the lag between the availability and general adoption of new technologies. Differences in factor prices will frequently dictate in favour of using earlier vintages of technology in developing countries (see below and Chapter 6). Imperfect capital markets obviate the use of new technology by many enterprises facing severe financial constraints. Often it is not feasible to reach a minimum threshold of scale of operations, below which new technologies do not pay. New technologies are accompanied by risks and uncertainty, including the unpredictability of the pace of technological obsolescence, which potential adopters sometimes find too daunting. Perceived transactions costs in learning about alternative technologies, screening alternative sources, and bargaining for new technologies may discourage some entrepreneurs. Similarly, the real or imagined costs of reorganizing production and managerial procedures associated with these technologies may appear excessive. Aside from these 'rational' economic conditions, introduction of the latest methods can be slowed by vested interests threatened by change, X-inefficiency, bounded rationality, or a high 'attention threshold' below which the firm will not act (Leibenstein, 1966; Simon, 1959; Schwartz, 1987.) This does not exhaust the explanations of why some firms stick with tried-and-true production techniques. The point is, however, that these conditions are likely to be more pronounced in developing countries.

A rough but imaginative exercise by Watanabe (1987) was designed to discover indicators for the rates of diffusion of microelectronics innovations. He compared the rate of diffusion with (a) a *demand* factor – GNP per capita, and the share of urban population and self-employed in the total economically active population (self-employed served as a proxy for the 'informal sector', which is assumed to have poor access to information); (b) a *demand-cum-absorption capacity* factor – share of metal engineering in total industrial employment; and (c) an *absorption capacity* factor – higher education enrolment as a proportion of population in the 20–24 age group. He found that the level of GNP per capita was a rather poor indicator of the diffusion potential of information technology. On the other hand, although there was considerable variation among developing countries at different income levels, the share of metal-engineering industry and higher education enrolment rates seemed to be more important variables.

Kaplinsky (1987) found that, as would be expected, major adoption, replication, and diffusion of microelectronics technology has so far taken place in the industrial sectors of both developed and developing countries. Diffusion in agriculture is either very limited or poorly documented. In the tertiary sector, banking and telecommunications account for the most rapid rates of adoption and diffusion, a tendency that holds for both industrialized and developing countries. In fact, the rate of growth of telecommunications in developing countries is similar to, or at times even higher than, that in the developed countries. This is explained partly by the fact that the sector has formerly been backward in developing countries, and the new technology adoption/diffusion does not involve much scrapping of old infrastructure. Secondly, the new technology (especially microwave and satellite technology) has reduced installation costs considerably, thus rendering it much cheaper to install in rural areas than the older cabling system.

Some generalities emerge from the literature. First, we find new technology diffusion primarily in a limited number of cutting-edge industries. Second, this localized pattern of diffusion does not yield the full productivity gains that are potentially available from the new technology (Freeman, 1987). Third, and particularly in the case of developing countries, the adoption of new technology has occurred more rapidly in routine administrative activities in government, public enterprises, banks, airlines, and railways than in production planning and control in industry. This has been shown for India where the transport sector (Indian railways, Indian airlines, and Air India) have introduced microelectronics-based information technology much more than has manufacturing industry (Khan, 1987). This may be due partly to the lower-level skills that the former sector requires for the application of new technologies.

We need to begin to learn more about which technologies, under what conditions, will encourage cumulative technical change either directly, through recombination with other technologies and application to new uses, or indirectly, through higher incomes and exposure to new technologies that create cultural and social conditions more conducive to innovation.

Constraints

A few specific factors, namely, product quality, skill requirements, requirements of infrastructure (including software), factor costs and market size, and information gaps, which may explain the limited adoption of new technologies in developing countries, are discussed below.

Product quality considerations

Though quality improvement may also seem to be a facilitating factor in the adoption of the new technology in the context of developing countries, the issue is more complex because the improvements in quality that are desired in high-income countries may not be those that the majority of those living in relatively poor societies would favour. The issue of quality considerations is further complicated by the increasing globalization of competition, which tends to impose uniform quality standards regardless of income differences across countries.

The problem is illustrated in the oversimplified form of Figure 2.1. In the initial situation, denoted by point 1, only the 'old' good exists and this

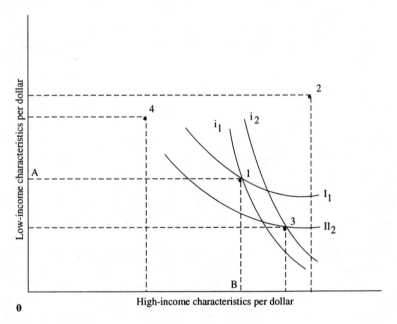

Figure 2.1   Product quality characteristics by income

allows consumers to obtain OA of 'low-income characteristics' per dollar and OB of 'high-income' characteristics. As a result of the new technology, the characteristics available per dollar will change. One case, represented by point 2, is where the new technology allows more of both characteristics per dollar than the previous technology. Here, of course, there will be no constraints on the diffusion of the new products even in low-income markets. Case 3, however, shows a situation in which the new product is preferred by those in rich countries but not by the majority of consumers in the low-income societies (who prefer point 4 to point 3 because it embodies a higher proportion of low-income characteristics).

This point is well-illustrated in Mytelka's study (1981) of technology choice among textile firms in Côte d'Ivoire. She concludes that

> to a large extent, the choice of technique in export-manufacturing is a function of international standards set for a given product – denim – in the case of COTIVO, polyester shirt fabric in the case of Gronfrevile .... *A far lower standard is acceptable on goods traded locally.* To meet that standard, less sophisticated production techniques are required. A wider choice of technique is thus available and the techniques tend to be more labour-intensive and less costly to purchase. The choice of more sophisticated techniques, moreover, increases the need for expatriate managers, reduces the learning effects and increases the water bill thereby raising the cost of production. (Mytelka, 1981, p. 78: emphasis added)

In one interesting example cited by Mytelka (1981), an Ivorian textile firm chose printing machinery that was more closely adapted to local (and other African) markets than those in Europe. What this meant was a process which did not stabilize the cloth nor sanforise it up to the levels that would be required for exports to Europe. As a result, costs were able to be held down.

Undoubtedly, some of the improvements in the quality of textiles and garments that are associated with microelectronics will be of type 2 in Figure 2.1, but there will also be many which are more like type 3 and which, in the absence of export markets to absorb this type of quality change, will impose a constraint on the adoption of the new technology in developing countries. (Sometimes even high-income *export* markets require the type of finishing quality that is only possible 'by hand'.) Côte d'Ivoire stands as a warning in this respect, for it was found that new technologies in the textile and wood industries, which were originally oriented to export markets, became too costly for domestic production when firms were forced, through changed circumstances, to reorient production to the local market.

Skill requirements

The adoption of new technologies imposes stringent requirements for additional and new types of skills at different levels. First, the demand for new types of sophisticated skills, for example, in programming and repair and maintenance, will need to be met. Second, many of the traditional types of skills and occupations which become obsolete will require readaptation and retraining for alternative employment. Third, for a strategy of blending (see Chapter 3) to work, the latest technical skills will need to be imparted to illiterate and semi-educated producers in rural and urban informal sectors through demonstration projects. Fourth, planners and policymakers will need to be sensitized to the potentials of new technologies for their application and integration with traditional production modes.

Skill requirements and occupational composition can change drastically as a result of the application of new technologies which generally demand greater skills of programming, control and logic, and much less of traditional craftsmen's experience and manual skill. Although there is no clear perception yet of the precise nature and kinds of skills that would be required to operate 'factories of the future', some indication can be given of the new types of emerging skills. For example, in engineering and maintenance fields, new skills and knowledge of new technologies involving logic, calculation and control function and dexterity to diagnose faults would be increasingly required. Microelectronics control systems and control room operation remote from production call for a total systems approach which is bound to involve changes in skill content for such occupations as operators, technicians and supervisors.

However, one redeeming feature particularly for the developing countries is the possibility that in some cases new technologies may perform the functions of skilled labour in short supply and thus be skill saving. Watanabe (1993) notes that it takes a much shorter time to train operators of FA (flexible automation) machinery than those of conventional machinery. He gives examples of saving of skills by the NC-wire-cutting machine which can be programmed by a college student after a few days of on-the-job training (p. 160). In this context a distinction between the use of new technology in producer goods or consumer goods production may be relevant. As Wood (1994) has noted many of the new consumer goods such as electronic toys and the assembly of CD players continue to require a high ratio of unskilled to skilled labour although some intermediate goods used in their production embody advanced technology. (p. 278). Furthermore, new technology displaces not only unskilled manual workers, but also many skilled occupations 'including a range of white-collar jobs, both technical (draughtsmen) and professional' (Wood, 1994, p. 279). The demand for some skilled occupations may also decrease because their productivity increased as a result of the application of new technology.

Requirements for retraining and adaptation of skills arise due to the process of deskilling or disappearance of traditional occupations (e.g. watchmaking) which is set in motion by the introduction of new technologies. Robots which replace both manual and intelligent human tasks are likely to lead to a general decline in education/training requirements. However, the question of deskilling is a complex one and the degree of deskilling will vary depending on the nature of industry and the extent and pace of new technology applications in it. For example, for food and drink industries, examples were found of both deskilling and skill enrichment for workers within the same process line but in different skill groups: the use of computer-controlled dough-mixing replaced the craft skills of the doughman whereas the computerized biscuit packet weighing complemented the skills and knowledge of the ovensman by giving him more information on production performance and demanding of him judgement and discretion in the control of the process.

Hoffman and Rush (1988) show that the impact of microelectronics-related innovations (MRIs) has considerable impact on deskilling and training costs. Taking the case of the garments industry, they demonstrate that the use of microelectronic equipment in an operation led to a saving of several months of training. Training times were reduced by between 10 and 90 per cent, thus leading to considerable saving in the costs of training, which was a principal factor motivating the firms interviewed to invest in the new equipment.

Exploitation of the potential of new technology to improve traditional technology and production would make it necessary to train small producers in the basics of the new technologies and the relevance of their use for enhancing their productivity and incomes. One of the difficulties is that most small producers in the Third World are unfamiliar with the potentials of new technologies like microprocessors, biotechnology and genetic engineering. It is therefore desirable that basic information on these technologies and the role of the small producers in utilizing them be imparted through what has been called the technique of 'training-by-doing'. It involves the launching of demonstration projects where trainees can observe diverse options that scientific research and new technologies can present. For example, it is noted that the utilization of rice biomass can offer good opportunities for income generation and training-by-doing for farmers in developing countries. The International Rice Research Institute (IRRI) and the University of the Philippines at Los Baños have established a demonstration-cum-training farm 'not only to educate students and farmers in the Philippines but also to impart training on optimization of rice yield and rice biomass to the staff of irrigation and other projects in areas having rice as a major component of the cropping system' (Swaminathan, 1983 p. 197).

Apart from the above micro-type training, an important element would be to sensitize and educate top planners and policymakers in the potentials of the new technology, their limitations and the prerequisites for their efficient adoption in the Third World. Our experience shows that the policymakers in developing countries are either totally ignorant about the scope for integrating new technologies with traditional production systems or are fully enamoured of these latest developments and their use without understanding the cost or the infrastructural requirements involved. One way of orienting the policymakers towards the new technology culture is to organize new technology clubs, not only for factory workers but also for senior policymakers. These clubs could use specially designed kits and home computers for general training and sensitization.

Infrastructure requirements

As we examine in Chapter 3, the highly skewed distribution of the benefits of the Green Revolution was due in large measure to the dependence of the HYV technology on a wide range of complementary inputs and infrastructure. Much the same problem besets the new microelectronics technologies. Microelectronics has much in common with the hybrid varieties of the Green Revolution in the sense that it is highly dependent on costly complementary inputs such as sensors, software and peripherals.

Microelectronics applications call for regular supplies of electricity and an even quality of raw materials like steel. Furthermore, skilled manpower with 'thinking capacity' and flexible education is required. These prerequisites are often missing in many developing countries. The Japanese experience shows that the successful use of computer numerically controlled (CNC) machines by small enterprises was due largely to the easy access to machine suppliers' advice and services, reliable supplies of electricity and materials, and the education and practical experience of workers with conventional machines which enabled them to master CNC programming and maintenance quite quickly.

In relation to computer-aided design (CAD) systems, users may require a great deal of back-up support with respect to software services from suppliers until the systems are able to function efficiently (especially when such equipment is unfamiliar to the user) (Kaplinsky, 1982). It is perhaps for this reason among others that the diffusion of computer-aided design and computer-aided manufacturing system (CAD/CAM) in developing countries is more limited than the numerically controlled machine tools (NCMTs). The NCMTs in developing countries started being used in the 1970s but their use gained momentum only after 1980. The bulk of the NMCTs is imported by the developing countries from suppliers in Germany, Japan and the United States. These imports have been concentrated mainly in a few NICs and Indonesia, Thailand and the Philippines. (Watanabe, 1993). As domestic production of new technology within developing countries expands (at present it is limited to three or four such countries) their diffusion is likely to spread more widely and rapidly.

Factor costs and market size

High capital costs have constrained the diffusion of the new technologies to smaller firms in the developed countries and in the Third World, where average firm size in industry is generally much lower, this constraint may be even more pronounced and the pattern of diffusion (and concentration) consequently even more skewed (for more details, see Chapter 4). Moreover, among developing-country firms of an equivalent size to those in developed countries that have been able to afford the new technologies, there will almost certainly be differences in rates of diffusion on account of differences in factor costs.

A number of studies on developing countries show that the price of new capital equipment constrained the diffusion of new technologies. For example, in a study of microelectronic industrial machinery in Malaysia and Singapore (Fong, 1989) the high cost of equipment was cited more than twice as frequently as any other perceived constraint on adoption. Similarly, in a study of the diffusion of CNC machine tools in the Brazilian automobile industry, the high cost of this technology was cited by the firms as the major constraint on adoption (Tauile, 1987).

As in the case of new products described in Figure 2.1 above, the new techniques may in some cases entirely dominate the old, that is, when they are more profitable at *all* relevant factor price ratios. But in other cases the new techniques will be profitable at the factor prices prevailing in the rich countries but not necessarily those in the poor, considering that many of the new techniques in garments and textiles are labour-saving and that the ratio of the difference in labour-costs between the rich and poor countries can be as much as 18:1 (for details see ILO, 1980, p. 109). The differential between the United States and the Republic of Korea is 10:1 even after allowing for efficiency differences (see Hoffman and Rush, 1982,). Evidence for the weaving industry, for example, indicates that 'research on improving production has not led to equipment that dictates the disregard of older methods of production in the developing countries. Indeed, the newer equipment is (privately) profitable only at wages considerably higher than market wages in the richer Latin American countries' (Pack, 1982, p. 27).

For the above reason, among others, the pace of new technology diffusion in the developing countries has been slower than was originally expected. But the cost of many microelectronics-based innovations such as CAD has been declining quite rapidly in recent years. This suggests that in future these innovations may be efficient and profitable even at the relative factor prices prevailing in developing countries (James, 1993).

Although the cost of many technologies is going down, at least for many developing countries it may still be high relative to the national per capita income and the availability of foreign exchange. The new technology hardware will remain rather too sophisticated for efficient and full use so long as the infrastructure, software and skill requirements are not met in these countries. Experience has shown that even though the use of new technology such as microelectronics may be capital-saving, the infrastructure (e.g. the telecommunications network) needed for its successful application, is highly capital intensive. In the case of biotechnology, Fransman (1991) notes the possibility that the upscaling of some biotechnological processes (e.g. fermentation) will raise barriers to the entry of developing countries in this field. He also notes that in some cases 'greater scale may not result in cost advantages' (p. 57).

Information gaps

Most empirical studies suggest that information is available for only a limited portion of the range of available techniques. From the standpoint of small-scale enterprises and in relation to new technologies, imperfect information is likely to present a particularly acute problem in terms of availability and the cost of search. In part, this is a question of demand for information and in particular, the varying extent to which industrial firms of different size find it profitable to search for information about new technologies. In the context of agricultural innovations, an argument along these lines has been used to account for the tendency for larger farms to adopt new technologies earlier than small farms, even when the innovations themselves are scale neutral (Feder, Just, Zilberman, 1985). Specifically, the argument is that larger farms have more of an incentive to search for innovations than small farms because the expected (absolute) gains to the former are greater. Similar reasoning may help to account for the tendency of many of the new microelectronics techniques to be adopted mainly by relatively large-scale industrial firms in developing countries.

Another explanation of this tendency, however, has to do with the supply of, rather than the demand for, information about the new technologies. What Edquist and Jacobsson (1988) emphasize in their study of the engineering industry in the NICs is that what (little) information is supplied to firms in these countries tends mainly to reach relatively large-scale enterprises with some kind of connection (e.g. through licensing) to foreign firms. It appears to be largely through such connections that information about new technologies is transmitted. For other medium- and small-scale firms, the problem is often that 'local suppliers do not exist and distributors of foreign-made machines may not be represented in the country. If they are, they may very well not put a great deal of emphasis on marketing etc.' (Edquist and Jacobsson, 1988). This problem, one might add, is likely to be especially pronounced in the least developed countries.

CONCLUSION

In this chapter we attempted to determine whether the new technologies were a myth or reality for developing countries. Our conclusion is that these technologies are being applied in many developing countries. However, at present all developing countries cannot take full advantage of them. A precondition for the successful use of these technologies is a minimum of technological capabilities which do not at present exist in many least developed countries.

New technologies will tend to find easiest application in the more affluent of the developing countries with domestic capabilities and substantial domestic and export markets. It is also likely that these technologies will in the near future be concentrated among firms that are large relative to the size of the economy and which most closely approximate medium- to large-scale firms in industrialized countries in terms of organization of work, management, etc. However, alternative models of industrial organization, such as that adopted in the Prato textile industry in Italy, seem to offer the potential for greatly enlarging the scope of new technology applications to traditional small producers in developing countries (see Chapters 3 and 4).

3 Technology Blending: Concept and Practice*

The concept of technology blending, to which we alluded earlier, originated from the growing recognition that the benefits of modern science and technology in the developing countries have not trickled down to the rural and the urban poor. In most of these countries, notwithstanding the development and availability of new and advanced technologies, age-old low-productivity techniques continue to be used. Can the application of new technologies to traditional activities in these countries – that is, the blending of new and traditional technologies – lead to a process of gradual modernization rather than of displacement? (Bhalla et al., 1984a; Bhalla and D. James, 1988, 1991). An answer to this question is the objective of this chapter.

Admittedly, in the process of technical change, at any given time, new and old technologies coexist. In this sense, there is nothing new – retrofitting at a micro-firm level takes place all the time. The novelty of the concept of technology blending lies instead in focusing on the application of new technologies to small-scale low-income activities, for meeting the basic needs of the bulk of the Third World's population. This chapter is concerned with the approach and analytical content as well as application of the concept in developing countries.

THE CONCEPT

Technology blending is defined as a *process* and a *development* strategy under which new technologies (e.g. microelectronics, biotechnologies, telecommunications, and new materials technology) are selectively

---

*This chapter is based on my several writings, most notably, 'An Approach Towards Integration of Emerging and Traditional Technologies' (with J. James) in Ernst von Weizsäcker, M.S. Swaminathan and Aklilu Lemma (eds), *New Frontiers in Technology Application* (Dublin: Tycooly, 1983); 'New Technology Revolution: Myth or Reality for Developing Countries?' (with J. James), *Greek Economic Review*, Vol. 6, No.3, Dec. 1984; *New Technologies and Development* (edited by A.S. Bhalla and D.D. James), (Boulder: Lynne Rienner, 1988), Chapter 2; and 'New Technologies, Rural Development and Employment' in Mohinder Singh et al. (eds) *Proceedings of the Third Asian Conference on Technology for Rural Development* (Asia Tech 1991) Kuala Lumpur, August 12–14 1991.

introduced in traditional economic activities of small farmers, craftsmen and manufacturers to ensure an increase in their productivity and incomes.

The process of technology blending can be interpreted in two distinct ways:

(a) *Coexistence* of new and traditional or old technologies in a given area and economic activity (there may be no resulting change in the character of traditional technologies);

(b) *Blending* of the two which leads to an improvement of traditional technologies, in terms of (i) cost per unit, (ii) productivity per unit of factor input, and (iii) quantity and quality of output.

In addition to these cases, there is also a real situation of disintegration, which may be defined as the displacement of traditional technologies by the new technologies over time. The historical experience of today's developed countries shows that as a result of rapid technological progress blacksmiths, carpenters and similar other craftsmen have gradually disappeared in the face of competition from modern cost-reducing technology. In fact, one of the objectives of development has been to transfer labour and capital out of agriculture into industry and services, which are the major driving forces of economic progress. Yet this model of development has not so far worked in many developing countries, where the rural sector continues to account for a substantial proportion of output and labour (Bhalla, 1992a). Traditional technologies and economic activities continue to exist side by side with modern technologies and products. This technological dualism is due partly to the fact that modern science and technology have either not been applied to improve traditional technologies (even when it is technically feasible) or the efforts made have been too inadequate to bring about the desired results.

Blending could be defined most meaningfully in terms of a fusion of traditional and emerging technologies into a new entity. However, even this type of blending can take a wide variety of forms depending upon the weighting of the two types of technologies in the fusion process. At the one extreme, the new entity will embody almost entirely the characteristics of the traditional technology and at the other, it will reflect mainly the elements of the new technology.

Institutional blending

Technology blending, to be successful, cannot consider only technological fusion. So far we have considered the hardware aspects of technology. However, there are circumstances when it is institutions rather than technologies that need to be adapted. Apart from improvements in available technologies and the development of new ones, new institutional blends, or what Brown (1986) calls 'partnerships', may be necessary. The roles of governmental and non-governmental organizations (NGOs), as well as the private sector, may need to be redefined, and new institutional structures developed to ensure a market for technology blends. As we shall discuss below, for some of these blends to be economically viable, a cooperative or cluster form of organization may be more suited instead of private ownership. This is particularly true in the case of public goods and services.

Different institutions perform different functions: markets to allocate factors and products, government agencies to promote favourable policy environments, the private sector to promote entrepreneurship and marketing, and grass-roots NGOs to provide delivery of goods and services, etc. A systemic approach to technology blending requires that the contribution of different institutions is harmonized and an adequate organizational framework provided. Technological innovations need to go hand in hand with social innovations – marketing, training, education, social and cultural adaptability and consumer acceptance. All these are essential prerequisites for successful blending. As noted below, the past experience of the Green Revolution offers lessons in this direction.

There are pros and cons of different types of institutional blends. As Brown (1986) has noted, the NGOs might act as 'catalysts, partners, or implementors of development partnerships, or some combination of all three'. However, their success in performing these roles can also create conflict situations and 'generate backlash from wealthy or powerful groups who prefer the previous status quo, or pressure from the newly empowered groups themselves'. Probably the main problem that has to be confronted here is of a socio-political kind. When incomes and assets are unequally distributed, emphasis on rural self-help and grass-roots participation may lead to the control of local organizations by the rural political élite, resulting in a disproportionate allocation of the scarce development resources in their favour (Lele, 1981). The failure of the Ujamaa village scheme in Tanzania and the *Panchayats* in India can be explained, at least partly, in these terms. And the more unequal the ownership of land, the more likely it is that rural cooperatives will be dominated or subverted by the élite groups. Consequently, if traditional producers are to be effectively served through cooperative organizations in such situations, a redistribution of land and political power in their favour may seem to be an essential prerequisite. However, the political feasibility of such measures is itself constrained if the government institutions themselves represent the vested interests of the élite. It is significant to note however that Taiwan (China) and the Republic of Korea succeeded in implementing a policy of radical equalization of rights in land through distributive reform. And rural credit was successfully provided to the small rural producers as a follow-up to these reforms (Lipton, 1981).

Land reform is likely to constitute a necessary condition for rural cooperatives to reach the poor, but it is certainly not a sufficient condition. For what is also essential is the adequate provision to these institutions of inputs, management, know-how, infrastructure, etc. These kinds of factors 'receive relatively little emphasis in cooperative development, in comparison with a rather amorphous and misdirected concept of existing grassroot organizations and of their potential for promoting participation and democracy' (Lele, 1981).

Most of the NGOs mentioned above tend to be involved in local relief or development projects. They tend not to be well endowed with managerial and commercial skills. It would therefore be necessary to supplement the efforts of the NGOs with the managerial skills of the private entrepreneurs and institutions to develop and market commercially viable technology blends.

In countries such as the Philippines, rental markets appear to be very highly developed, as evidenced by the fact that 'harvesting and threshing equipment, tractors, and motor vehicles, are used on about five to seven times as many farms as those who own them'. (Binswanger, 1982; Binswanger, Pingali and Bigot, 1987). In an analogous manner, institutions such as service bureaus could play an equally important role in the adoption and diffusion of some of the new microelectronics-based technologies, such as computer-aided design (CAD). Existing service bureaus in the garment industries of a number of developed countries (Sweden, Japan, United States) and developing economies (Hong Kong, Singapore) offer one specific institutional model that may be relevant in the future when expanding markets and globalization of production and trade might make it particularly suitable. What these service bureaus offer is microelectronics-based equipment which performs all functions up to marker making on behalf of garment producers, thereby reducing their investment, maintenance and managerial costs (Tulsi, 1985). All that the manufacturers have to do is to supply the bureau with a sketch of the garment to be produced. The case of Borås in Sweden (a district with the highest concentration of garment producers) illustrates the functioning of the concept of the service bureau in actual practice. The Borås bureau services about 200 customers out of a total of 300 firms (in 1985). The ten bigger firms possessed their own pre-assembly equipment, which suggests that the bureau customers were mainly small firms who could not afford to instal this equipment.

Institutional innovations need not, however, be confined to one or another form of rental market. They may involve, in addition, a change in the *level* at which choice of technique decisions are made and more specifically a change from individual to communal patterns of ownership. The latter are in fact already prevalent in areas such as irrigation and sanitation, where adoption decisions necessarily involve the community as a whole. And the experience with these decisions (especially the pronounced problems that they have so frequently encountered) offers much that may be relevant to a 'communally-oriented' approach to the diffusion of microelectronics innovations among small-scale enterprises (including, as we note in Chapter 5, the flexible specialization approach). In any case, however, what is clear is that choice-of-technique decisions made at the community level cannot be understood in terms of the traditional choice of technology model, which generally presupposes the existence of a single decision-maker (Enos, 1985; James, 1985). Instead, an analytical framework is needed which, on the one hand, incorporates a variety of possible modes of individual interaction and which, on the other hand, makes it possible to understand how conflicts between individuals arise and ultimately get resolved.

Potential technology users

Four potential users of traditional and new technologies, and technology blends, are likely to be the most important, namely traditional agriculture and rural non-farm activities; rural cooperatives; clusters of artisanal workshops in the rural sector and urban small-scale producers (small-scale organized sector and urban informal activities); and large-scale industrial firms in the urban sector.

These four groups of users are distinguished by a number of criteria, namely, scale of production, social and economic organization and work patterns, modes of employment (self-employment or wage-labour), nature and quality of products, and market and income characteristics. The requirements for successful blending of traditional and new technologies are likely to vary in relation to each of the above four user groups. We discuss below these requirements for each group.

In the rural sector of developing countries the traditional farmers are clearly the dominant group. (It is necessary, however, to recognize that there are diverse groups of non-farm producers in the rural sector – such as cobblers, blacksmiths, carpenters and other craftsmen – whose traditional technologies are also often sorely in need of upgrading because they result in incomes that are very low.) The requirements for successful application in the case of traditional farmers (who comprise much of the Third World's agriculture) derive from their special socioeconomic characteristics. Most importantly, these farmers are usually very poor, often even in relation to average income in the developing country. Indeed, in some countries traditional producers in the rural areas comprise a relatively high percentage of those classified as living in poverty. In many, if not most cases, moreover, they are illiterate and produce mainly for subsistence needs rather than sale in the market. Finally, we need to mention the paucity of infrastructural facilities (such as irrigation, repair and maintenance, etc.) that are typically available to this kind of traditional farmer.

The importance of the above characteristics of peasant farmers is that they impose highly stringent requirements for successful blending of traditional and new technologies. First, the innovation must be close to the traditional practice in the sense that it must not demand cash outlays that are large relative to the farmer's highly limited resources. Secondly, the innovation must not impose a high degree of risk on the farmer. This is particularly true of subsistence farmers who earn only a limited amount of cash from market sales, and who are understandably reluctant to venture these resources for new techniques of production whose outcome is by no means certain and may even be hazardous. Thirdly, the new technique must be comprehensible to the peasant farmer. That is, it must not presuppose knowledge that he does not (and often cannot) possess and it must be recognized by him as 'do-able'. This condition is more likely to be satisfied the more closely the innovation fits in with the prevailing ecological system (e.g. the pattern of local resource use, waste collection, etc.). Finally, the new technique must not pre-suppose the existence of facilities – for power, transport, repair and maintenance and so on – that are simply not available to traditional producers.

So far we have been discussing only the *demand* side of the requirements of successful blending with respect to small farmers. But the special characteristics of peasant farming also pose requirements on the *supply* side. What is important to recognize here is that the mere supply of blended technologies is not sufficient – the fact of their existence and information about them also has to be communicated to the traditional producers. And the location of these farmers (who, as noted above, are frequently illiterate) in scattered and isolated rural localities often makes this a formidable problem.

A stringent set of requirements for the successful blending of traditional technologies in rural areas with the new technologies is based on the assumption that traditional producers are organized along essentially individualistic lines. One way in which the stringency of the requirements may be relaxed is the organization of production on a cooperative basis, which allows the resources of individual farmers and artisans to be pooled for the purposes of communal investment in productive equipment, inputs and infrastructural facilities. To this extent, it becomes possible to exploit some of the technologies which, from the standpoint of the individual producer, would be inaccessible. Cooperatives appear to have been successful in a number of countries. It would be a mistake, however, to conclude that cooperatives are a panacea for all the difficult problems that are associated with the application of new technologies in rural areas. Particularly in countries without a strong communal ethic, these types of organizations can often only be implemented with considerable difficulty and many have failed. The most that can therefore be concluded is that cooperatives offer one possible way of relaxing the severe constraints on the application of new technologies to traditional activities that are imposed by the nature of traditional agriculture. The other two ways are 'sub-contracting' by large industrial enterprises to small and 'cottage' (rural) producers, and the clustering of workshops. These latter cases are examined below.

Many producers in the small-scale urban sector share the characteristics of peasant farmers and rural craftsmen described above. In particular, many of these producers live in absolute poverty, are self-employed and uneducated or school drop-outs. One of the main distinctive features of the urban small-scale sector is its capacity to generate income-earning employment opportunities. One way in which applications of new technologies in the urban small-scale sector seem feasible is through the formal large-scale sector subcontracting some work to the former, and providing technology, skills and other types of assistance. Organization of small-scale producers (e.g. knitters and weavers) in cluster-type workshops might for example facilitate an economic use of simple numerically-controlled machine tools (NCMTs) in the manufacture of some consumer goods (see Chapters 4 and 5). Nevertheless such applications, even if they can be successfully organized, may be socially undesirable if they displace employment in the sector.

Small-scale producers in the industrial sector are differentiated from producers in the urban informal sector in a number of respects that are relevant to discussing the requirements for the successful blending of disparate technologies. At the risk of over-simplification, the former can be said to be differentiable from the latter by virtue of more closely resembling the model of the firm in industrialized countries. That is, small scale producers in industry tend to operate according to the principles of profit-maximization on the basis of wage labour. Compared to most firms in industrialized countries, however, they produce on a very small-scale using relatively old technology. Though their incomes are usually very low in relation to average earnings in industrialized countries, small-scale producers in the industrial sector are rarely among those classified as living in poverty in the Third World.

It may seem surprising that we include large-scale firms as the final source of traditional technologies, for it is well-established that the size of firm in a given industry is positively correlated with the degree of modernity of the technology that it employs. However, since some production processes (or sub-processes) are much more resistant to technical change than others, this general association does not exclude the existence of traditional techniques in *some* aspects of the large firms' behaviour. (Equally, it is often possible to find elements of modernity within the production processes of small firms in the industrial sector.) For example, transport functions within large firms may sometimes be conducted manually rather than with the use of a conveyor belt. It is these more traditional aspects of the production of large firms that offer the promise of blending with the new technologies.

A matrix approach to technology blending

The above four users of new and traditional technologies can be cross-classified by different types of new technologies (e.g. microelectronics and biotechnology). Such a matrix is presented in Table 3.1 which shows various possibilities for the four groups of new technology users.

The microelectronics technology is now sufficiently developed for use in agriculture and industry. This does not seem to be the case with biotechnology and genetic engineering, where much R&D still remains to be done before the technology can be applied effectively to solve the food, nutrition and other problems of developing countries. The case of new energy technologies, like photovoltaics, seems to be somewhere in between the other two: although some scattered applications are already noticed in developing countries, new solar technology and new biotechnology have not yet achieved any major breakthrough.

Technology blending vs. appropriate technology

Like that of 'appropriate technology' (AT), the concept of technology blending does not refer to a *choice* from an existing set of techniques, but

Table 3.1 A matrix of blending possibilities

Users/ New technologies	Microelectronics	Biotechnology
1. Traditional agriculture, rural non-farm activities and rural services	– measuring of fat content of milk – microcomputers in primary and secondary schools – microcomputers in primary health delivery services	– nitrogen-fixing (substitute for chemical fertilisers) – SCP (substitute for grain in tissue culture) (crop yield increases)
2. Rural cooperatives	– food storage control – moisture control – sprinkler control in irrigation	– recovery from agricultural wastes
3. Small-scale industrial producers	– mini-computers (for management, marketing) – quality control (through the use of computer numerically controlled devices) – computer-aided design	
4. Large-scale industrial firms	– self-monitoring factories: computer-aided design, manufacture and control; – numerically controlled machine tools	– microorganisms (mining and extraction) – pharmaceuticals (e.g. vaccines) – recovery from industrial wastes

Source: Bhalla and J. James (1984).

rather to the *development* of new technologies that would be more suited to the needs of the poor developing countries. Technology blending (or blends) may be best analysed in terms of the *objectives* sought and the *characteristics* of the new technological variant. As noted above, the objective is simple enough, that is, to bring the benefits of new technology revolution to bear on the improvement in the standards of living of the rural and the urban poor. To some extent this objective determines the required characteristics of technology blending.

As infrastructure and repair and maintenance facilities and skills are very scarce in urban and rural milieus where the small producers are concentrated, the technology blends would be required to be simple, easily comprehensible, and easy to maintain and repair. Thus, in terms of characteristics, technology blends are somewhat similar to appropriate technologies. It is this similarity which seems to have led some authors (Kaplinsky, 1989) to describe technology blending simply as a variant of the concept of appropriate technology. Of course on the surface there may appear to be a parallel between the two since blending represents an intermediate stage between conventional and new technologies in a process of continuous technical change. Also improvement of traditional technologies is the objective common to both technology blending and appropriate technology. But the similarities end here.

There are substantive differences between the two approaches to improvements of traditional technologies. First, while the concept of appropriate technology refers mainly to incremental innovations, blending of new technologies with traditional activities implies a quantum jump on the part of developing countries who do not necessarily have to go through all the stages followed by the technological leaders of today (Colombo, 1989; Soete, 1985, 1990).

The new technologies require a systemic approach to their application which is different from the promotion of individual technologies that many of the protagonists of AT promoted in developing countries. This is well illustrated by the experience of ENEA (Italy) in launching technology -blending projects in Argentina, Paraguay and Uruguay, discussed below. Rather than promoting individual firms, the objective of these projects is to raise the productivity of a number of traditional industries through the combined impact of a number of technologies as well as institutions, both governmental and non-governmental (Colombo, 1991).

Furthermore, in contrast to 'appropriate technology' new technologies are being developed and applied at a very rapid rate particularly in the industrialized countries. They entail capital costs which far exceed those involved in the development and commercialization of appropriate technologies. Thus the pace of development of technology blends can be more rapid and their commercialization perhaps easier if the industrialized countries – the main producers of these technologies – take account of the potential needs of the developing countries. The role of networking between research institutions of industrialized and developing countries can be fruitful here.

Whereas the developing countries are both producers and users of appropriate technologies, in the case of 'technology blends' most of them (with very few exceptions) will remain mere users for the foreseeable future. The new technologies will continue to be produced mostly in the industrialized countries. While appropriate technology was inspired by a development strategy of national and local self-reliance, technology blending may tend to reduce such technological autonomy. In the absence of a national/domestic capacity to develop new technologies, most developing countries will have to depend on the industrialized countries which are the main sources of supply of these technologies. This technological dependence may be particularly serious in the case of the least developed countries with limited capabilities to create or absorb new technologies (see Chapter 8). In fact, with increasing globalization of production and competition in world markets, the issue of access of developing countries to the new technologies will in future become even more important.

We noted in Chapter 2 that the capacity of developing countries to be able to create and absorb new technologies varies a great deal which may mean widening technological gaps not only between developed and developing countries but also within the developing countries. In other words, a growing divergence of Third World interests may be explained in the future partly in terms of the technological factor.

The concept of blending is being increasingly recognized as a useful practical tool for focusing attention on the relevance and application of new technologies to meet the basic needs of developing countries (Colombo, 1989). However, the critics find fault with the analytical merits or utility of the concept. The first legitimate criticism has to do with the difficulty of drawing any clearcut dividing line between new frontier technology and blended technology (Kaplinsky, 1989). This was indeed recognized by the proponents of the concept (Bhalla and D. James, 1988). The problem of boundaries cannot be solved in any process of *continuous* change. However, to the extent that technical progress is *discontinuous* (which corresponds more to reality), the boundaries between different technology sets or trajectories can be perceived by analysing their distinctive characteristics and properties.

Secondly, some authors (Rosenberg, 1988; Kaplinsky, 1989) see utility in defining technology blending only narrowly in terms of retrofitting and not in any more macroeconomic sense. Kaplinsky (1989) suggests an alternative definition to technology blending. Pursuing the line that blending is a variant of AT, he would like to identify and distinguish between the following sources of AT: downscaling of large-scale production, the improvement of existing/traditional technologies and the production of new technologies.

BLENDING IN PRACTICE

Serious investigation of technology blending only began in the early eighties. Therefore instances of practical experience with blending are still rare. Furthermore, deliberate blending experiments *de novo* with adequate data collection during the project planning phases are not plentiful. Therefore it is not always possible to evaluate technical performance and organizational efficiency of blending and to determine whether an alternative use of resources would have been more beneficial. But recent initiatives in a few Asian and Latin American countries described below suggest that the concept of technology blending has slowly come of age.

Biovillages in India and China

Projects on 'biovillages' currently in progress in India and China were initiated in February 1991 as a follow-up to the Dialogue on Biotechnology organized by the MS Swaminathan Research Foundation based in Madras (see Swaminathan, 1991).

The concept of 'biovillages' aims at taking 'the benefits of biological technology research to the rural poor...', 'integrating the principles of ecological sustainability and those of economic profitability with equity...' and seeks to 'promote skilled employment through integration of traditional and frontier technologies' (M.S. Swaminathan Research Foundation *Second Annual Report, 1991–92*, p. 89).

Three villages were chosen in the Union Territory of Pondicherry on the east coast of peninsular India. In China, the biovillages project was initiated in Hebei Province by the Chinese Academy of Sciences, with the selection of six villages in the Qianxian Township in Yuanshi county. An interesting feature of the project is a close collaboration between China and India, through the M.S. Swaminathan Research Foundation and the Chinese Academy of Sciences.

The major thrust of the projects is technological as well as institutional blending. The latter is being promoted through different types of group action. For this purpose it is proposed to set up a biovillage society and two bio-centres at the village level. These institutional arrangements are made in order to test and evaluate new technologies and organize regular participatory meetings attended by scientists, local extension workers and target beneficiaries such as small farmers, landless workers, women and youth. The meetings aim at identifying local needs (e.g. for food production and employment generation), infrastructural and marketing requirements and feasible technological options in consultation with the local population. For example, at these meetings the small and medium farmers in the Pondicherry villages selected for the project expressed their inability to afford the required quantities of inorganic fertilizers. Experiments were therefore undertaken to determine the feasibility of using biofertilizers by selecting marginal farmers in each village to introduce Azolla in the paddy fields. The results of these trials show that the use of this new technology is feasible with some worker training in trampling of the Azolla fronds during weeding. The development of biofertilizers provides an alternative source of nitrogen and can reduce the use of inorganic nitrogen by 10 to 20 per cent.

The biovillage centres will be run and managed by the biovillage society consisting mainly of educated unemployed youth. The centres will be equipped to provide facilities 'for the testing, evaluation, adaptation and demonstration of new technologies and for self-supporting production units for planting and breeding materials' (Hopper and Nair, 1993). They will also serve as information and training centres.

Under the project some progress has already been made. A baseline survey, covering qualitative and quantitative analysis of the local resource base in the selected villages, was completed in September 1991. A farming system survey to assess the potentials and constraints for sustained productivity growth under different resource and management conditions was also completed in October 1992. Thirdly, different technological and institutional interventions have been identified (Hopper and Nair, 1993). A feasibility report has been prepared for the Asian Development Bank which is one of the sponsors of the project.

The organization of the biovillage project in India also includes a consortium of government institutions such as the Department of Biotechnology, Government of India, Tamil Nadu Agricultural University and National Bank for Agriculture and Rural Development, whose contributions are essential for the success of the project. The project concentrates on a core of 16 income- and employment-generating activities designed to reach the resource poor in the project area. Three main target groups covered are women in landless households, women on small farms, and small farmers in general.

In China six villages have been chosen for the project. They belong to the Qianxian Township in Hebei province. The area covered includes a resource-poor mountainous region. The main constraints of the region are: scarcity of arable land – average size of farm is only 0.37 hectares; low rainfall and thus short growing period; and degradation of mountain lands through grazing. However, potential exists for biomass production from barren lands, for fruit growing and processing, and for shifting production from crops to livestock farming. Accordingly, the project envisages apricot and pomegranate orchards, a fruit-processing unit and rabbit farming to utilize crop wastes.

Although the social and political systems and organization of rural production are different in China from those in India, a similar approach to the biovillages has been adopted in the two countries. One of the main differences is that while Indian villages suffer from social and economic inequalities due largely to an uneven distribution of land and the presence of landless labour, in the case of China the problems faced are largely ecological due to the very poor land resource endowment and environmental degradation due to grazing. In China, thanks to the massive and effective land reforms in the early fifties, access to land is fairly equitable.

As in India, under the Chinese Academy of Sciences, a consortium of scientific institutions and research organizations has been established to provide technological support to the biovillages project. A management committee, consisting of representatives of research organizations, Yuanshi county and Qianxian township, has also been established.

Information technology in the Indian and Malaysian rural areas

Although examples of technology blending in industry through the use of information technology in small and medium enterprises are more rare, some beginning has been made in this direction in India and Malaysia.

In India, a Dialogue on Information Technology organized under the auspices of the MS Swaminathan Research Foundation (see Swaminathan, 1993) led to the initiation of a project on 'information villages'. The project aims at combining the traditional sources and channels of information (e.g. folk media and demonstrations) with new technology information networks and computer-aided extension systems to meet the information needs of farm-related and off-farm activities in rural areas. In addition to this, information on quality of life indicators of the rural population – namely sanitation, drinking water, primary health care and primary education – will also be collected and processed.

As a follow-up to the Dialogue, a consortium of interested governmental and non-governmental agencies was established to formulate specific project proposals. At present feasibility studies are underway in six administrative districts in different states of India which are chosen in order to examine the diversity in existing farming practices and varying agro-climatic regions. In each of these districts a computerized profile of villages is being developed. Such a profile will include information needs for farm and non-farm activities, sources and channels of information (e.g. friends, extension workers, teachers, shopkeepers) and linkages with producers of information (e.g. agricultural and rural universities, meteorological services, Indian Council of Agricultural Research) (see Swaminathan, 1993, Appendix 2, 'Establishment of Information Villages').

It is proposed to set up computer-based 'information shops' which will consist of computers and communication facilities to help the villagers to 'monitor their agricultural assets and environment with the help of remote sensing studies'. These shops will be managed by unemployed graduates and/or schoolteachers from the village.

It is expected that the project on 'information villages' will gradually form part of a larger programme: Small Farmers' Agri-business Consortium, which the Government of India initiated in 1993. This consortium will be an autonomous corporate entity, funded by the Reserve Bank of India and the National Bank for Agriculture and Rural Development, aiming at rural development for the benefit of resource-poor small and marginal farmers (see Swaminathan and Hoon, 1993). It is too early to assess the information village project. However, the success of such an endeavour will depend largely on how successfully required information can be packaged in a form that is directly useable by the resource-poor and often semi-literate or illiterate farmers.

Another recent initiative to use information technology for small and medium enterprises has been undertaken by the Government of Malaysia. In 1992, the *Bumiputra* National Congress held in Kuala Lumpur endorsed the concept of technology blending for improving the economic and social situation of the *Bumiputra* Commercial and Industrial Community. As a follow-up to this decision, the Malaysian Agricultural Research and Development Institute (MARDI), a government-funded institution, organized a national seminar on technology blending which was attended by representatives of research institutes, government departments, universities, banks, chamber of commerce and industry.

The seminar discussed at length the scope of blending in Malaysia in different industrial sectors through, *inter alia*, the clustering of economic activities and sub-contracting under which parent companies can ensure access of small producers (sub-contractees) to new technologies. The seminar recommended the launching of a few pilot projects on blending in such sectors as food processing, textiles and garments, and furniture. It also recommended the establishment of a network of individuals and agencies for the exchange of information and experiences. Studies are currently underway to determine the feasibility of different technology options in food processing. The use of new technologies in the small-scale production units is being examined with a view to raising the quality of the product, the design capability of the producers, and their competitiveness in the market.

The Malaysian government is clearly committed to the use of new technology to achieve the goal of reaching the status of a developed nation by the year 2020. It is equally committed to improving the standard of living and quality of life of *bumiputras* (the native community of Malaysia which is engaged mainly in small-scale traditional activities). The establishment recently of a high-tech unit in the Prime Minister's Office is a clear manifestation of this commitment.

Conditions for the success of technology blending seem to be particularly favourable in Malaysia. The economy has been growing rapidly for a number of years. The growth of investments, both foreign and domestic, has also been impressive. The outward-looking nature of the economy makes it imperative for industry and other sectors to raise their competitiveness through the use of new technology. New investments are an essential precondition for successful blending. Similar conditions have been missing in India and many other developing countries, particularly in Africa. However, in the case of India the recent economic reforms and the introduction of an open-door policy should in principle provide a more favourable climate for technology blending in the future.

Technology blending in small industrial sectors in Argentina, Paraguay and Uruguay

In the Latin American region also some initiatives have been undertaken to promote technology blending – in Argentina, Paraguay and Uruguay – in such specific small-scale industrial sectors as textiles and garments, leather and footwear, and furniture. Two projects are underway. The first is a bilateral project in Argentina on the improvement of textiles, leather goods and furniture sectors funded by the Italian Ministry of Foreign Affairs and technically supported by the Italian National Commission on Environment, Energy and New Technologies (ENEA). This project has identified the use of robotics, irradiation technology and separation technology as important means for improving Argentinian small and medium enterprises in the above industrial sectors. The second project, funded by the Commission of the European Union with technical support from ENEA, covers Argentina, Paraguay and Uruguay and deals with technological upgrading of leather goods production (see Colombo, 1991).

Under the bilateral project with Argentina, ENEA has already undertaken feasibility studies of traditional sectors – textiles and clothing, wood and furniture, and leather goods. The Argentinian business confederation participated in the choice and selection of these enterprises to be covered by the project. As a second step, suitable Italian enterprises were identified as having relevant skills and expertise in these sectors and knowledge of the use of such new technologies as computer-aided design (CAD), advanced cutting systems for cloth and quality control systems for wood products. As a third step, Italian industrial partners – engineers and manufacturers – were identified to design the required equipment and technology suitable for Argentinian enterprises.

Local scientific communities and local manufacturers in Argentina and Italy are working in close collaboration to identify existing shortcomings of current processes and products, to examine the feasibility of raising the quality and competitiveness of products, and to ensure the supply of adapted equipment designs and machinery.

The second project which deals with MERCOSUR countries (viz. Argentina, Paraguay and Uruguay) is confined only to the leather goods sector and is intended to improve the technological levels of the sector so that the exporting countries have greater access to the markets of the industrialized countries. Apart from technological improvements, the project also promotes industrial partnerships – through joint ventures for example – between the Latin American countries on the one hand and European countries on the other.

EXPERIENCE OF THE GREEN REVOLUTION

The experience of the Green Revolution technology introduced in the rural/traditional agriculture in developing countries should offer lessons and a parallel for the application of new technologies to traditional activities in general. The development and use of this technology required laboratory research in international and national centres, arrangements for its diffusion to the farmers in developing countries and the provision of a package of inputs like seeds, fertilisers, pesticides, machinery, irrigation water, fuel and remunerative pricing policies. The application of high-yielding varieties (HYVs) in the 'alien' environment of developing countries involved a number of consequences which are relevant to technology blending in other sectors. We examine these consequences below.

One can argue that at the time of the introduction of HYV seeds, the technology was not fully mature in the sense that its effects on the ecology and environment were not foreseen for several years. It was discovered that HYVs were not disease-resistant, unlike the local varieties. Another ecological danger of the HYV technology is the excessive use of water and synthetic fertilisers and insecticides, dangers recognized much later than the development of the technology.

The HYVs did not emerge endogenously from traditional technologies used by the farmers in developing countries. Instead they were specifically created in international and national scientific research centres. The laboratory research was designed to suit the environmental conditions of countries and regions in which it was to be applied. The practical experience with the use of the new technology shows that it called on 'the cultivator to amend too many distinct aspects of his technology all at once, and to attempt a radical leap forward in which there is discontinuity between the existing and the new' (Pearce, 1980, p. 180). This type of discontinuity puts a major burden on the small farmers whose capacity to undertake the risks involved is generally low given the limited economic means at their disposal. This factor may partly explain why the yields attained in the laboratory experiments were not actually matched by the results at the field level.

HYV technology is highly dependent on a wide range of supporting services and infrastructure (e.g. irrigation machinery, fertilisers, pesticides) which are needed to reap the full benefits. Most of these physical inputs and services originate from the urban industrial sector, thus leading to the dependence of the rural communities on the modern sector.

There is some parallel here to the situation regarding the application of new technologies like microelectronics, biotechnology and photovoltaics. They are deeply rooted in the modern modes of urban industrial organization and their maintenance and repair may also call for exogenous inputs into the traditional rural areas. Furthermore, their contribution to the alleviation of poverty presupposes the supply and equitable distribution of a software package consisting of modern skills, appropriate management and organizational structure and extension services, and so on.

In order that the new technologies are easily assimilated into the prevailing cultural patterns of traditional societies, it is essential that they be in keeping with local customs and traditions. The experience of the Green Revolution shows that this new technology was biased in favour of the larger farmers and landlords who had better access to factor inputs, credit and other supporting services required. Since the HYV technology requires several complementary inputs, it would seem that it could benefit the smaller farmers more within the framework of cooperative modes of production under which better access to these inputs could be assured.

Whether the utilization of certain new technologies (e.g. small-scale satellite communications systems) can be better exploited through cooperative organization needs further examination.

CONCLUDING REMARKS

To promote technology blending in developing countries three policy areas need to be pursued: (1) measures and policies designed to facilitate the adoption of new technologies; (2) those needed to adapt the new technologies to the needs of traditional producers; and (3) reorganization of traditional production which may be necessary and may call for new institutional blends involving cooperation between a number of entities such as government agencies, banks and private entrepreneurs as well as grass-roots NGOs.

With respect to the industrial sector, the problems of altering the way production is, for the most part, now organized seem to be no less formidable. For although sub-contracting relationships were an important feature of the development of many countries that industrialized in the previous century (and more recently also in Japan and the Republic of Korea), there is in most developing countries 'a tendency towards vertical integration rather than a reliance on either sub-contracting or market relationships with suppliers' (Rao, 1974). While the nature of the reasons for this divergent pattern of industrial development are not altogether clear, it does seem that an alteration of this tendency in the direction of providing greater linkages between large and small firms will require a policy of active encouragement of the latter. Our discussion of the Prato Textile Industry in Italy (where sub-contracting is fairly common) in Chapter 4 shows that considerable protection and assistance is granted to the many small firms in the industry. Similar encouragement (in terms of access to credit, foreign exchange, technical assistance, etc.) will need to be given to small-scale enterprises in developing countries; at the same time, the existing discriminations against these firms should be eliminated. The Prato experience also underlines the importance of providing a package of centralized services and utilities. It is unlikely that the new and emerging technologies could be effectively used in developing countries without some provision of government support and/or infrastructural facilities like the teletext network introduced in Prato.

So far we have described some of the problems involved in altering the organization of traditional production so as to facilitate the adoption of the new technologies. These technologies may also need to be adapted to fit in with the requirements of traditional small producers. This is the second broad area of policy which deserves attention.

There are several good reasons for the developing countries to undertake the research required for adaptation of the new technologies themselves (though, of course, one does not wish to exclude some form of supportive international role). First, the learning effects of the research could be captured within the developing countries. The second reason has to do with our insistence on the need for research to be closely related to the needs of the target groups of potential users. Though this objective will not necessarily be achieved merely by the location of research in developing countries, it seems more likely since the necessary close links with traditional producers will then be easier to forge and maintain.

Finally, some types of traditional production may not be ready for technology blending. In other cases, the straightforward introduction of new technologies without a blending aspect may be a superior choice. Therefore scope and feasibility of technology blending needs to be considered along with other alternatives.

4 Microelectronics for Small-Scale Production: Some Evidence*

In Chapter 3 we considered some examples of technology blending. The application of microelectronics-based technologies at small scales of industrial production – another form of blending – is the concern of this chapter.

Many developing countries have grappled with programmes and policies relating to small-scale production to ensure employment expansion. With few exceptions, these programmes and policies have not been very successful with respect to either output or employment generation. In the past, the industrial development strategies in the Third World have rarely given any prominence to rural and small-scale industrialization. Whenever they have done so, not enough emphasis was placed on the issues of complementarities or competition between large-scale and small-scale industries.

With few exceptions, the performance of rural industry programmes in developing countries has not been very successful. These programmes have suffered from lack of markets resulting from a low local purchasing power, poor infrastructure, inadequate credit facilities and competition from large-scale industry. The last factor has particularly become more acute in recent years with privatization and the liberalization of economic policies in both developing and developed countries. More liberal economic and trade policies are being adopted which may further aggravate the problems of weak small enterprises, at least during the period of transition.

In the following section, we present arguments in favour of new technology applications to small-scale production. Another section is devoted to a discussion of the experience of the application of microelectronics-based technologies by small and medium enterprises (SMEs) in a selected number of industrialized and developing countries.

---

*A revised and updated version of an article originally published in *Economic and Political Weekly*, 29 November 1986.

THE CASE FOR HIGH-TECH COTTAGE INDUSTRY

New technologies can enable small and medium enterprises to improve their efficiency by raising the quality of their products and by introducing flexibility. This flexibility, made possible by new technologies, is in sharp contrast to the complexity and large-scale operations typical of modern conventional technologies. In microelectronics, for example, equipment can be put to new uses fairly easily through reprogramming. Furthermore, by enabling de-scaling, new technologies may reduce the importance of product and plant-related economies of scale (see below) and lower entry barriers. We examine below this issue of scale economies on which there is no general agreement for lack of adequate empirical evidence.

Scale economies

The question of scale economies is a complex one since it relates to different dimensions (e.g. products, plants, firms and industries) which are often not distinguished in the literature. Generally, scale economies are considered only in relation to the size of plants and output of individual products per unit of time. There may indeed be divergent trends in scale economies relating to these different dimensions. For example, Alcorta (1992) argues that 'although NT (new technologies) may have a significant scale reduction effect at product level, it is not clear they would have a similar impact at plant level'. Indeed some empirical evidence relating to automobile, bicycle and process industries suggests scaling-up rather than de-scaling. However, many authors (Dosi et al., 1988; Kaplinsky, 1990) have argued that flexible production (made possible by new technologies) would tend to reduce the optimal size of plant and firm.

Whether the scale factor will be less important in the future industrialization of developing countries will depend in part on the nature of the industry and the product-mix. Whether new technological developments are likely to give rise to an increase in CAD adoption rates by small firms in developing countries also remains unclear. For example, Kaplinsky (1983) estimated that 'CAD design systems based upon minicomputers are unlikely to be profitable (in relation to the choice of technique rather than the design of product) with fewer than 10 designers; those based upon mainframe have even greater effective economies of scale'. Much will depend, apart from the scale factor, on the evolution of relative factor prices, the cost of acquiring new technologies and the terms and conditions at which these technologies are likely to be available to developing countries, particularly those which do not produce these technologies themselves.

Miniaturization of new technologies and simplicity in use make it possible for small enterprises to adopt them. It is not clear however whether these enterprises can efficiently use these new technologies at full capacity. Whether new technologies offer a competitive edge to small enterprises over larger ones is also not easy to determine, since large enterprises are also able to avail themselves of flexible production. In manufacturing industries small firms may have an advantage over large firms in exploiting the potential for innovation and employment generation, especially if workers in smaller enterprises are less unionized than those in larger enterprises. However, it does not necessarily follow that on this account alone the use of high technology would be easier. Only in the cases of family ownership of small enterprises, where the distinction between workers and employers is much less significant, might this factor facilitate the application of new innovations. But even in this case a shortage of requisite skills, noted in Chapter 2, may pose a problem.

There are as yet very few studies on the comparative costs of conventional versus new technologies and diffusion by firm size (Bagchi, 1986; Dodgson, 1985; Edquist and Jacobsson, 1988). In the developed countries, empirical evidence on the adoption of new technologies by size of firm (measured by numbers employed) tends to conform to what one might expect, namely, that the larger firms, because of their greater technical and financial resources, know-how and information, have adopted these technologies to a greater extent than relatively small-scale enterprises. The Policy Studies Institute (London), for example, undertook a detailed survey of a total of more than 3800 factories in France, Germany and the United Kingdom to 'measure across the whole range of manufacturing industry, the form, extent and effects of the use of microelectronics in products and production processes'. (Northcott and Rogers, 1985). The study noted that the microelectronics applications (e.g. CAD/CAM, CNC machine tools and robots) were concentrated mainly in large-scale mechanical and electrical engineering and automobile industries.

Evidence on patterns of adoption by firm size in developing countries is more difficult to attain. Some of this evidence conforms broadly to the developed-country patterns noted above. The Edquist–Jacobsson study (1988) of the engineering industry in the newly industrializing countries (NICs) found that, with few exceptions, it is mainly the larger firms which adopt CNC machine tools in these countries. Fleury's study of the adoption of microelectronics technologies in the Brazilian metal-engineering industry appears to come to a similar conclusion (Fleury, 1988). In the Indian machine tool industry smaller firms have 'often catered to customers who demanded low quality but cheap products' (Bagchi, 1986), while the larger firms would supply customers with more stringent quality requirements. And since CNC machine tools tend to be associated with high (or at least more precise) standards of quality, they are demanded to a correspondingly greater extent by the large, rather than the small-scale firms in the industry. It is perhaps at least partly on account of this scale factor that the rate of adoption of CNC machine tools often appears to be relatively low, even in the more advanced regions of the Third World.

USE OF HIGH-TECH BY SMALL AND MEDIUM ENTERPRISES

We noted in Chapter 2 that new technology diffusion is confined largely to the industrialized countries, and within these to large-scale industry, banking and services. However, there is growing experience on the part of small and medium enterprises (SMEs) in these countries in the adoption of new technologies like microelectronics, which has revived the traditional industries like textiles and footwear in such countries as Italy, Germany and Japan. Although the examples are not as numerous as one might have expected, they point to the growing scope for revitalizing traditional industries.

The experience of dynamic growth of small firms in Italy discussed below suggests the important facilitating role played by new technologies. Although all their dynamism cannot be attributed to the adoption of these technologies, there are good examples of how small firms, say in the Prato region (see below) have successfully adopted computer-based technologies to respond to rapidly changing market requirements (Colombo, Mazzonis and Lanzavecchia, 1983; Colombo and Mazzonis, 1984). The question arises whether this model of an industrialized country can be replicated to improve the efficiency of craft production in developing countries and thus expand output as well as employment. Scattered empirical evidence discussed below shows that at least some small and medium firms in developing countries are taking advantage of new technologies to improve product quality and international competitiveness.

Of course, the conditions for 'flexible specialization' and small-scale production in the industrialized countries are different from those in the developing countries. In the former it was a response to stagnating and competitive mass markets. Although similar conditions of demand may also apply to developing countries, the supply constraints – viz. lack of access to raw materials and spare parts due to foreign exchange scarcity – are likely to pose major bottlenecks. As we noted in Chapter 2 surplus labour conditions and resulting low labour costs in many developing countries are likely to discourage the rapid adoption of new technologies. However, the situation of NICs such as the Republic of Korea, suffering from a growing labour shortage, is rather different. As we argue in Chapters 3 and 5, to benefit most from new technologies, developing countries may need to establish agglomerations of small firms or similar other institutional innovations for promoting cooperation among firms.

The experience of developed countries

Italy

The experience of Italy is now well-known but it is worth recapitulating, especially that of the Prato textile industry which withstood recession much more successfully than many other areas, particularly in maintaining employment levels in a climate of general decline in employment. Contrary to what may be expected the Prato small enterprises were favourable to the adoption of new technologies. In fact, even the smallest enterprises have adopted innovations, which may be explained partly by the prevalent sub-contracting system (under which the parent companies provide assistance to raise the technological levels of small enterprises working for them) and what we called 'institutional blending' in Chapter 3 (that is, a combined role for the state, the private sector and NGOs).

Sub-contracting between large and small firms, in respect of different operations, is quite common. According to some estimates, the share of sub-contracting by the woollen mills in some operations may be as high as 70 per cent of total production if account were taken of the role of the 'trade brokers' (*impannatori*) who keep track of the worldwide textile markets, and designs and fashions.

Sub-contracting started in the region during the economic crisis in the 1950s when redundant workers set up their own small shops, leasing or buying old machines from larger firms. However today the relationship between the parent companies and the sub-contractors is based much more on the proper division of labour and decentralization of operations. Hardly any firms in Prato are fully integrated in the sense that they specialize in all operations ranging from the processing of raw materials to the finished product.

In Prato, a distinction is made between two types of sub-contractors, namely, the 'pure' ones, who are set up independently of the parent firm (which does not supply any initial capital), but work for it in carding, weaving, finishing, etc. The second category of sub-contractors is more dependent on the parent firm for initial establishment, supply of equipment, technical assistance, etc. The latter type of sub-contractors is promoted by large woollen mills with a 'working partner' who is a technically qualified person capable of running the production unit. This unit is like a small company with several shareholders including the 'working partner', whose fortune is thus directly linked with that of the parent company. The market for the output of the sub-contractors is fully assured by the woollen mills, thus reducing management, organizational and marketing problems.

The growing demand for the products of the Prato textile industry has maintained a healthy and mutually beneficial relationship between the contracting parties. In a few cases longer runs of work have been offered to sub-contractors, with the aim of securing the services of those with greater expertise (Lorenzoni, 1989). The parent companies are satisfied with the technical expertise of their sub-contractors of both artisan and non-artisan types, and with their ability to adapt to changing fashion requirements.

The sub-contracting arrangements also provide insurance against risk for small-scale firms, and stimulate them to introduce technological modernization which may be partially financed by the parent companies. The plant modernization (the introduction of modern looms and spindles, for example) is known to be quite impressive among small-scale firms and artisans. Of the total stock of looms more than 50 per cent are new shuttleless looms including a few air and water jet looms. Although open-end spindles are less common, they are being increasingly used by the larger-scale firms. In the case of finishing and dyeing, the technique of press dyeing in small volumes has replaced traditional techniques. These two processes are computerized. However, computer applications seem to be more widespread in marketing, banking and information exchange.

A teletext experiment has also been introduced. Under this project computers are used with terminals in all strategic points like banks, 'trade brokers' (*impannatori*), customs and transportation. These terminals supply information on raw material and product prices, fashions, new products and designs, foreign currencies, and so on. The objectives of the project include: information processing (typical of informatics), information transmission (typical of telecommunications) and meeting user or consumer needs (typical of consumer electronics) (see de Brabant, 1989, p. 247). The telematics experiment is intended to integrate these three aspects.

Thanks to sub-contracting and cooperative forms of organization, the new technologies have been introduced in the Prato region despite the predominance of small-scale firms. However, the speed with which the new innovations are applied is rather slow on account of the geographical dispersion and smallness of firms, and their lack of knowledge about the existence and usefulness of these technologies. Although the small firms cannot afford the high cost of new technologies individually, their organization into associations, clusters and cooperatives enables them to take advantage of these innovations. Close cooperation among producers is ensured by such associations as the Industrial Union, Association of Artisans, and the Association of Traders. Furthermore, fiscal measures and social security legislation protect small firms which are entitled to medium-term loans at subsidized rates. These loan funds have enabled the financing of investments in new machinery.

The provision of centralized services by a government agency – *Sistema Prato Innovazione Technologica (SPRINT)* established by the Italian Agency for Atomic and Alternative Energy Sources (ENEA) – in several areas partly accounts for the success of small enterprises in applying new technologies. These areas on which SPRINT has initially concentrated are:

(a) *process and product innovation*: automation, control systems, product design and new production technologies;
(b) *organizational innovation*: rationalizing information flows and communications, electronics and information technologies;
(c) *raw materials and energy conservation.*

SPRINT monitors an experimental project on the use of computer-aided design (CAD) for worsted fabrics. This technological innovation is intended primarily to reduce costs and improve product quality.

In Prato, the introduction of new technology does not seem to have led to any labour displacement. In fact, in contrast to the widespread decline in textile employment in most industrialized countries since 1973, the Italian woollen textile industry (concentrated mainly in the Prato region) registered an increase in its employed labour force. Between 1970 and 1975, the number of textile employees increased by 12 per cent in Prato but declined by 7 per cent in France, 15 per cent in the UK, and 26 per cent in the former Federal Republic of Germany (Balestri, 1982). More recently, Mazzonis noted that the 'gains in productivity have not been based on cuts in the labour force: on the contrary, the labour force has expanded (Mazzonis, 1989, p. 237). The factors explaining this exceptional situation in Italy are not very clear. However, it is plausible that sub-contracting and the small-scale family-based mode of organization, clustering of activities in industrial districts, and inter-firm cooperation, ensured flexibility and adaptation of production to changing demand patterns and fashion requirements. Furthermore, the apparently successful use of discarded rags blended with reclaimed wool (thus improving yarn quality) may have enabled the industry to expand production and exports at relatively low costs.

To conclude, the experience of the Prato textile industry described above is generally valid for the dynamic growth of small firms particularly in northern Italy. Apart from the factors noted above, the changing character of technical progress has shifted the emphasis from in-firm R&D to scientific research in the universities and public or government institutions whose role has become important (see Becattini, 1990). That the Italian experience described above is of relevance to many developing countries is demonstrated by the launching of pilot projects by ENEA in Latin America (see Chapter 3).

United Kingdom

Although small firms are less important in the United Kingdom than in Italy, their number has grown thanks to the low labour costs and increased production flexibility resulting partly from the use of new technology, and favourable government policy (Marsden, 1990).

The use of new technologies (e.g. CAD/CAM, CNC machine tools and robots) by small firms employing 1–19 and 20–49 workers is not insignificant. The Policy Studies Institute (PSI) of London undertook a detailed survey of a total of more than 3800 factories in France, Germany and the United Kingdom to 'measure across the whole range of manufacturing industry, the form, extent and effects of the use of microelectronics in products and production processes'. The survey shows that in the case of process applications, the percentage of the largest firms using microelectronics is about three times the percentage in the smaller firms. The percentage of the smallest firms using microelectronics varies from 25 per cent in France to 28 per cent in the United Kingdom and 34 per cent in Germany. In the case of product applications, the use of the new technology by the smallest firms is less marked – ranging from only 4 per cent to 7 per cent of the firms (see Table 4.1).

Despite the handicaps faced by the UK small firms the adoption of microelectronics has increased over time, due perhaps to the growing awareness of the potential benefits including the declining cost of new technology. It is noted that 'between 1983 and 1985 diffusion has spread more to the smaller establishments, somewhat reducing the disparity between the ones in the largest size band and those in the smallest' (Northcott, 1986, p. 41). This situation refers to product applications: in the case of process applications, the 'disparity between those in the largest size

Table 4.1 Use of microelectronics by size weighted for percentage of all establishments in manufacturing industry in each size range (France, Germany, United Kingdom)

Employment size	Product applications			Process applications		
	UK	*Germany*	*France*	*UK*	*Germany*	*France*
1–19	5.5	–	–	18	–	–
20–49	6	7	4	28	34	25
50–99	9	11	8	41	48	34
100–199	12	18	9	54	59	47
200–499	13	22	9	67	67	67
500–999	23	34	18	83	87	80
1000–	35	45	33	94	93	90
All Sizes	10	13	6	43	47	35

Sources: Northcott and Rogers (1985); for 1–19 employment size, Northcott and Walling (1988).

bands and those in the smallest has diminished from nine times the user ratio in 1981 to three times in 1985' (Northcott, 1986, p. 41).

In the first three surveys undertaken by the PSI in 1981, 1983 and 1985, the smallest firms covered were those employing 20–49 workers. Yet in the United Kingdom, firms employing fewer than 20 workers account for more than three-fourths of all manufacturing firms and 12 per cent of total manufacturing employment. Therefore in 1987 PSI decided to undertake an additional sample survey of 200 of these very small firms. These firms were asked the same questions as those in the earlier sample. Thus at least for the United Kingdom the data for the very small firms (1–19 workers) are comparable with those for the next group of firms (see Table 4.1). Over 5 per cent of the very small firms accounted for microelectronics applications in their products whereas a much larger percentage (18) accounted for process applications. The applications are noted to be limited for the following reasons: small production volumes, limited variety of products and lack of cost effectiveness (Northcott and Walling, 1988).

Japan

The importance of small enterprises and inter-firm cooperation through sub-contracting is proverbial for Japan. It is noted that the diffusion of microelectronics technology has further encouraged the growth of small businesses (see Koshiro, 1990, p. 199). Even many of the traditional local small businesses, which have suffered from falling demand for their products and rising labour costs, have started adopting new technologies. Koshiro (1990) notes 'new technology is penetrating this area... computer graphics and a direct jacquard weaving system with electronic punching have been introduced by some innovative small firms in Nishijin'. Similar innovations – new wood lathes for lacquer products and painting robots for mosaic wooden food container production – have also been introduced.

According to a survey undertaken in 1980 by the Japanese Medium and Small Enterprise Agency, small-scale units invested in CNC machines in order to save labour costs and overcome a shortage of skilled labour, to cope with increasing demand for precision and to produce efficiently small lots of different products. Although there were other reasons (e.g. to save energy and materials and produce new products) the above factors seemed to be the most important. A survey by Watanabe (1983a) of Japanese small enterprises using CNC machines in the small town of Sakai in the Nagano Prefecture also confirmed these findings.

The Japanese wood products industry (furniture and furnishings), which consists mainly of small enterprises, has been fully automated. The industry uses CNCs and industrial robots because of the increased costs of craftsmen's labour time and shortage of milling apprentices. Furthermore, a new and unique type of CNC equipment has been developed which eliminates the need for programming of the wood-working operation. One of the companies in Kagoshima on Kyushi island, employing 25 workers, had actively introduced CNC machines for wood working. The level of investment made by the company was unusually high due to the cost incurred in the development of the CNC parts jointly with the CNC equipment suppliers (Heian and Fanuc) which are two of the world's leading suppliers of CNC units.

Three main reasons explain the increasing use of CNCs by the Japanese small enterprises. First, a fairly high standard of education in Japan which facilitates mastering of simple CNC programming techniques. Secondly, the CNC manufacturers have introduced a marketing innovation in the form of low-cost training schools to develop markets for their products. Thirdly, the Japanese machine tool dealers offer hire-purchase schemes which are widespread. Notwithstanding these favourable factors, many small enterprises in Japan face difficulties in the use of CNC which are summarized in Table 4.2. The survey noted that some small enterprises had to get rid of CNCs since they failed to find suitable work for them. Others did not need these CNCs since they either specialized in the mass

Table 4.2   Problems encountered by small and medium enterprises in using
CNC machine tools (Japan)

Problem	Percentage of total respondents
Financial burden due to high cost of machinery	36.5
Underutilization of capacity due to inadequate programming ability	36.0
Underutilization of capacity due to inadequate amount of work	29.1
Shortage of maintenance ability	20.3
Limited reliability of the machinery	8.5
Mismatch between machine capacity and user need	7.9
Resistance from employer	2.5
Other	1.8
No problems	16.4

Source: Japan, Small and Medium Enterprise Agency, Ministry of International
Trade and Industry (MITI), *Survey on Technology Development by Small and
Medium Enterprises*, Tokyo (1981 p. 183).

production of a limited variety of products or in the production of very
small quantities of miscellaneous items.

The experience of developing countries/areas

We describe the experience of the industrialized countries above to
ascertain if it guides the future evolution of applications in the developing
economies at present at a lower stage of development. There is another
aspect which makes the developed country experience relevant to the
developing countries. A technological renewal of traditional industries like
textiles in the industrialized countries (due to the adoption of new
technologies) is likely to erode the comparative advantage of the
developing countries based on lower labour costs. The problems faced by
the industrialized countries in using new technologies (noted above) may
offer a breathing space to the developing countries in the short run
(Zanfei, 1989). However, in general the developing countries facing
increasing international competition from the North will be forced to gain
access to the new technologies, and to attempt technology blending to
maintain or capture market niches.

   In Chapter 2 we noted that at present the adoption of new technologies
is limited largely to the NICs which have the technological capability,

manpower and infrastructure to take advantage of them. This is confirmed by the experience of the countries and areas described below.

Brazil

The development and use of 'high tech' in industry and banking is fairly advanced in Brazil, thanks to a vigorous government policy in this direction. But empirical evidence of technology diffusion is at present quite scarce. In the case of small and medium enterprises (SMEs), a representative survey of 19 such firms in the mechanical industry of the state of São Paulo, carried out by the National Bureau for Industrial Manpower Development, revealed important findings on the profile of firms more likely to adopt new technologies, the reasons for adopting them, and their impact on employment (Leite, 1985).

The survey included interviews with 43 employees in management and higher technical occupations and 57 employees in operation, programming and maintenance of new technologies, as well as direct observations of work activity involving the use of new technologies. The majority of firms which had adopted any of the new technologies were of medium size, 22-years-old on average, largely controlled by foreign capital and producing mainly for the domestic market. The use of new technologies was largely confined to CNCs. In 1985–86, 17 out of the 19 firms were also considering investments beyond CNCs by 1987–88.

It is worth mentioning that only three out of the 19 firms had carried out feasibility studies as a basis for decisions on the choice between the new technologies and conventional ones. Reasons given by the managers and higher-level technicians for the use of new technologies included: higher quality, precision and productivity. Status and prestige associated with the new technologies were also important factors detected by the interviewers, although the respondents in general did not admit this explicitly. Most employees in conventional manual programming (still predominant in the sector) saw the new technologies as an opportunity for 'moving up'. Nearly all the CNC operators were once operators of conventional machinery who had acquired new skills, although in some cases they were supplemented by NC computer technicians. Furthermore, practically all the maintenance and technical assistance employees using new technologies had previous experience as mechanics, electricians and electronic technicians. Only about 43 per cent of the employees who had moved up from the conventional to new technologies had relative wage increases which were very small (10 to 20 per cent) and were found to be mainly related to the quality of the workers rather than the transition *per se*.

The survey also assessed whether the adoption of the new technologies had a negative impact on employment. Conventional machine tools were totally or partially phased out in eight out of the 19 firms and were replaced. by numerically-controlled machine tools (NCMTs) at a replacement ratio of 3.5 to 1. In these eight firms, however, the managers said that all the operators were kept to work either with the new NCMTs or with the conventional equipment. Only in four out of the 19 firms was it possible to find that between 1980 and 1984 output had increased more than employment. By and large, however, employment losses were not problematic and seemed to be partly compensated by additional demand for labour resulting from work reorganization and training activities.

Mexico

One study of Mexico examined the use of flexible automation (FA) equipment in the following industries: automobiles and parts, electrical appliances and machine tools. It found that 'at the beginning of the 1980s over 80 per cent of the FA machines were used by small and medium-sized firms, but their share fell to 45 per cent in 1983 and to 28 per cent by mid-1987' (Dominguez-Villalobos, 1987). At the same time, the share of large firms using the technology actually increased, thus widening the gap between the large and small firms.

The rapid growth of the domestic market for machinery and consumer durables during the first sub-period is noted by the author to be a possible explanation for the small-scale adopters. During the second sub-period, the liquidity problem of the small firms (with little access to export markets) is proposed as a factor explaining a decline in their share among the adopters. The larger firms adopted FA equipment to compete in the export markets. Other factors explaining a decline in the share of small adopters in Mexico may be the fact that most new technology equipment is imported from abroad. The increasing debt crisis and the erosion of the national currency must have made these imports extremely expensive, with the result that the large firms alone could afford them (Boon, 1986).

Republic of Korea

Until recently the Republic of Korea (henceforth Korea) was dominated by a few large-scale industries and business groups (*chaebol*). Thus the role of SMEs might have been somewhat neglected. The Korean heavy industry was also dependent on foreign capital, technology and markets, with the result that the large industries' linkage with traditional small industry was rather weak (Cho, 1992). According to an Asian Productivity Organization

(APO) study (Ho, 1988), in 1987 the Korean Government recognized the weaknesses of the SMEs and the Economic Planning Board decided to assist them through massive industrial investments. It is reported that 1000 SMEs were selected for financial assistance and another 500 for technology assistance (Ho, 1988, p. 111). In 1991, 1100 large firms were reported to maintain supply–demand channels with 12 500 small firms (Cho, 1992).

In the eighties with the rapid economic growth and increasing investments – particularly in high technology industries such as microelectronics, automatic processing machines and transport equipment – demand seems to have grown for new small firms to supply spare parts and components to large firms. The market share of small firms (employing 20–199 workers) has expanded from nearly 21 per cent in 1980 to about 27 per cent in 1987, whereas the share of large firms (employing 500 or more workers) declined from 59 per cent to 53.4 per cent in the same period. The proportion of small firms subcontracting for large firms has also substantially increased (Cho, 1992); the proportion of small firms sub-contracting for large ones in manufacturing increased from 30 per cent in 1980 to a little over 59 per cent in 1988.

The textile industry is a good example of small firms using new computer-based technology. More than 90 per cent of the Korean textile firms employ fewer than 100 workers. The increasing shortage of labour (particularly skilled labour) has induced these firms to install such labour-saving equipment as advanced weaving machines fitted with computer-control systems. The Korean government offers incentives to firms (in the form of subsidies) to introduce new technology in the industry. As a result of this policy, in 1992 the 'share of automated weaving machines in the total stock has risen to 65 per cent, near to the level of advanced countries like Italy' (Cho, 1992). Software houses also play an important role in assisting SMEs to introduce computer numerical control. However, it appears that in general the use of microelectronics-based technologies by the Korean SMEs is only a recent phenomenon.

Malaysia and Singapore

A small sample survey of firms in Malaysia and Singapore in machine tool, electrical machinery and automobile industries examined the diffusion of flexible automation (FA) machinery (NCMTs, robots and CAD/CAM) (see Table 4.3). In Malaysia, a greater percentage of very small firms used NCMTs than the larger firms; these firms also used CAD/CAM, although not as much as the large firms. In both Malaysia and Singapore, robots are used mainly in large firms, since large lot sizes are required for their efficient utilization.

Table 4.3   Use of flexible automation machinery in sample firms (Malaysia and Singapore) (percentages)

Country/employment size	Total respondents	Respondents using		
		NCMTS	*Robots*	*CAD/CAM*
Malaysia				
<20	6	6	–	1
20–49	6	6	–	1
50–199	6	5	–	4
200–999	4	–	1	3
1000+	3	2	2	1
Singapore				
<20	2	2	–	–
20–49	3	3	1	–
50–199	–	–	–	–
200–999	5	2	3	2
1000+	2	2	2	2

Source: Fong (1993).

An unusually large use of NCMTs by the small firms may have been due partly to a rapid decline in their prices. One respondent in the sample firms noted that prices of NCMTs declined by 50 per cent in terms of the local currency *ringitt*, between 1975 and 1980. Another factor is the formal education of the local entrepreneurs, which created an awareness of the potential benefits of the use of microelectronics technology.

In Singapore the Small Enterprise Bureau, responsible for the development and promotion of SMEs, offers several incentives to local industry, grants and loans for the purchase of CNC machine tools. In 1986, a small Enterprise Computerization Programme was started to raise the competitiveness of local SMEs through the use of microelectronics-based technologies. Under the Programme, financial incentives are offered for hiring consultants and for meeting the hardware and software costs (Ho, 1988, p. 64).

Hong Kong

Hong Kong is suffering from growing labour shortages which induce a switch to new technologies. The factor costs and prices in this territory are likely to be much more favourable to the rapid diffusion of these technologies than in the non-NICs.

Several examples of CNC and robot applications have been observed in Hong Kong. However, the use of CNC lathes is at present not so common in SMEs. In 1979, a subsidiary of an American company manufacturing aerospace parts introduced a computer numerical control machining centre. The firm also introduced CNC lathes, automatic grinding and heat treatment equipment. One of the reasons for the use of CNC machines was the relatively small lot sizes which made it necessary to reduce costs by the lowering of setting-up time through the use of CNCs. It is noted that as a result of the use of CNCs, the rate of defects had fallen from 35 per cent to less than 10 per cent, and the productivity index rose from 50 to 89 (Lee, 1986).

Textile and garment industries are among the oldest industries which have continued to grow during the last thirty years. The industries still consist of relatively small and medium enterprises – those employing 100–500 workers account for over 30 per cent of the workforce and 40 per cent of output. These enterprises have a comparative advantage for several reasons. First, because of land shortage factory buildings are high-rise, which encourages separate small factories rather than big ones. Secondly, the factory workforce, which is largely of Cantonese origin, prefers small enterprises for cultural and historical reasons. Thirdly, smallness seems attractive since 'buyers are increasingly seeking variety coupled with decreasing volume per order' (Taylor, 1984). Fourthly, the use of small computers and microprocessors helps overcome such disadvantages of small enterprises as low productivity. These enterprises tend to concentrate on fashion-oriented work, requiring a wide variety of small-batch products. The Hong Kong Productivity Council assists these enterprises in the use of computers to undertake many repetitive and time-consuming tasks. Special emphasis is placed on the development of suitable software to enable small producers to increase their production in fashion work without raising managerial skill requirements.

As a result of research by the above Council on the local implications of the use of CAD/CAM in pattern grading and marker making, a low-cost CAD system has been developed with a Chinese character display. This system enables the user quickly to grade and plot his/her patterns, which can subsequently be laid up by hand in the user's own factory to make markers. Alternatively, an optional facility is available to transfer to the central marker's bureau the graded pattern information and marker's requirement over the telecommunications network. This service bureau enables the typical small factory to dispense with the space required for a marker's lay-up table.

The Council has also developed an integrated garment management information system which is claimed to be superior to imported systems in terms of performance and maintenance (Ho, 1988). The system is said to be suitable for small and medium enterprises since it can be used with a stand-alone personal computer.

Several benefits have accrued from the process of computerization described above, for example elimination of production bottlenecks, reduction in material costs through timely feedback on consumption, and identification of unaccounted-for rejections between stages of production. In general, the managerial and financial efficiency of small and medium firms has improved.

CONCLUSION

The above discussion suggests that at least for some advanced developing countries, the use of microelectronics-based innovations can encourage small-scale and decentralized production. Particularly in the export-oriented small and medium enterprises, which increasingly have to compete with their counterparts in the industrialized countries, adoption of the technology is becoming particularly necessary and attractive. In the developing countries in general, the application of new technologies by the small and medium enterprises is likely to be facilitated under situations in which the large-scale firms sub-contract work to small-scale firms, thus guaranteeing the supply of technology and skills, infrastructure and other types of technical assistance. This seems to be the case in Italy and Japan discussed above. (Of course, in the industrialized countries small enterprises which do not sub-contract work also use new technologies.) Yet the experience with sub-contracting arrangements in developing countries has not generally been as successful, presumably owing to a less advanced stage of industrial development.

The illustrations of new technology adoption noted in this chapter give some indication of the scope for using microelectronics efficiently at lower scales of production. However, empirical data on the links between microelectronics and decentralization of production are not yet very evident, particularly in the developing countries. More empirical research is therefore necessary to explore such issues as the type of communications infrastructure necessary to facilitate production away from large urban centres, the measures required to reduce the cost of new technology to small producers, and the scope for changing the production structures to facilitate the effective use of new technologies.

Most of the benefits from new manufacturing technology come not so much from the technology itself but from the way in which it forces firms to reorganize to manage new technology efficiently. To the extent that small firms demonstrate organizational flexibility and skill in management, they can exploit the potential offered by new technologies. These issues of industrial organization and management are the subject of the following chapter.

5 New Technologies, Flexible Specialization and Industrialization*

In this chapter we extend the analysis presented in Chapters 2 to 4 to examine whether new technology applications and approaches such as flexible production and specialization (briefly mentioned in Chapter 4) can be fitted into the choice of technology framework. Under this framework, the new technologies simply widen a choice set at a given point in time. Actual selection of the new technology would depend on whether it is cheaper and ensures a better quality product, or is simply technologically superior in the sense that it uses less of all factor inputs or produces maximum output for given inputs. The chapter also discusses the manifold institutional mechanisms required to promote a more flexible smaller-scale industrialization in the Third World.

THE CHOICE OF TECHNOLOGY FRAMEWORK

In Chapter 4 we discussed how firm size could influence the rate of adoption of the new tecnologies. This relationship, as we shall see, depends not only on the characteristics of the new technologies themselves but also on a number of institutional variables as well as on the nature of the industry considered. To begin with, though, let us consider the simplest textbook version of the choice of technology, according to which the individual firm is confronted with a range of alternatives and a choice is made at a particular point in time. In this version of the model, the new technology will be chosen on the basis of whether or not it reduces the costs of production in comparison with existing techniques.

To an important degree, the issues relating to the demand rather than the supply side of the choice of technology are likely to be significant. These issues are briefly discussed below.

*This chapter is a revised version of J. James and A.S. Bhalla, 'Flexible Specialization, New Technologies and Industrialization', first published in *Futures*, Vol. 25, No. 6, July–August 1993, and is published here with the permission of Butterworth–Heinemann, Oxford, UK.

The demand side: products and markets

Much of the standard choice of technology debate tends to focus on questions of efficiency and costs: that is, on the supply side of the issues. Yet, when it is viewed from the standpoint of the characteristics that are embodied in products (as we noted in Chapter 2), the demand for products may also have a major influence on the returns that can be expected from a new (process) technology. The reason is that changes in technology often cause changes in the product and these in turn may shift the firm's demand curve to the right.

In the case of many of the new microelectronics-based technologies, these product changes often seem to be of overriding importance to the choice-of-technique decisions. Consider in this regard Table 5.1 which mostly contains a summary of the results of a series of studies conducted by/for the Technology and Employment Programme of the International Labour Office (ILO) on the adoption of a variety of the new technologies. Other case studies have also been included in the table. In each case demand factors appear to be decisive to adoption decisions, whereas factors related to costs of production on the other hand were not regarded as being very influential at all.

The demand dimension of technology choice is likely to have different implications for large-scale as against small-scale firms in developing countries. In general, small-scale firms in industry tend to serve particular and fragmented markets. Thus whereas 'Large units tend to sell mainly to high-income markets – most small units mainly sell low-income products to the informal sector' (Stewart; Ranis, 1990). By 'low-income' products what is meant here is essentially products embodying a relatively high proportion of essential (e.g. food nutrients) characteristics and a relatively low proportion of unessential characteristics (or what are sometimes referred to as 'frills'). Yet, it is precisely the opposite combination of characteristics that may often define the products associated with microelectronics innovations, such as CAD and CNC machine tools. The reason is that these innovations comprise part of what historically (in the industrialized countries) has been a close relationship between innovations in products and innovations in processes (Stewart, 1977).

Supply and demand combined: a technology decision matrix

The discussion so far has dealt for the most part separately with the demand and supply sides of the choice of technology decision. Before going further with these issues, however, it is worth emphasizing that, in

Table 5.1   The role of demand in the choice of microelectronics-based innovations in selected developing countries

Author (year)	Country	Sectors	New technologies	Determinants of the choice of technology
1. Onn (1989)	Malaysia/ Singapore	General machine manufacturing; electrical and electronics; auto-mobile assembly and component manufacturing; computer and computer component manufacturing	NC machine tools, CAD/ CAM, robots	'Despite the much feared labour-displacement potentials of the new technology, labour saving was by no means a major motive of its adoption. Of the 24 Malaysian firms ... 14 reported that their main objective had been to improve the quality of their products or work, while another 12 had introduced the new technology to enhance their competitiveness.' (p. 53)
2. Pyo (1986)	Republic of Korea	Automobile; electronics; industrial machinery and shipbuilding	NCMTs, robots, CAD/CAM	'The firms in our survey introduced it (FA machinery) for three main reasons: for better quality control (22 out of a total of 30 firms), to compete in export markets (18 firms); and due to product standard imposed by domestic buyers' (15 firms).' (pp. 94–95)
3. Dominguez Villalobos (1988)	Mexico	Electrical; electronics; automobile; machinery and tool	CNC machine tools, CAD, robots, machining centres	'By far the most frequent purpose of using NCMTs ... was to attain a higher or more regular quality of work ... followed by a higher speed of production/reduced downtime. Flexibility was the third important consideration.' (p. 24)

Table 5.1 Continued

Author (year)	Country	Sectors	New technologies	Determinants of the choice of technology
4. Fleury (1988)	Brazil	Metal engineering	Electronic data processing equipment, CAD, NCMTS, programmable logic controllers	'Although the degree of emphasis varied from one industry to another, the adoption of FA equipment was primarily motivated by the desire to improve the quality of products or work and to increase productivity for the purpose of strengthening the firm's competitive position in export markets.' (p. 81)
5. Tauile (1987)	Brazil	Automobiles	CNC machine tools	'Motivation for introducing NC machine tools is – quality control, flexibility in production and the characteristics of certain products.' (p. 171)
6. Boon (1986)	Colombia	Bottling plant	CNC machine tools	'The adoption of the CNC machine took place to achieve a better quality in order to maintain and enlarge export markets. In addition the size of the lots (fluctuating between 25 and 200 pieces) facilitated the adoption of the machines.' (p. 38)
7. Boon (1986)	Peru	Metal-working industry	CNC machine tools	'The acquisition reasons which the seven (adopting) firms gave, were as follows: to reduce costs, to improve quality, precision, piece complexity, increment in production and volume.' (pp. 36–7)

Sources: For 1 to 4, Watanabe (1993); for 5, Watanabe (1987); for 6 and 7, Boon (1986).

practice, the decision to select one technology instead of another is based on a combination of both supply and demand factors.

In fact, since both costs (supply) and demand (products) may increase, decrease or remain unchanged following the adoption of a new technology, the decision can be depicted in terms of the nine cells shown in Table 5.2. Thus, whereas some combinations give rise to an unambiguous decision about whether to accept or reject the new technology, others are indeterminate and depend on the relative strengths of the opposing influences on profitability. These indeterminate cases appear in the upper right and lower left cells of the matrix.

As we noted in Chapter 2, capital cost is one of the factors explaining a low or slow diffusion of new technologies. This factor does not, however, bear only on the profitability of the new technologies. For, even if this factor does not render the new technology unprofitable (in terms of the decision matrix shown in Table 5.2), a formidable problem of indivisibility or 'lumpiness' may nevertheless still confront the small-scale (though perhaps not as much large-scale) enterprises.

THE FLEXIBLE SPECIALIZATION PARADIGM

Another mechanism through which the benefits of the new micro-electronics-based technologies are transmitted to industrial enterprises is what is known as flexible specialization. This concept, associated most

Table 5.2   Combining supply and demand determinants of adoption

| | | | *Demand* | |
		increases	*remains constant*	*falls*
Supply	*Costs fall*	+	+	–
	Costs remain constant	+	X	X
	Costs increase	–	X	X

+ = the new technique is adopted;
X = the new technique is not adopted;
– = the outcome is indeterminate, depending on the relative
        influences of supply and demand on the profits of the firm.

closely with the work of Piore and Sabel (1984), represents a new paradigm of industrial organization, which,

> In contrast to mass production – uses a series of general resources to produce a constantly shifting mix of specialized products. It depends upon the increasing generality of the resource base: finding new uses for existing skills and equipment and extending the range of products which the economy can produce. This form of production was typical of the craft communities which existed throughout Western Europe and North America in the first half of the nineteenth century. (Piore, 1985)

New microelectronics technology is one of the factors that has given rise – in the 'new dynamic' form that is known as flexible specialization – to the revival of craft production. These technologies are flexible in the sense that they allow a greater range of output to be produced, as well as in the sense that they permit a more rapid response to changes in consumer demand (a form of flexibility that is especially relevant to industries such as textiles, footwear and automobiles, which are prone to demand changes).

The concept of technological flexibility means different things to different people however. First, it may mean 'the possibility of producing simultaneously on the same line different alternative products' (what is labelled as 'mix flexibility' by Gerwin and Leung, 1980). In a discussion on different types of flexibility, Boyer and Coriat (1986) make a distinction between product differentiation and product variety. While the former refers to minor modifications in existing forms of production organization (e.g. annual changes in car models), the latter refers to a case when a firm decides to introduce a new product which involves more substantial changes in organization of production. Flexibility may also imply that the whole production process can be simplified or complicated without involving much additional cost. It may also mean (as noted above) the ease with which production can be adapted to fluctuations in market demand. The programmability of new computer-based technologies makes it possible to take advantage of the above elements of flexibility.

With the utilization of microelectronics-based innovations – viz. numerically controlled (NC) and computer numerically-controlled (CNC) machines – the disadvantages can be overcome of handicrafts and small-scale industries in developing countries (poor quality of the product and low output and productivity). For example, CNC machines can ensure quality control in two ways. First, they can be programmed to diagnose faults in the control system and the machine. Secondly, often the new technology can remove the causes of defective production altogether. Revival of some craft production is therefore facilitated. It has also been suggested that de-scaling facilitated by new technologies can lead to new patterns of decentralized industrialization (see below).

The CNC machines enjoy several advantages which should be of particular interest to small and medium enterprises. These are:

(i) *flexibility*, that is, capacity to alter parts very quickly which enables production of varied and complex components in small batches;

(ii) *greater accuracy and predictability*, which reduces the requirements of working capital and factory space;

(iii) *reduction in down time*, through reduction in number of machines, greater consistency in quality, and improved and standardized tooling; and

(iv) *savings in capital*, through significant reductions in door-to-door time (between receipt and fulfilment of an order) and of consequent reductions in costly inventories of raw materials, work in progress and finished stock. This releases considerable amounts of working capital and can help small firms with cash flow problems.

As Piore and Sabel (1984) emphasize, however, although it has increased the flexibility of production, the computer alone cannot account for this revival (partly because computers can be used in a 'rigid' manner and partly because Piore and Sabel cite cases where flexible production does not depend on computers). Nor are the new technologies (in the hardware sense) the only form of innovation that is emphasized by the concept of flexible specialization.

The concept and definitions

The concept of flexible specialization is often described as a contrast to the mass production paradigm. Whereas the latter is characterized by high output and the large size of firms, hierarchical management, specialized dedicated machinery, and fragmented and routinized tasks, flexible specialization is associated with large or small firms, small-batch production, varied and customized products, and general or multi-purpose machinery and a flexible or multi-skilled labour force.

The term 'flexible specialization' has been defined in several different ways in the literature. In addition to the technological flexibility of CNCs noted above, flexibility is often used, for example, to refer to changes in working practices that are required by flexibility of production. Another meaning has to do with labour markets, both internal and external. For example, 'task flexibility can be facilitated by a greater use of internal labour markets, reducing labour turnover, increasing training in a range of skills, winning flexible working practices and a willingness to move within the firm in return for job security' (Sayer, 1989). Still another meaning of flexibility refers to organizational innovations within and between firms. Within firms, for example,

> Factory outlets need to alter, from mass production's dedicated lines and functional layouts to flexible production cells. 'Families of parts' need to be composed, each family being allocated a separate 'factory' to itself; these are based on the principle of modular-designs and involve a process of what has come to be called 'design for manufacture'. (Kaplinsky, 1991a)

Changes in the nature of the relationships between firms are frequently also discussed; some of these discussions focus on the relationships between small-scale firms (notably in industrial districts) while others are concerned with the relationships between large- and small-scale firms (often in the context of sub-contracting relationships).

Some writers like Schmitz (1990) and Piore and Sabel (1984) have focused on the concept of flexible specialization in the context of small and medium enterprises, their clustering (to provide for collective efficiency) and inter-firm division of labour, assuming that these factors account for their dynamism. Others argue that the concept is scale neutral and that the size of firm is not important for reaping the benefits of flexible production.

The concept of flexible specialization seems to have had its origins in the industrialized countries with the recognition that many small and medium enterprises (organized in the so-called industrial districts) succeeded (during the seventies and eighties) in facing the economic crisis and in obtaining market niches in conditions of saturated markets (Schmitz, 1989, 1990; Nadvi, 1992). In contrast, large-scale industry, based on the system of mass production, showed declining rates of productivity growth (Kaplinsky, 1990). It is assumed that the resilience of small enterprises was due to their flexibility in responding to fluctuations in markets.

Despite the numerous shades of meaning attached to flexible specialization, noted above, its basic features seem to be concerned with (a) technology and product characteristics; (b) industrial organization; (c) labour flexibility, the segmentation of the workforce into core and periphery and informalization of work, and (d) social and institutional cooperation and division of labour between firms. As we noted above, greater flexibility of technology enables production in small batches and with a greater variety and differentiation. New forms of industrial organization are designed to reduce costs through dispensing with inventory stocks. Just-in-time, lean production and changes in factory layout are all intended to achieve this goal.

Whatever the definition of the concept of flexible specialization, in future production in both industrialized and developing countries the pattern of industrialization is likely to be characterized by new forms of labour utilization, thanks partly to the greater use of new information technologies. A changing pattern of employment, its 'flexibilization', a shift between core and periphery workers, flexible working hours and so on are already becoming a reality in industrialized countries. These characteristics of the new flexible labour markets are likely to be a model of the future particularly for the newly industrializing countries (NICs). Their influence on industrial productivity, skill structures and human capital formation is bound to be of important concern for industrial firms facing the challenge of quality as well as price competition. This is already emerging from the spectacular economic success of most East Asian economies.

If there are, therefore, a variety of meanings that attach to the concept of flexible specialization, even further meanings (and one might add, in many cases, further confusion) are created by the numerous ways in which these dimensions can be combined. Some dimensions can of course exist separately from the others: adoption of the new technologies, for example, can be effected without changes in the other dimensions and the same is true of organizational changes. On the other hand, there are a number of powerful complementarities between the various dimensions that are ascribed to the concept of flexible specialization (Hoffman, 1989; Kaplinsky, 1990).

Innovational complementarities

The choice of technology literature tends to focus on a single innovation which, typically, is an innovation in the hardware of technology. (This, of course, is a general observation and is not meant to deny the existence of untypical contributions.) Those who have contributed to the flexible specialization literature, in contrast, emphasize (as noted above) organizational as well as technological innovations and some of them deal also with relationships (especially those of a complementary kind) between these innovations. It is widely recognized, for example, that organizational changes within an industrial enterprise are required if all the potential gains from the new technologies are actually to be realized. This recognition owes much to the Japanese experience. 'They have built on their already highly flexible production organization, to develop the management structure and practices necessary to extract the full benefit of flexible automation' (Hoffman, 1989). In the industrialized countries, this recognition is supported by a large number of empirical studies; in developing countries, in contrast, such studies are relatively few and of these, the best documented is Kaplinsky's analysis of a medium-scale garments firm in Cyprus (Kaplinsky, 1990). He shows that through essentially three mechanisms – reorganization of the production line, the introduction of a computerized information processing system and the closer integration of marketing and production – the firm has experienced a 'substantial enhancement' of its competitive position.

It bears emphasizing, though, that complementarity between innovations does not mean that they need to be simultaneously adopted (Feder, Just and Zilberman, 1985). In fact, there are several reasons why organizational change may be undertaken *prior* to the adoption of the new process technologies. One reason is that organizational change may stimulate or facilitate the adoption and effective operation of the latter forms of innovation. A second reason why organizational innovations may precede those of a technological kind is that, in certain circumstances – such as an acute scarcity of capital and foreign exchange – the former may be the only feasible option for small-scale enterprises in developing countries (Kaplinsky, 1991). What occurred among small firms in the light engineering industry in Argentina during the economic crisis of the 1980s may be illustrative of just such a possibility. In particular, the 'Japanese' organizational model (of inventory minimization, reduction in setting-up time of machinery etc.) appears to have been combined with old, non-sophisticated physical technologies; this experience, according to Roldan (1991), suggests that 'the Japanese "classical model" may be successfully emulated by a small firm, in small batch or custom-made production, with traditional physical technologies, in a crisis situation'.

The model of the industrial district

The concept of flexible specialization is perhaps most commonly understood to refer to regional clusters of small enterprises located in geographically contiguous areas or industrial districts and specializing in specific sectors of economic activity. A number of external economies are claimed from such clustering, such as sharing of knowledge, technology and skills on the basis of a division of labour, reduction in the cost of job search, etc. (Nadvi, 1992a). Within the scope of the industrial district concept thus defined, it is important to distinguish between two very different strands of literature.

One of these strands is concerned specifically with developing countries and, in particular, with the notion of 'collective efficiency', which denotes the various types of gains that accrue collectively to small-scale enterprises clustered 'around a set of related activities' (Schmitz, 1990). Schmitz did not seek to link the concept to the adoption of new (microelectronics) technologies (or, for that matter, to any form of technical change). In the early nineties other case studies have emerged on small firm clusters in a number of countries at different stages of economic and industrial development, e.g. Brazil (Ruas et al., 1994), Indonesia (Smyth, 1992; Smyth et al., 1994), Zimbabwe (Rassmusen and Sverrisson, 1994), Pakistan (Nadvi, 1992). Fairly common to these country case studies are the following main manufacturing activities: textiles and garments, footwear, furniture and metal working. These studies do not explore the use of new technologies in these countries and industries.

The neglect of links with new technologies renders the concept of flexible specialization as employed by Schmitz and others (Rasmussen, 1992; Smyth, 1992) open to the criticism that it lacks novelty. For without any such dimension, it is difficult to see what is in fact novel about this approach, or to discern what new hope it offers to existing clusters of small-scale producers in developing countries who are reliant on traditional (and usually unproductive) technologies. After all, not only have regional clusters of small firms (such as at Kumasi in Ghana, an example that is frequently quoted by Schmitz) long been in existence, but they have also been actively promoted by governments in a wide variety of developing countries through the establishment of industrial estates and workshop clusters (see below) (UNIDO, 1978; Mytelka, 1993).

In sharp contrast to the concept of flexible specialization that has just been described, the second (albeit less extensive) strand of literature seeks explicitly to *incorporate* the new microelectronics technologies. This concept of flexible specialization, which can appropriately be described as 'high-technology cottage industry' (Sabel, 1982), is much closer to the model of the industrial district that is found in the so-called 'Third Italy', and especially to the many small firms in that region that make use of, for example, CAD and CNC machine-tool technologies (see Chapter 4).

In the context of Italy, this concept is defined as 'a fragmented cycle of production' which 'can assume different forms, ranging from a pattern of decentralization of production within larger firms to a constellation model of small firms' (Mazzonis and Pianta, 1991). In the case of the 'Third Italy' the latter interpretation and experience has proved to be much more successful in responding 'to the ups and downs of demand and to the introduction of innovations' (Mazzonis and Pianta, 1991).

One recent study on the Republic of Korea classifies clusters of firms by three technological levels: upper (referring to microelectronics), middle and lower (Cho, 1992). It argues that three regional clusters have been emerging in the Republic of Korea in line with these three levels of technology. Cho concludes: 'given that each cluster has its own pattern of inter-firm relations and resultant flexibility, the sum of three flexible techno-spatial clusters gives rise to a flexible regime of accumulation ... There is no single pathway to a flexible specialization industrial paradigm' (p. 21).

From the standpoint of the concept of the industrial district, the key question takes a normative rather than a positive form, namely, whether 'high-technology cottage industry' represents a model of the industrial district that is capable of replication in the Third World context either now or in the future. The answer to this question depends on what preconditions will need to be met.

Some of these preconditions are likely to involve precisely the types of problems that have so frequently undermined the efficacy of various forms of collective action in developing countries. The literature is replete, for example, with frustrated collective outcomes in areas such as irrigation and sanitation, while the historical experience with cooperatives on the whole provides a no-less-discouraging record (Johnston and Clark, 1982). Common to many of these disappointing experiences is an inherent and formidable problem that Mancur Olson (1965) described so forcefully many years ago, namely, the problem of the 'free-rider'. One well-known form that this problem takes is that when the community is large no single individual has an incentive to participate in a communal venture. 'For by definition, he cannot make a perceptible contribution to the group scheme, and since no one in the group will react if he fails to contribute, there is no economic incentive for him to do so' (James, 1989). The industrial districts of the 'Third Italy' appear to have been able to overcome this type of problem largely through the countervailing pressure that is exerted by very powerful communal ties. Piore and Sabel (1984) suggest for example that 'the fear of punishment by exclusion from the community is probably critical to the success of the explicit constraints on competition' that seem to be so important in these districts. Comparable mechanisms are known to exist in some Third World communities but in general they cannot be relied upon. Indeed, even in the Brazilian footwear industry that is so approvingly cited by Sabel, it is doubtful that anything like the strength of communal ties as in the 'Third Italy' can be found. In fact, according to one recent description of this industry, smaller firms 'do not find in Brazil a propitious environment in which to operate, which seems to exist in the case of the Italian model – there exists a climate of *distrust* in the inter-industrial market' (Prochnik, 1992).

Other types of preconditions that need to be met if the Italian model is to be replicated are likely to revolve to an important extent around the role of government. For, as is frequently acknowledged in the literature on the 'Third Italy' local government institutions and municipal authorities have been key to the adoption and utilization of the new technologies (the use of CAD in Prato, the textile industry, is one of the clearest examples of this, as was noted in Chapter 4). Whether governments in developing countries will be willing (and able) to emulate this behaviour depends, among numerous other factors, on how far they can overcome, in Kaplinsky's words, 'their fixation with large-scale production' (Kaplinsky, 1990). This form of production often appears to have been favoured directly and indirectly by governments, even when more profitable (in private as well as social terms) small-scale technological alternatives were available. Still, as Kaplinsky indicates, the governments of at least three relatively small developing countries – Cyprus, Jamaica and the Dominican Republic – have already modelled their industrial development strategies on the basis of the small-scale clusters found in the 'Third Italy'(Kaplinsky, 1990).

Industrial districts versus industrial estates

On the surface, the concept of the industrial district in the industrialized countries like Italy seems to be similar to that of industrial estates promoted in developing countries for over three decades now. They both represent a constellation or agglomeration of small firms. However, one important distinction between them concerns size: whereas the industrial districts of Italy typically comprise between 1000 and 3000 firms (Brusco, 1990) industrial estates are usually concerned with a very much smaller number of firms. Moreover, while the industrial districts of Italy have developed more or less spontaneously, the industrial estates are by their very definition 'tracts of land and (possibly) buildings developed by the State, presumably on favourable terms, for industrialists' (Shinohara and Fisher, 1968). In the Indian industrial estates, for example, several incentives were granted to attract small-scale firms: favourable terms for hire purchase, improved terms for small loans and the supply of equipment and materials and common facilities.

An important question is whether existing industrial estates in the developing countries can provide an appropriate model for the government to disseminate and promote the use of new technologies like CAD/CAM and CNC machines among small and medium firms. It would seem that, to date, governments have not made wide use of the estates for the sake of improving small-scale technologies, reflecting perhaps the more general absence of a technological component in measures to promote small-scale industries in developing countries (Livingstone, 1991).

In at least some countries (e.g. Kenya) this neglect is apparently being redressed. (Kenya Ministry of National Development and Planning, 1990; Nadvi 1992). Nadvi (1992) found that small light engineering firms in an industrial estate in Gujranwala (Pakistan Punjab) were using NC and CNC machines, but there was no inter-firm cooperation in their use as would be expected by the proponents of industrial districts and flexible specialization. On the contrary 'new technology was ... considered a guarded secret whose benefits could only be realized if such firms retained monopoly over its availability' (Nadvi, 1992, p. 22). This suggests that clustering of small firms *per se* may not necessarily lead to 'collective efficiency' or dissemination of new technologies.

DECENTRALIZATION

The spatial dimension of production is generally neglected in the standard choice of technology approach. Yet location, in the specific form of agglomerative clusters of small-scale firms, is central to the flexible specialization paradigm. Locational issues arise also in a different, but no less important way, in the notion that the new technologies might permit a more decentralized pattern of industrialization than has hitherto been possible on the basis of 'mass production'

One way in which this might arise relies on the tendency towards diminished plant size and greater flexibility of production that is associated with some of the new technologies. These characteristics of the new technology, so the argument runs, may alter the regional concentration of production that has been so prevalent under import-substituting industrialization in developing countries. More specifically, what is envisaged is the alteration of a pattern of industrialization that has been characterized by production in a few large-scale (usually imported) plants, of goods embodying characteristics in proportions very similar to those found in the developed countries. The new technologies may be able to alter this pattern through the dispersed location of a larger number of small-scale plants which are able to serve the heterogeneous preferences of a much wider group of consumers. (Kaplinsky refers, in this context, to an 'ability to "niche" output to the specific conditions of individual markets, without sacrificing quality and price', which, he contends, 'opens the prospect of developing appropriate products for developing country markets' [Kaplinsky, 1991].) The extent to which this type of locational change actually materializes, however, will depend (among other factors) on the numerous supply- and demand-side determinants of adoption of the new technologies that were described above. On the demand side, an especially important question arises as to whether effective demand will be sufficient in the decentralized (particularly rural) locations to make adoption profitable. More specifically, the question is whether the new products that are associated with the new technologies embody characteristics in proportions that are desirable and accessible from the point of view of low-income rural households. While this may indeed occur in some cases – thereby validating the view that the new technologies are able to produce 'low-income' or appropriate products – there are likely to be many other cases when the new products are suitable instead for 'high-income' markets (see Chapter 2). After all, many of the examples cited earlier suggested that the new technologies are often adopted precisely to be able to compete in the export markets of the industrialized countries.

This form of demand-side issue does not, however, apply to applications of micro-hydro power to rural areas, because a given demand (for energy) is here simply being met more cheaply. What has nevertheless still to be overcome in most such schemes is the problem of lumpiness of investment, since even relatively low-cost versions of this form of power will be inaccessible to most individual households in rural areas. If, on the other hand, adoption decisions can be made *communally,* micro-hydro projects appear to represent one important way in which the new technologies can promote a pattern of industrialization that is based on small-scale producers in rural areas. A project in a small rural village in central Colombia that used the power from a micro-hydro plant to establish a small sawmill illustrates this potential (*Appropriate Technology,* 1983; Bhalla et al., 1984; Bhalla and D. James, 1988). The community in that village was able (with the assistance of a non-government rural development organization) to commit itself not only to the joint ownership of the sawmill hydro plant, but also to planning and building the sawmill. Evidently, therefore, the problems of collective action are not insuperable, and the incomes of even very isolated rural communities can, under the right conditions, be increased by the adoption of the new technologies.

Still another way in which the new technologies might facilitate decentralization exploits the ability of (some of) these technologies to overcome long distances. Unlike the two previous possibilities which were based on 'stand-alone' adoption by individuals or communities, this third possibility involves communication *between* the geographically fragmented elements of a system of production or distribution of goods and services. In the context of public goods provided by governments, one can point to a variety of examples of this model in developing countries (e.g. the way in which computers at different levels of government are linked together in information systems). In the context of the privately owned enterprise, aspects of the Benetton experience provide probably the best example (especially when they are compared with the case of Prato, the Italian textile industry).

The Benetton retail shops are to be found in locations throughout the world. The Prato case, on the other hand, as noted above, comprises a cluster of large numbers of small-scale firms in one particular region. It would seem that the production structures of Benetton and Prato are similar, but not their distribution structures. For, while Benetton producers are, like their counterparts in Prato, centralized in a particular area, the retail outlets are very widely dispersed. This dispersion is based on a telematic network (combining information processing and transmission) which Benetton introduced in 1978 to provide communications between the headquarters and the sales outlets. The network has proceeded through different stages of sophistication since then. In 1985, the basic telematic network was linked to the different Benetton agents through the provision of a personal computer to each. As a result, the agents are able to receive information about consumers, goods and prices very rapidly. At the same time, 'The pattern of sales and extent of re-orders are regularly fed back from the shops to Benetton, and in this way the time required for the final decision of distribution among subcontractors is markedly reduced. This allows for an optimization of the total production cycle and a better utilization of capital equipment of the whole system' (Belussi, 1987).

As with Prato, it is difficult to conceive of Benetton as a model (for incorporating small-scale enterprises into the new technology system) that is easily replicable in developing countries. On the supply side, for example, Benetton requires a highly complex communications infrastructure which for many, if not most, developing countries simply does not exist. On the demand side, it is worth emphasizing that the complex information system is used by Benetton to communicate with retail outlets which are overwhelmingly concentrated in the developed countries. The reason is that it is in these countries that the major markets for Benetton are to be found and it is information about these markets (and changes therein) that the company requires (so precise is this information, in fact, that Benetton 'almost directly interacts with its customers') (Belussi, 1987). Correspondingly few developing countries participate in the communications network of retailers; in fact, according to one study, the Benetton experience casts doubt 'on the general applicability of the thesis which suggests the progressive displacement of labour intensive "mature" products to LDCs' (Belussi, 1987, p. 16).

CONCLUSION

This Chapter has examined the various economic and institutional mechanisms through which the benefits of the new microelectronics-based technologies are, or might be, transmitted to small-scale enterprises in developing countries. We have suggested that although there is a tendency in the literature on this topic to emphasize the 'newness' of these technologies, many instances of adoption can be understood with reference to the received choice of technology framework (albeit one that differs in some ways from the neo-classical model). There are, for example, a number of similarities between the patterns of adoption and diffusion of agricultural innovations and those that are associated with the new microelectronics-based technologies.

On the other hand, there are numerous other mechanisms through which the benefits of the latter might be transmitted to small-scale enterprises that cannot (or at least not easily) be fitted into the choice-of-technology framework. This was shown to be mainly because the framework tends to focus on the individual rather than the group or community; because it neglects relationships between and within enterprises; because it tends to deal with the hardware rather than the organizational dimensions of technology; and because it lacks a spatial dimension. In each of these areas, we have compared the choice of technology with two other analytical frameworks, namely, those associated with flexible specialization on the one hand and with decentralization on the other. The outcome of these comparisons is contained in summary form in Table 5.3. We wish to emphasize, however, that our approach to these alternatives has been essentially comparative rather than exhaustive; by no means, that is, does our discussion purport to review the substantial literature on them that already exists.

None of the mechanisms we have considered suggests that the complex of new technologies is likely to constitute a major alternative to previous

Table 5.3   New technologies and small-scale industrialization: alternative economic and institutional mechanisms

	Choice of technology	Flexible specialization	Decentralization
Technological focus	New technology as an expansion of the existing range of techniques	New technology as part of the new flexible specialization paradigm	New technology as an expansion of spatial technological possibilities
Unit of analysis	Individual firm	Individual firm as part of well-defined cluster of firms	Individual firm/community
Organizational change	Not major area	Innovational complementarities	May involve changed relationships between central and dispersed units of production (distribution)
Geographical focus	None	Agglomerative clusters	Dispersion
Inter- and intra-firm linkages	Only insofar as differential rates adoption by small and large firms affect the competitive position of the former	Central issue, competitive and cooperative relationships between small-scale firms and between large and small-scale firms	Unimportant (with dispersed 'stand-alone' adoption), or important (where dispersed units interact with centrally-located unit)
Benefits	Increased profits by individual adopting firms	'Collective efficiency', dynamic gains in export markets, externalities	Regional decentralization, dynamic increased equality
Main constraints	Factor prices, skills, information	Problems of collective action, 'government failures' to induce cooperative behaviour	Lack of infrastructure and effective demand in dispersed locations
Examples	CAD/CAM in NICs, microcomputers in Africa	Prato textile industry in Italy	Benetton (Italy), electronic load controllers in Sri Lanka, Colombia, Thailand and Nepal.

patterns of industrialization, at least in the short-run (though particular types of small firms have and will benefit from these technologies).

6 Socioeconomic Implications of New Technologies*

In Chapters 2 to 5 we examined the pattern of new technology diffusion in different sets of developing countries, and the scope and limitations in the adoption of new technologies at both large and small scales of production. We also attempted, in Chapter 5, an analytical framework within which new technologies could be analysed along with flexible specialization and decentralization. In this chapter it is therefore appropriate to examine the socioeconomic implications of the adoption of new technologies in the Third World.

THE IMPACT OF NEW TECHNOLOGIES: SOME GENERAL CONSIDERATIONS

As may be expected, there are very few impact studies which examine the effects of new technologies such as microelectronics and bio-technologies on employment, the labour market and income distribution, and international competitiveness. One of the difficulties in undertaking these types of studies is the all-pervasive and global impacts of the new technologies. Yet from a policy point of view these effects and their direction (whether they are favourable or not) are very useful to determine a case for or against new technologies (James, 1993).

There are both analytical and methodological problems in tracing the effects of new technologies on output and employment. Most of the empirical studies available, some of which are discussed below, fail to point out explicitly the difficulty in isolating the effects in terms of gains or losses resulting from (i) structural adjustments, (ii) organizational innovations and (iii) technological change (Bhalla, 1987). For example, for policy making in the field of education and training, it would be useful

---

*This chapter is based on: A.S. Bhalla, Assessments of the social effects of new technologies, *ATAS Bulletin*, No. 4, October 1987; A.S. Bhalla and D. James, 'Integrating the technologies with traditional economic activities in developing countries: An evaluative look at technology blending', *Journal of Developing Areas*, July 1991; and A.S. Bhalla, 'On technology blending and rural employment' in M.S. Swaminathan and Veena Hoon (eds.) *Ecotechnology and Rural Employment*, Proceedings No. 7, Madras, April 1993.

126

to know whether employment/occupational changes resulted mainly from organizational changes or new technologies, or both. This identification problem, apart from the partial nature of the studies, often vitiates the usefulness of the existing studies. Furthermore, the fact that the results of different studies move in opposite directions limits their usefulness in guiding policy and action.

The partial nature of studies may not pose much problem if the new technology is localized in a particular sector or industry. In this case, its effects on the rest of the economy may be limited and could well be ignored (James, 1993).

When the extent of new technology diffusion is widespread across sectors, only more general analyses – tracing the effects throughout the economy as well as globally – become relevant. Three such analyses have been considered mostly in the context of the industrialized countries, viz. (a) a general equilibrium approach, (b) the Keynesian approach, and (c) the Leontief input–output approach (see Freeman and Soete, 1985; Lipton and Longhurst, 1989; and Fransman, 1991). The general equilibrium approach, which considers the effect on prices, markets and resource allocation, suffers from an unrealistic assumption of perfect competition (Fransman, 1986). The Keynesian approach, which traces the multiplier effects of expenditure on incomes, though useful suffers from a lack of discussion of the supply considerations. The input–output approach examines intersectoral dependence and the interrelationships between inputs and outputs. Leontief and Duchin (1986) studied the effects of automation on employment in the United States from 1983 to 2000. However, few studies exist on technology/employment-oriented macroeconomic or input–output interrelationships in a developing country. Measuring the indirect effects (which can often far outweigh the direct effects) of investments can be very hazardous in the absence of input–output or macroeconomic analyses. The indirect employment effects of the microelectronics-based technologies are likely to occur mainly through backward linkages, creating jobs in industries producing computers and related capital goods. However, many Third World countries (particularly the least developed ones) are importers of these technologies and thus cannot hope to generate such additional employment. There are several other indirect effects, namely: (a) secondary income and price effects resulting in increased demand for existing as well as new products; (b) investment demand and multiplier in capital goods and other supplier industries; (c) the long-run growth effects of capital accumulation (that is, increase in capacity effect as opposed to aggregate demand effect); and (d) better product design and more sophisticated products which raise the competitiveness of an economy (see James, 1985).

Since the above three approaches suffer from some limitations, it may be desirable to combine them. But as Lipton and Longhurst (1989) noted, even if it is possible to combine neo-Walrasian, Keynesian and Leontief GE (general equilibrium) analysis of 'directional effects', the process of combination may conceal important historical inter-relationships between new technology (modern seed varieties) on the one hand, and the state, class structures, population change, and land distribution on the other.

Having presented some general considerations on the socioeconomic effects of new technologies, we shall review, in the following three sections, evidence regarding the introduction of new technologies into developing countries in terms of whether the technology provides (i) a cost-effective method of production of goods or services; (ii) a net positive effect on employment levels; and (iii) whether it leads to a more equitable sharing of any resulting benefits.

COST EFFECTIVENESS

New technologies would be applied by individual enterprises and producers if they were economically viable; that is, if their use was cheaper and more productive (in terms of both quantity and quality of the product) than the available technological alternatives. It is not easy to determine the cost effectiveness or efficiency of new technologies since their diffusion, particularly in the Third World, has been quite recent. Also very few studies are available on cost comparisons between new technology and conventional or traditional technology. Whatever limited empirical evidence is available is analysed below for both agricultural and manufacturing sectors. The empirical evidence described is confined only to the use of microelectronics-based technologies. We are unaware of any comparative cost studies relating to the use of new biotechnologies.

Agriculture

In the agricultural sector, the examples of cost comparisons are more abundant than those in manufacturing and related sectors. The following examples relate mainly to laser levelling, microelectronic and photovoltaic power generation for production or street lighting.

Table 6.1   Benefits and costs per 1000 *feddans* (hectares) in Egypt

	Benefits (Egyptian Pounds)	Costs (Egyptian Pounds)	
Private			
Land preparation	80 775	Rental price	60 000
Water savings	6 760–12 600		
Yield increase	24 720–675 550		
Social			
Water savings		Unemployment	N/A
Average	4 072–5 023		
Marginal	18 113–10 006		
Returns/feddans		*Costs/feddans*	
Private	112–768	Private	62
Social	159–822		

N/A = not available.
Source: Jonish (1988).

Major applications of laser-guided land levelling are found in civil engineering functions in agriculture and construction. Jonish (1988) investigated land-levelling activities in Egypt for agricultural purposes and found that this new technology reduces survey time, saves labour, improves accuracy and speed, and increases crop yields.

In Egypt, laser levelling has been resource-augmenting by saving water (more uniform land plots require less water) through better drainage and slope characteristics. At a number of cooperatives, farmers reported time savings of up to 50 to 60 per cent. Also, reduced irrigation time lowers labour and pumping costs for the farmers. These private benefits need to be compared with the private costs of capital installation, training, maintenance costs, and so on. In addition, the social cost of labour displacement and foreign-exchange loss through machinery imports need to be weighed against social benefits such as water savings and output increases. Table 6.1 attempts to quantify these costs and benefits of laser levelling for Egypt.

It is clear from Table 6.1 that the benefits far outweigh the costs. As for employment, Jonish calculated that if the water conserved on existing farms is used to bring more land under cultivation, the additional employment generated will more than offset the reduction in labour used in land levelling. The cost for laser-guided land levelling is less than 50 per cent of the cost using conventional techniques.

Cost comparisons of solar photovoltaic (PV) energy with conventional sources of energy appear to be somewhat more abundant. A comparative-cost analysis for two farm sizes and three crop rotations in Ghazipur (northern India) shows that photovoltaic-powered water pumping (under the least-cost and highest-efficiency assumptions) is much cheaper than the four cost-efficiency alternatives for two crop rotations, although this option is much more expensive for a third crop rotation involving sugarcane because water requirements for the critical month of May are very high (Bhatia, 1988). A detailed analysis of the cost effectiveness of lighting from photovoltaic power compared to power from a diesel generator in Fiji shows that the photovoltaic system is technically and financially viable as a means of providing limited lighting to household and commercial establishments (Bhatia, 1988a). This is particularly true for outer islands where light is abundant and the cost of providing benzene or kerosene is higher. Many consumers liked the PV lighting system and found it particularly attractive when a set of two or three panels could be installed in a shop-cum-residents complex. Photovoltaic-powered street lighting in an Indian village also shows the attractiveness of the photovoltaic method, and three grid power alternatives showed that the PV system was less costly. Bhatia (1988), however, emphasizes that cost effectiveness depends on a number of variables; thus grid power will be the logical choice for many villages.

One of the more successful cases of cost effectiveness involves the electronic load controller, a sophisticated electronic device that makes possible hydropower generation on a relatively small scale (Whitby, 1984). The load controller is being used in the Colombian community of Dormila for saw-mill operations as well as for household lighting and cooking. The annual costs and benefits for the community show the benefit-to-cost ratio to be positive and high. Costs and benefits were also calculated for refurbishing a hydropower installation in Sri Lanka, where the power was used for drying tea. An annual cost of US$542 yielded yearly savings of US$14 117 to US$29 410 in grid power use with additional saving from eliminating tea spoilage resulting from grid power failures during the tea-drying stage.

In the field of biotechnology, according to pilot projects undertaken in Mexico for SCP production from sugarcane bagasse, attempts to reduce overall costs have been pursued and a reduction of about 10 per cent in capital investment seems to be possible. This will permit the SCP to be marketed at a price lower than US$1000 per tonne. Further cost reductions are being pursued through the application of biotechnological advances to the fermentation technology (Bifani, 1992). However, this process is still not economically feasible for all countries. Perhaps it may be viable in sugar exporting countries where molasses is produced as a by-product of sugar refining. The existence of this 'free' raw material is an indispensable requirement for SCP production. The price of the SCP is very sensitive to the price of the raw material. In many cases raw material costs are dominant, sometimes contributing up to 70 per cent of the total cost of producing low-value commodities such as SCP (Hacking, 1986). This dependence on raw material can be illustrated by the termination of the majority of the SCP projects based on petroleum products in the Western world after the oil crisis of 1973–4.

In the final analysis, the degree to which the potential of biotechnology is actually realized for the benefit of developing-country producers will depend on the cost at which these techniques can be made available to poor farmers and small producers, which in turn depends partly on the amount of research devoted to this specific problem.

Industry

In the case of the manufacturing sector, two examples of the comparative costs of using microelectronics technologies or more conventional technologies relate to the printing industry and the engineering industry in India.

In a study on the microelectronics-based technologies in India Bagchi (1986) includes a detailed set of cost calculations for different types of printing technologies in the country. Of the three printing modes considered, the one using microelectronics technology shows the lowest cost of printing (see Table 6.2). The new technology seems to enjoy a cost advantage particularly at larger scales of output. The calculations suggest that for the firms producing small batches, the low wages and low initial investment costs associated with the conventional letterpress method may enable this technology to retain a cost advantage over the new technology.

Another Indian study (Tulpule and Datta, 1990) compares the costs of purchase and use of CNC machines and conventional machines in the engineering industry. Three large companies based in Bombay, one of which is a subsidiary of a multinational enterprise, were considered. Between 1982–3 and 1987–8 all three companies witnessed an impressive growth in gross fixed assets, the value of plant and machinery and annual sales. In all three, total employment declined steadily during the same period. The number of CNC machines used in the three companies is

Table 6.2 A comparative estimate of the initial capital requirements and the cost of production in three different modes of printing (India, 1985)

	Letterpress with power driven handfed platen machine (Calcutta)	*Sheet-fed offset printing (one-colour) press (Calcutta)*	*Typesetting on word processor in a research institution (Bombay)*
Initial investment			
(a) Machine	Rs. 15 000	Rs. 650 000 (second hand; imported from the UK)	Rs. 180 000 (8-bit word processor purchased in 1983; plus printer)
(b) Types English and Bengali	Rs. 10 000	Nil	Nil
(c) Composing sticks, galleys and other furniture	Rs. 3 000	Nil	Nil
(d) Cost of installation	Rs. 1 000	Rs. 10 000	Rs. 40 000
Cost of printing (1000 impressions)	Rs. 7.00	Rs. 1.25	Rs. 1.00
Suitable production runs (printing)	100	3 000	3 000

Source: A.K. Bagchi and D. Banerjee, 'The Impact of Microelectronics-based Technologies: The Case of India', *ILO/WEP Working Paper Series, No. WEP 2–22/WP. 169*, Geneva, September 1986.

estimated to be between 40 and 45; all these machines were imported. All three companies made some cost-benefit assessments before introducing CNCs. The two common methods used were the marginal rate of return and the net present value of total cash outlays. A cost comparison between conventional machines, local CNCs and imported CNCs showed that labour costs saved (based on labour requirements of 16, 10 and three workers) were Rs.864 thousand, 540 thousand and 102 thousand respectively. The total capital cost of CNCs (including the cost of tools, accessories, transport and customs duties) was about 2.2 times that of conventional machines of equivalent capacity. The cost effectiveness of the use of CNCs would vary from operation to operation and is likely to depend on the relative capital and labour costs involved. In operations in which the CNC use does not lead to a substantial reduction in labour input, the cost per operation may turn out to be higher than that with conventional machines.

Some general considerations

The above examples concentrate on straightforward aspects of cost effectiveness. Reporting the bottom-line figures, however, can conceal useful insights for assessing the full economic impacts of a technological change. First, even successful cases will entail some problems. Although from a narrow economic view laser-guided land clearing and preparation is beneficial, there is the problem of some loss of the small farmer's freedom to choose the dates of planting and, relatedly, the crop (owing to the necessarily centralized provision of the laser technology in order to minimize unit costs). These types of costs are, of course, not quantifiable and can only be netted out of measurable gains in a subjective fashion.

Second, often the technical soundness of the technology is not the controlling variable in the analysis of cost effectiveness, as is shown by the experience of the Indian satellite communications for rural education. Here the technology *per se* functioned well, but an urban demand for entertainment, a lack of imaginative programming for rural-aimed broadcasts, and the incredible cultural, linguistic, topographical, and meteorological diversity of rural India seriously reduced the effectiveness of the educational effort (Bhalla, 1984).

Third, although some new technologies may be ready for fairly wide replication in the Third World, for most the safest approach will be a case-by-case assessment of cost effectiveness. Nowhere is this better exemplified than in an examination of Indian village street lighting (Bhatia, 1988). Is PV power a more efficient way of providing street lighting? Among the important considerations are: how far the village is located from grid power, whether the PV-lighting power is in addition to existing grid-supplied electricity already going to the village, and how much non-lighting power the village requires. It is not possible to make any meaningful generalization about the cost effectiveness of PV technology since circumstances vary from case to case and according to changes in PV capital costs and other cost parameters, such as prices of oil products or grid electricity.

PV technology also provides the basis for a fourth observation. Consumer preferences will influence the cost effectiveness of new technology applications. In assessing PV power for lighting in Fiji, some consumers preferred the PV systems even after taking into account the restricted number of hours of lighting from the technology; others did not. Given some economies of scale in the distribution and installation of systems (leaving production aside in the case of Fiji), consumer tastes and preferences can impinge on unit costs (Bhatia, 1988a).

Finally, a reduction in costs does not always seem to be a major motivation for the introduction of microelectronics technologies in developing countries. Empirical evidence shows that quality improvement is a far more important factor than the reduction of costs *per se*. This for example was the case (cited above) for the three Indian engineering companies whose managers indicated that higher quality, a larger volume of output and the achievement of greater technological capability were the main reasons for choosing CNCs.

EMPLOYMENT IMPACT

Interest in examining the relationship between technical change and employment can be traced back to Adam Smith, Marx, Ricardo and Keynes (for a brief review, see Kaplinsky, 1987). But causation, that is, the employment impact of technical change, especially in the developing countries, is rather difficult to determine because a number of non-technological factors (e.g. organizational innovations, economic recession and a slowing of demand for goods and services) are also simultaneously at work to influence the quantity as well as quality of employment created or destroyed.

The contradictory nature of the employment consequences of the use of new technologies also arises due to the different assumptions made about the growth of output and demand, different levels of aggregation (sector, industry, plant) and the inclusion and exclusion of indirect and multiplier effects. Much of the empirical evidence reviewed below relates to the industry and plant level studies in the case of the microelectronics technology. These partial (sectoral or industry-specific) studies suffer from several limitations that need to be borne in mind. The varying employment effects of microelectronics from one industry to another and from one firm to another are also due to differences in the levels of automation and organizational efficiency attained prior to the introduction of a new technology, the process-wise distribution of equipment intra-firm and inter-firm, the flexibility of the employment system, and worker adaptability.

Below we concentrate on a brief review of a few sectoral/industrial studies on the employment impact of microelectronics technologies and advanced biotechnologies in developing countries. The above caveats need to be borne in mind in interpreting this empirical evidence.

Some Empirical Evidence

1. Microelectronics

Kim (1986) attempted to quantify the employment impact in the Republic of Korea of new industries – computers, semi-conductors, and electronic switching systems – made possible by new technologies. Two approaches were followed to generate the data shown in Table 6.3. First, data were collected through interviewing a sample of firms taken from published directories. Second, industrial employment was estimated on the basis of industrial output. The Table indicates that employment (estimated on the basis of both aggregate and disaggregated data) expanded quite rapidly from 1981 to 1985.

The study on CNCs in three Indian companies cited above concludes that 'there is little doubt that the rise in value of output per employee and consequent stagnation of employment is largely the result of advancing technology of which CNC machines are an important part'. (Tulpule and Datta, 1990). The study on the printing industry in India (also cited above) asserted that 'there is little doubt that in large establishments the introduction of photo-composing and other microelectronics technologies could lead to labour displacement. In 1981, the workers' union of a leading newspaper in Calcutta calculated that the replacement of a hot metal system of composing on linotype by photo-composing and consequential changes in other departments would lead to displacement of 514 persons out of the existing 706 workers in the composing and printing department.' (Bagchi, 1986, p. 22). Although the study itself did not make

Table 6.3   Estimates of employment creation by new industries: Republic of
Korea (1981–1985)

Industry	1981	1982	1983	1984	1985
Results based on disaggregate data[a]					
Electronic switching system industry	805	3 256	2 603	5 719	7 102
Semiconductor industry[b]	–	11 729	15 233	18 023	21 406
Computer industry	–	–	9 869	14 781	19 490
Results based on aggregate data[c]					
Computer industry	1 979	3 168	10 678	17 220	20 803
Semiconductor industry	–	42 768	43 555	50 799	46 194

[a] Figures are the sum of disaggregate employment data from individual firms.
When a firm makes products that are based on both old and new techologies, the
total employment size of the firm was multiplied by the proportion of total value
accounted for by microelectronics to make a rough estimate.
[b] Of 23 semiconductor firms, employment figures for 12 small- and medium-sized
firms could not be obtained.
[c] Figures here are rough estimates based on aggregate industry employment data
multiplied by the proportion of industry production value accounted for by
microelectronics-based products. This method overlooks differences in labour
intensity in production among various product lines in the electronics industry.
Source: Kim (1986, p. 33).

any quantitative estimates, it recognized the possibility of at least some
compensatory increase in employment if the growth in newspaper and
glossy magazine readership occurred.

A study in Mexico, based on a 1987 field survey of firms producing
electrical consumer goods, electronic machinery and automobiles, made
assessments of both the direct and indirect employment effects stemming
from the adoption of microelectronics innovations. (Dominguez-
Villalobos, 1987.) Estimates were generated by using the responses of
firms regarding the labour-saving effect of microelectronic machinery *vis-
à-vis* the conventional machinery it displaced, time-series data provided by
the sample firms on the evolution of employment, and the relationship
between microelectronics and productivity.

An average labour-saving effect of the adoption of various computer-
numerically-controlled machine tools (CNCMTs) was determined for the
sample. Multiplying this average by the number of units and subtracting
electronic specialists, engineers, and technicians in charge of CNCMTs'

maintenance, labour saving was about 1323 workers or 3.2 per cent of the sample. These labour savings cannot be attributed entirely to the application of new technology since improved plant layout and reorganization of production processes also occurred.

The Mexican study noted that despite a drop in output for all three industries considered, the sales in the user figures either grew or declined more slowly than non-users. This suggests that the adoption of the new technology compensated, to some extent, for the labour-saving effects of microelectronic machinery. Other positive compensating effects occurred through the increased export share of these firms, as well as through the introduction of new production lines and the creation of entirely new products. These indirect effects, however, could not be quantified.

A survey of the Mexican footwear industry in 1989–90 by Dominguez and Grossman (1992) examines the employment impact of new technology applications (mainly CNC machinery and CAD) by 18 firms (see Table 6.4). In an effort to increase efficiency, most firms were interested in either reducing the number of workers or increasing production with the same number of workers employed. Table 6.4 shows that between 1989 and 1990 the firms that introduced new technologies suffered a decline in employment. Interviews by Dominguez and Grossman also suggested that changes in work organization, even in the absence of new machinery, enabled the cutting of some posts, the reduction of downtime and an increase in overall productivity.

A Brazilian study by Tauile (1987) was based on the assumption that numerically controlled (NC) machine tools on average substituted for three to five conventional general- purpose machines, a figure determined by questionnaires and field visits to automobile manufacturers. Since there were about 190 NC machine tools in Brazil in 1984, it is estimated they replaced between 570 and 950 conventional machine tools and their use resulted in a loss of jobs for about 1140 to 1190 conventional operators on two shifts.

A study by Hewitt (1992) of employment and skills in the Brazilian electronics industry notes that the ' electronics equipment industry, which formed some 21 per cent of the whole sector in 1984, reached a peak of employment in 1980, then declined in the following year. By 1984 the total employment in electronics had surpassed the 1980 level' (p. 188). The growth of employment continued to be impressive in the computer industry, thanks to the entry of new firms and the expansion of existing ones. During the 1980–4 period the consumer electronic firms suffered a loss of employment of over 12 per cent (Hewitt, 1992, p. 191).

Table 6.4 Production, labour productivity, employment and plant utilization in a sample of 18 footwear manufacturers in Mexico, 1989–90

	Production pairs/week			Productivity pairs/week/man				Employment			
	1989	1990	Per cent increase	1989	1990	Per cent increase	Number of models	1989	1990	Per cent increase	Per cent plant utilization
All sample firms	176 794	188 550	6.65	31	33	5.28	167	5 619	5 692	1.30	78.57
High quality segment	20 050	30 300	51.12	14	17	27.34	325	1 483	1 760	18.68	72.00
Medium quality segment											
All firms	156 744	158 250	0.96	38	40	6.20	123	4 136	3 932	-4.93	79.58
Firms with technolgical changes	146 744	148 250	1.03	39	41	6.74	126	3 811	3 607	-5.35	82.78
Firms without technological changes	10 000	10 000	0.00	31	31	0.00	107	325	325	0.00	70.00
Export-oriented firms	101 644	103 500	1.83	36	38	5.97	183	2 810	2 700	-3.91	78.80

Source: Dominguez and Grossman (1992).

2. Biotechnologies

In Chapter 2 we noted that the advanced biotechnologies are likely to exercise a significant influence on agricultural and rural development in the developing countries. There are a number of ways in which new/advanced biotechnologies can influence rural employment and incomes in these countries. These are summarized below:

(a) Biotechnologies can enhance employment opportunities by contributing to an increase in output; by raising agricultural productivity (by enhancing crop resistance to pests and diseases and lowering the unit costs of production); by allowing extension of cultivation into marginal or unfavourable areas; and by making new and improved crop varieties possible.

(b) Biotechnologies contribute to generating additional rural employment by enabling multiple cropping. Through the use of these technologies (e.g. micropropagation techniques for potato growing) year-round cultivation of crops becomes possible. Thus the seasonality of agricultural operations is reduced, and additional incomes and employment are generated.

(c) Biotechnologies can also lead to the displacement of labour (especially women's employment). Weeding is one of the most labour-intensive operations in which women are primarily engaged. The introduction of genetically-engineered plant varieties leads to a substitution of chemical herbicides for manual weeding (Ahmed, 1992).

(d) At a global level, the use of advanced biotechnologies in the industrialized countries may lead to substitution of new products (e.g. high fructose corn syrup (HFCS), biotechnologically produced sweetener) for the traditional crops/products of developing countries (in this case, sugarcane). Apart from the substitution effect, the price effect – that is, the decline in the price of traditional traded crops resulting from the superior yield and quality characteristics of the new products – can also have adverse employment and income effects in the developing countries (Galhardi, 1993).

A preliminary assessment of the impact of new biotechnology applications in selected subsistence and export crops of developing countries, presented in Table 6.5, suggests their positive effects through a lowering of production costs, an increased labour demand and greater benefits to small farmers. But as noted above, both gains and losses in employment are likely to occur as a result of the use of new technologies. Given the present state of knowledge, it is difficult to determine conclusively the direction of the *net* employment effect. The trade-related

Table 6.5 Impacts of some biotechnology applications on selected subsistence and export crops

Crop	Bio-techniques	Cost of production	Effects on rural growers	
			Labour requirements	Scale of production
Maize and beans	Biological nitrogen fixation	cost saving through reduced input of expensive chemical fertilizers (in Brazil savings of US$60/ha. in the case of beans is expected)	increased demand for traditional labour due to enhanced land productivity; increased demand for more skilled labour at the laboratory stage and at factory level	small-scale production is feasible (in Mexico, the maize yields of small holdings could be increased by 26 per cent and incomes, by 55 per cent)
Cocoa	Enzyme technology for fractionation of oils and fats for high quality 'cocoa butter alternative' production	decline in costs of cocoa butter production due to substitution of palm oil for cocoa, for example	job losses in developing countries producing cocoa	small producers will suffer from declining demand for cocoa bea74ns

Table 6.5   Continued

Crop	Bio-techniques	Effects on rural growers		
		Cost of production	*Labour requirements*	*Scale of production*
Soybeans	1) Biological nitrogen fixation	reduction in use of nitrogen fertilizers which results in cost reduction (savings in Brazil are about US$500 million per year)	increased demand for labour due to the increased yields and soil fertility (through the surplus of nitrogen that remains in the ground after harvest)	small farmers in developing countries will benefit through an increase in incomes (in Thailand income is expected to increase by 17–42 per cent due to increase in yields, reduction in nitrogen fertilizer, etc.)
	2) Biological control of caterpillars, weeds and bedbugs	reduction in costs due to reduced use of chemical pesticides (in Brazil, a saving of 80 billion cruzeiros per harvest was reported)	increased demand for labour (for collecting the dead caterpillars and for spraying plants)	has the potential to benefit small farmers in developing countries

Source: adapted from Galhardi (1993).

possible negative effects due to a declining demand for the export products of developing countries are real for many primary-producing countries. On the basis of data on production, consumption and exports as well as technical and labour coefficients for cocoa and coffee in Costa Rica, and assumptions about decline in demand and imports of the industrialized countries for these crops, Galhardi (1993) shows that a decrease in employment is likely to result 'even if production and internal consumption increases at rates expected' (p. 35). However, caution is needed in interpreting such results since the decline in import demand may result from factors other than biotechnological breakthroughs.

The substitution of HFCS for sugar in the industrialized countries may also threaten employment in sugar-exporting developing countries. The replacement of sugar by isoglucose is most substantial in the United States, where the latter accounts for 57 per cent of the total sugar use. This substitution has adversely affected the following traditional exporters of sugar to the United States: the Dominican Republic, with a reduction in exports of 39 per cent; El Salvador, with 72 per cent decline; Nicaragua, with 46 per cent decline, and Argentina and Brazil recording 34 and 35 per cent decline respectively (Bifani, 1992). It is estimated that the sugar exports of the Dominican Republic to the United States accounted for nearly 60 per cent of the foreign exchange earnings of the country (Crott, 1986).

The decrease in the price of sugar resulting from a substantial rise in consumption of sweeteners in the industrialized countries had a negative effect on the sugar-exporting countries of the Third World. For example, sugar exports from the Philippines to the United States dropped from US$624 million in 1980 to US$246 million in 1984. The resulting shift away from sugarcane to less labour-intensive crops is known to have accounted for a loss of half a million jobs on the Filipino sugarcane plantations (Hobbelink, 1987).

An interesting contrast in the results of cloning palm oil trees in Malaysia and Costa Rica (Elkington, 1984) also demonstrates possible employment implications of crop substitution. In Malaysia, direct employment is about the same per unit of land planted with cloned and non-cloned plants. Thus, if cloning techniques continue to progress, no direct displacement of labour is expected. Costa Rica's efforts are similar as far as the promise of reduced plantlet cost and enhanced oil yields. Owing to a slack in the market for bananas, however, palm oil trees are already replacing banana plantations. Any improved efficiency resulting from cloning will reinforce incentives to cut banana production. Since a given area planted in bananas requires about three times as much labour as is needed for palm trees, if cloning continues to progress on schedule, it will eventually exacerbate the problem of finding productive jobs for the labour force.

Even in the case of Malaysia, we still do not know the ultimate impact on global employment. If there is a substantial increase in productivity, even though direct employment per hectare is unaffected, employment may drop if demand for palm oil lags behind productivity gains or there is a decreased output of competing products. The effects would need to be traced through a host of impacts that depend on price elasticities of supply and demand for the product, elasticity of demand for labour, cross elasticity of demand for close substitutes, and so on.

The ILO undertook/sponsored a number of case studies in Mexico, Kenya, Malawi, Nigeria, and the Philippines to shed some light on the direct and indirect employment effects of new advanced biotechnologies (see Ahmed, 1992). These studies suggest that although the use of labour in some agricultural processes would decline, it might increase in the case of other processes. For example, in Mexico the net employment effect of the use of micropropagation techniques in citrus cultivation was positive, since the decline in labour input was more than offset by a more intensive labour use in weeding, pruning, irrigation and harvesting (Eastmond and Robert, 1992). Similar conclusions were reached for Kenya and Malawi, showing increased labour intensity per unit of land and increased yields resulting from the introduction of new practices (Mureithi and Makau, 1992; Chipeta and Mhango, 1992).

The indirect employment created through backward linkages to crop production can be supplemented by employment generated through forward linkages, to processing industries for example. In the case of Mexico, expansion of the production of juice processing plants generated additional employment; in Nigeria poultry production expanded as a result of the use of biotechnology; and in Kenya the tea industry recorded an increase in employment indirectly.

In Mexico it is estimated that the application of nitrogen-fixing bacteria in maize could increase the yields of small holdings by 26 per cent and income by 55 per cent, assuming constant output prices. Considering, however, both the direct and multiplier effects of the additional farmers' income generated, the income improvement leads to an increase in Mexico's gross domestic product of 1.0 per cent, which would create 200 000 jobs (Gilliland, 1988).

Some general conclusions

Despite the initial fears of massive unemployment due to the use of information technologies, several studies suggest that the direct and indirect employment effects of information technologies may in fact have been marginally positive (ILO, 1985; Watanabe, 1993; OECD, 1988, 1992).

The limited empirical evidence from developing countries is however inconclusive. In discussing the employment effects one needs to distinguish between the short-run and long-run effects and the time lags before the effects materialize. These effects will also vary among countries depending on whether they produce or purchase new technology. The present state of knowledge is inadequate to justify any predictions of the net employment effects of new technologies. And whatever predictions may be made are also likely to become obsolete rapidly in view of the radical rate of technological advance. But one thing is clear: the new technologies affect not only the occupational composition and quantity of employment but also its quality: they promote flexible types of employment and its informalisation, shorter working hours, home-based work and a higher quality of working life.

Optimism about the positive employment effects of new technologies arises largely from the assumption that any negative impact in the short run would be more than compensated by the positive 'compensation effects' resulting from the development of new products and an increase in the demand for existing products resulting from a reduction in price and improvement in quality. As we noted above, quantification of these indirect effects in developing countries remains to be done. The size of the positive effects will, *inter alia*, depend on the length of time lags over which investments in the new technologies will be realized in terms of essentially long-term benefits.

Table 6.6 speculates on the divergent impacts of microcomputers and new biotechnologies on agriculture and rural development. It suggests that the proportion of the sectors affected by microcomputers would be rather low, whereas the potential of biotechnology to influence them would be high. In terms of the employment impact, the qualitative aspects are likely to be more important than the quantitative ones in both cases.

Since biotechnology deals directly with the production process, the locational and institutional considerations are likely to be important. Farming and related activities are a result of complex economic, institutional and organizational factors much more than factory production. The climatic considerations and the different production cycles, the seasonality of operations, the institutional structure and organization (e.g. family or cooperative modes discussed above) set the agricultural sector apart from other sectors.

DISTRIBUTIONAL IMPACT

The new technological revolution is also likely to have a tremendous potential influence on the distribution of income within and between

Table 6.6 The impact of new technologies on agriculture and rural development

Impact on products	Impact on processes	Proportion of the sectors potentially affected	Potential employment effects	
			Quantitative	Qualitative
I. MICROCOMPUTERS[1]				
Agriculture				
Minor, or mainly quality, improvements	Minor (mainly safety, reliability, efficiency improvements, replacement of scarce skills, improved management and control)	Low	Minimal losses, small improvement in labour productivity	Skill level required likely to rise, need for polyvalent skills e.g. mechanics/ electronics
Rural Development				
Minor, or mainly quality improvements	Major/minor – mainly in improved management but in production impact may be major if pace of computerization improves in small-scale rural production.	Low	Low improvements in productivity	High skill requirements and nature of skills will change significantly

Table 6.6 Continued

Impact on products	Impact on processes	Proportion of the sectors potentially affected	Potential employment effects	
			Quantitative	*Qualitative*
II. BIOTECHNOLOGY[2] *Agriculture*				
Product quality improvement (e.g. protein content) quality improvement of inputs (better fertilizers and pesticides; improved animal feed and improved seed quality). New products (inoculants, biopesticides, new seeds and plantlets), new and improved products for animal protection and health (drugs, vaccines).	Increased effectiveness of disease and pest control and of fertilization; higher yields; resistant and tolerant varieties; saving of energy and other resources; increasing efficiency in animal reproduction, health and production; efficient use of crop residues.	High	Slight increase in agricultural production; generation of new employment in fermentation activities; improvements in productivity	High skill requirements to exploit the use of new biotechnology products (e.g. inoculants, biopesticides and new micropropagated plantlets); but no particularly high skills for applications on the farm.
Rural development				
Greater availability of health products: pharmaceutical products; vitamins, vaccines, antibiotics and food products (single cell protein, isoglucose (HFCS)).	General improvement of environmental quality (e.g. application of biotechnology for pollution and sanitation control, and health improvements); waste recycling.	High	Slight increase in rural services (health and pollution control) agroindustries (SCP production, biopesticides production)	No particularly high skills required but improvements in existing skills necessary

Sources: [1] Adapted from Bessant and Cole (1985), pp. 108–9.
[2] Provided by Pablo Bifani.

countries (James, 1985a; Bessant and Cole, 1985; Cole, 1986). Yet empirical evidence on the nature of these distributional implications is even more sparse than the employment implications. For example, little is known about the effects of microelectronics technologies on the personal and size distribution of incomes, on the distribution between producers and consumers, and between producers and workers. Also it is not clear whether the effects of microelectronics on income distribution will be different from those of the Green Revolution. James (1985a) argues that microelectronics is much more likely to be producer-biased than the Green Revolution and that the bias is likely to be weighted in favour of large producers and multinational enterprises which wield a comparative advantage in large-scale production and exports. In the case of the consumers, the gains may accrue mainly to the rich consumers in developing countries who can more easily afford the products incorporating microelectronics (e.g. watches and clocks, and passenger cars).

This hypothesis remains to be tested empirically. While at a macro level it may be valid, in individual cases the situation may be quite different. For example, the use of microelectronics-related innovations can raise productivity and reduce the production costs of very small enterprises; their use further tends to improve the competitiveness of these establishments *vis-à-vis* large-scale enterprises (see Chapter 4). To the extent that this occurs, poor consumers are also likely to benefit from cheaper and better-quality products (e.g., garments and textiles, where the use of new technologies has reduced costs and improved quality). In a survey by the Policy Studies Institute (London) of industrial establishments in the United Kingdom, about one-half of those adopting microelectronics reported lower production costs as an important benefit (Northcott and Rogers, 1984). It is a moot question as to whether these benefits are passed on to consumers and, if so, in such a manner that the general public shares in the gains.

We stated in Chapter 3 that the entire rationale of introducing new technologies should be to increase the standards of living of the urban and rural poor who are generally engaged in small-scale activities. Increasing the effectiveness of, and at times access to, education and health care of a wide complement of the population of developing countries translates into higher potential productivity. *A priori* some of the potential should find release and result in higher incomes. In the absence of perverse demand conditions, cost-effective increases in small farmers' agricultural or livestock output should translate directly into higher incomes. This should ordinarily be true regardless of whether the technology involves remote-sensing techniques, computer planning at a district, regional, or national level, hydropower or laser technology.

To take some examples: the use of PV technologies can contribute to a reduction in rural–urban inequality by reaching remote rural areas without requiring large infrastructure and distribution systems. Quality of life can be enriched by household and street lighting and by PV-powered irrigation accessible to small and marginal farmers who can maintain the technology cheaply. We receive a cautionary message, however, from the observation that in the Indian village of Achheja there was a suspicious concentration of street lighting units around the residence of the village headman and the homes of his friends (Bhatia, 1988)! Such clout in controlling the use of new technology by the more powerful and wealthier groups also conjures up memories of the Green Revolution, with its distribution of producer gains generally benefiting larger farmers.

From the foregoing evidence it is not possible to draw any clearcut conclusion on the distributional impact of new technologies which would depend, *inter alia*, on their effects on the labour markets and earnings, changes in the demand for skilled and unskilled labour, and the way in which relationships between labour and leisure, and market production and home work, are altered (see James, 1993, pp. 425–6).

Apart from the distributional impacts of new technologies within developing countries, there is the broader consideration of inequalities among countries. We know of only one study estimating the employment and income distribution effects of new information technologies taking the world economy as its framework of analysis (Cole and Bessant, 1985; Cole, 1986). The world economy is divided into six groups of countries, that is, technologically progressive; technologically declining; centrally planned; newly industrializing; resource exporting; and less industrialized and other developing countries. Essentially however the country classification based on income per capita is reduced to the more conventional high-income, middle-income and low-income categories (see Bagchi, 1987, 1987a). Within each of these country groups, using a social accounting matrix, the authors work out employment and associated income effects for skilled and unskilled labour and for capital.

Within countries the effects of information technology are disaggregated into eight sectors: agriculture, extractive industries, basic industries, intermediate manufacturing, advanced manufacturing, utilities, basic services, and advanced services. Both systemic (involving reorganization of production) and non-systemic (involving no reorganization) technical changes are examined. Taking non-systemic changes first, Bessant and Cole (1985) show that income distribution worsens in industrialized countries and improves slightly in the low-income developing countries. On the employment front, there is a loss of jobs for skilled workers in the latter countries which results from a loss of comparative advantage in industry and services. There is however a net marginal gain in the employment of unskilled workers.

The impact of systemic technical change is shown to be drastically different from the above. In this scenario, the income of the high-income countries increases most rapidly, and that of the low-income countries, most slowly. Income distribution worsens more in developing than in high-income countries; it also gets worse both between various groups in the economy as well as within groups.

Caution is needed to interpret the above results. The simulation exercises used are based on a number of assumptions which may or may not conform to reality. These assumptions are about changes in relative factor prices, propensities to consume, factor intensities by branches of production and so on. A variety of results are foreseen depending on the variations in the parameters. There are limitations of the Bessant–Cole model, namely, the short-term nature of the analysis, the limited account of structural change in industry, a lack of recognition of demand failures as well as of macroeconomic capabilities of particular economies reflected in literacy and education, R&D, etc. (Bagchi, 1987a).

CONCLUDING REMARKS

We conclude our discussion of new technologies in this chapter by noting that these technologies are no longer a myth for developing countries. They will affect developing countries no matter what policies are adopted. These may be indirect impacts, such as those entailing the creation of manu-factured substitutes for natural resources or technology-driven trade reversals for manufactured exports of developing countries, as is the likely case for biotechnology, discussed above. Or, of course, the effects may result from the direct employment of new technologies within the Third World. This technological revolution (or these revolutions) cannot be avoided; the trick is to exercise influence on the uses to which these technologies are put, the sectoral balance that devolves, and who gets what as a result of their deployment. A strategy of technology blending has a part to play here as is shown in Chapters 3 and 4. Having concluded our discussion on new technologies in this chapter, we move on (in the following chapters) to broader issues of cleaner technologies and production, technological dependence, technological indicators and capability, and the national development goals which technology is supposed to serve.

7 Cleaner Technologies with Special Reference to Small Enterprises*

Issues of environment and sustainable development are today in the forefront of both global and national debates. Some of the most oft-quoted concepts in this context are the green accounts, cleaner production and environmentally sound technologies. In this chapter we concentrate mainly on the application of cleaner technologies particularly in small and medium enterprises (SMEs).

The first section of the chapter deals with conceptual issues on which there is some ambiguity. The second section then discusses the status of cleaner production and technologies in both the industrialized and the developing countries. The special case of SMEs is the focus of the third section. The fourth section discusses the impact of environmental protection measures on labour – in terms of employment, education and training requirements, and health and safety of workers. The concluding section speculates on the role of different social partners and action groups in mobilizing public opinion, and producer and consumer acceptance of cleaner technologies and products.

DEFINITIONS AND CONCEPTS

A number of terms are often used interchangeably: environment-friendly or environmentally sound technologies, cleaning vs. cleaner technologies, and low and non-waste technologies. Are the clean or cleaner technologies the same as 'environmentally sound technologies'? The concept of environmental soundness is not unambiguous. As Perrings (1994) has noted, most of the debate on the concept relates to the disciplines of engineering and biological sciences, not to that of economics. The concept

---

*This chapter is an abridged and revised version of a paper entitled *Clean, Green and All That,* which was presented at the Commonwealth of Scientific and Industrial Research Organization (CSIRO) Australia and UNIDO Conference on *Economic Growth and Clean Production* (Melbourne, 6–9 February 1994). It appeared in *Science, Technology and Development,* April 1995.

can be defined in two different ways. The biological interpretations refers to some notion of safety with respect to the external environment. Environmentally sound technology is any technology which does not threaten ecological services at current levels of resource use and conditions of application. The engineering interpretation, on the other hand, uses the assessment criterion of 'the relative volume of environmental inputs or outputs in some process ... without reference to the external environment' (Perrings, 1994, p. 308). Thus any technology that reduces environmental inputs (emissions, waste, etc.) per unit of output will be cleaner than the existing technology. Cleaner technologies may require characteristics of lower pollution, lower energy intensity and lower resource intensity, a greater use of renewable resources and more recycling of waste products.

Much of the current effort in industry seems to be to control pollution through incremental changes in processes and technologies (the so-called 'end-of-pipe' solutions) and by such measures as waste management, air quality control and noise control. But preventive measures and technologies are also needed to avoid pollution and environmental hazards in the future, which may require more radical innovations and changes in processes and product composition and characteristics to eliminate waste (Almeida, 1993). Preventive measures are different in nature from the corrective ones and entail different implications for product and technology development as well as for related educational and training requirements (Schmidheiny, 1992). For example, the corrective end-of-pipe technology will call for specialized manpower to design and maintain it, whereas preventive measures such as the manufacture and consumption of cleaner products will require environmental education and literacy for the entire population to sensitize it to change consumer behaviour.

It has also become commonplace to look for cleaner products (e.g. electric cars and energy-saving light bulbs) in a search for a better environment. This implies changes in producer and consumer behaviour, alteration of the product mix and new styles and patterns of consumption. Such measures as eco-labelling and banning of harmful products are designed to improve environmental standards as well as the health of the population. However, the dividing line between cleaner products and processes may not always be that clearcut, especially when some final products may also be used as inputs for other processes (e.g. plastics for auto components).

The question arises whether clean technologies, as defined above, already exist and are generally applied by industry, including small-scale industry. This is an empirical question, the answer to which is likely to vary from industry to industry and country to country. While in some cases such technologies may already exist, in others they may have to be developed involving high resource cost. Much of the environmental policies (introduced mainly in the industrialized countries) in the past have concentrated on the diffusion of the available best-practice technologies as a short-run solution. The development of new and cleaner technologies can be considered only in a medium- to long-term perspective.

All best-practice technologies need not necessarily meet all the criteria to qualify as 'environment friendly'. In the past, many advanced technologies/industries have been polluting – they generate chemical emissions, waste and noise, besides being energy intensive. According to some estimates, 'an increase of 25 times in per capita GNP is accompanied by an increase of about 150 times in per capita hazardous waste generation. It is estimated that in the United States, the chemicals industry accounts for over half of hazardous waste generation' (Hirschhorn, 1990). Yet these polluting technologies/industries have contributed to the growth of output and employment.

Any policy towards cleaner production will need to ensure that both the objectives of growth and environmental quality are compatible. And it is not growth *per se* that is bad, but its *pattern* that needs to be changed. Economic growth is clearly a necessary but not a sufficient condition for achieving environmental protection. Indeed, one can argue that countries that grow more rapidly and that are more developed are also in a better position to develop cleaner technologies than those which are slow growing or stagnant. Thus, as Beckerman (1992) states, 'although economic growth usually leads to environmental deterioration in the early stages of the process, in the end – the best and the only – way to attain a decent environment in most countries is to become rich' (p. 482).

STATUS OF CLEANER TECHNOLOGIES IN DEVELOPING COUNTRIES

The environmental problems of developing countries and those of economies in transition in Central and Eastern Europe seem particularly acute. In these countries can cleaner technologies and products be developed in the short run when capital, human, and foreign-exchange resources are in serious shortage? Almost all cleaner technologies are developed and used in the industrialized countries. Therefore, they have to be imported at high cost. Competing claims on scarce foreign exchange and other developmental resources may imply relatively less immediate concern for environmental protection in the developing countries.

It is sometimes argued that poorer developing countries at lower per capita incomes are likely to generate a relatively lower demand for cleaner products and technologies than the richer countries. In other words, although people in poor countries may value clean air and water as much as those in rich countries, they may be less able to afford it. In a study sponsored by the ILO, Panayotou (1993) finds, on the basis of cross-section data, that a U-shaped relationship between income distribution and per capita income, so that income distribution first gets worse before improving after a certain stage of development is reached (Kuznets curve), also applies to the environment. Thus, using data on deforestation from a number of developed and developing countries, and assuming that deforestation depends on per capita income and population density, Panayotou shows that deforestation first rises with an increase in per capita income and then drops. A similar U-shaped relationship is found between air pollution and income.

Some developing countries, even at low levels of development, have introduced environmental standards. For example, in India the Environment Act and Rules of 1986 have established a set of minimum standards of discharge which compare favourably with those in the developed countries. In China, certain industrial pollutants are subject to emission fees which are collected by local Environment Protection Bureaux (Bhalla, 1992). Some examples of the adoption of cleaner technologies by individual firms in Brazil, China, India and Zambia are given in Table 7.1.

Technology access

Developing countries, with few exceptions, are unable to develop cleaner technologies and must therefore depend on the import of these technologies. Thus the problem of their access to available clean technologies and pollution abatement equipment becomes important. While many such technologies do exist, these countries often do not enjoy access to them either because they are of a proprietary nature and may not thus be in the public domain, or because these technologies (e.g. coal for residential heating) are no longer in use in the industrialized countries.

In 1991 the OECD undertook a survey of producers of a selected number of cleaner technologies (not necessarily the most advanced but those in which trade does take place) in order to assess their experience in exporting these technologies to developing countries as well as to the countries in Central and Eastern Europe. Some firms in developing countries were also contacted. The OECD study (1992a) concluded that trade-related factors including intellectual property rights did not hinder

Table 7.1 Examples of cleaner technologies in industry in developing countries

Country	Technology	Sector	Advantages
Brazil	Technologies that promote better use of the laminator Water and gas emissions treatment Coal (from trees) management system	Steel	Reduction of emissions on water, air, decrease consumption of coal Annual savings $1.5 million Prevented exploitation of 1 000 hectares of forest a year
India	Technology which allows recycling of emissions Re-use of chlohydric acid and caustic soda Utilization of solid waste called willow dust	Polyfibres Textile	Considerable savings Production of biogas Savings in energy consumption
China	Utilization of organic wastes	Small straw pulp mills	Production of agricultural fertilisers
Zambia	Technologies to filter dust from the stove	Cement	Net annual savings $40 000 Pollution inside the factory avoided Productivity raised Reduction of investment in equipment

Sources: Celso Almeida, 'Development and Transfer of Environmentally Sound Technologies in Manufacturing – A Survey', *UNCTAD Discussion Paper No. 58*, Geneva, 1993, p. 22.

the transfer of environmentally sound technologies to developing countries in any significant manner, and that other barriers such as a lack of access to financing and low environmental standards (limiting demand for cleaner technologies) were more important. This is not to suggest that such trade-related factors as tariff barriers, local content requirements and foreign exchange restrictions by the developing countries do not act as barriers to the more liberal transfer of technologies. The OECD study (1992a) is somewhat inconclusive since it deals with only a small sample of cleaner technologies. Neither does it cover more consumer-oriented final products for which trade practices may be more important.

There are other barriers to the access of developing countries to clean technologies: multinational enterprises, which are the main technology-transfer agents, may perceive low profits from sales of clean technologies to developing countries because of the limited markets (the demand for clean products and technologies is likely to be limited due, *inter alia*, to the lower environmental standards in these countries); the relatively high cost of clean technologies (compared to the conventional polluting ones) may also limit demand.

How can the access of developing countries to cleaner technologies and products be improved? First, stricter environmental regulations and standards and their enforcement would be necessary to generate greater demand. Secondly, environmentally based development aid and technical cooperation can be targeted directly towards the production and proper utilization of cleaner technologies. The donor community can help in the monitoring of and compliance with environmental standards by assisting in the establishment of appropriate institutions and monitoring mechanisms. But this alone will not be adequate. Access of developing countries to financing the acquisition of cleaner technologies may be far more important. Such access can be improved through bilateral and multilateral assistance and concessional financing by the governments (e.g. tax and export credits), as well as by new international funds like the Global Environment Facility and the Nordic Environmental Financing Corporation.

THE CASE OF SMALL AND MEDIUM ENTERPRISES

The small and medium enterprises (SMEs) represent a substantial proportion of industrial production in both developed and developing countries. It is therefore important to determine whether these enterprises are more polluting than the larger ones. In other words, is the scale of production inversely related to the extent of pollution? And how best can the needs of these enterprises be met for environmental protection through cleaner processes and products?

The most polluting industries are generally chemicals, textiles, pulp and paper, leather and footwear, and cement. With the exception perhaps of chemicals these branches of industry also tend to be operating at small and medium scales of operation. For example, in China most of the 5000 pulp and paper mills are categorized as small and very small and they account for an estimated annual effluent discharge of about 15 per cent of the total industrial discharge. Some of these industries (notably textiles, leather, and pulp and paper products) have been growing much more rapidly in the developing than in the industrialized countries. This is particularly true of leather and textiles, both of which registered an annual rate of growth of over 5 per cent for the developing countries during 1985–92, while there was a decrease of -0.2 per cent for leather and zero growth for textiles for the industrialized countries during the same period. For these two industries the share of value-added for the developing countries in the world total also substantially increased (ILO, 1992). Between 1978 and 1990, employment in leather and footwear (including wearing apparel) also increased substantially in developing countries, whereas it declined for the developed countries during the same period (UN, 1990).

These data suggest that output, employment and pollution may have been growing in the developing countries, thanks to a dynamic growth of small and medium enterprises. But it does not necessarily follow that there is an inverse relation between firm size and pollution. To determine such a relation, empirical studies would be necessary of industrial firms at different scales – small, medium and large – in given industries. At present such studies are rare in both developing and industrialized countries. Whatever anecdotal evidence is available is briefly summarized below.

In **India**, a preliminary estimate shows that 'the small-scale industrial sector contributes about 50 per cent of industrial output and 65 per cent of industrial pollution' (Nyati, 1988, Kent, 1991). This implies that the large-scale sector is less polluting per unit of output. In India the small-scale sector is usually defined in terms of firms employing up to 50 workers whereas in other developing countries it is generally defined in terms of up to 20 workers. A recent World Bank report on industrial pollution in India also concludes that pollution problems are more acute among small and medium enterprises (World Bank, 1991). In the case of non-manufacturing sectors, an Indian study suggests that small-scale enterprises such as roadside stalls and restaurants and bakeries contribute to deforestation by using firewood (Centre for Science and Environment, New Delhi, 1985).

In **Indonesia**, although small enterprises are abundant, especially in the leather tanning industry, their contribution to output is far less (only about 18 per cent of the total manufacturing value added) than that of large enterprises. Thus in relative terms (unlike the Indian SMEs) the Indonesian small enterprises account for only a small proportion of total industrial pollution. Nevertheless, small tanning enterprises may pollute more per unit than the large ones because they are less efficient in measuring chemical inputs or because they tend to process in batches which requires frequent discharge of effluents. These tanneries are also known to cause water pollution by discharging untreated effluents. Polluted water, used to irrigate rice fields, causes high levels of salinity and a reduction in crop yields.

In **Thailand**, a study by the Thailand Development Research Institute states that smaller factories do not have their own waste treatment facilities due to a lack of space or of funds. Thus they may be more polluting. A significant proportion of organic effluents in Thai rivers originated in tapioca and sugar-processing factories, many of which operate on a small scale.

Even for the industrialized countries information on the relationship between small enterprises and environmental degradation is very hard to find. One of the earliest studies dealing explicitly with environmental problems caused by small enterprises is that undertaken by Japan over 20 years ago (Japan External Trade Organization, 1972). This survey found that 34 per cent of smaller enterprises had experienced an increase in pollution over the previous year. The noise pollution caused by machinery, printing and binding shops in cities and suburbs with limited space, and by metal-fabricating enterprises, was found particularly serious. Other types of pollution included air and water contamination. Pollution resulted largely from overcrowding, lack of space and urban congestion. The survey noted several difficulties faced by the SMEs in controlling pollution: lack of low-price and high-quality equipment affordable by the SMEs; technical problems which involved prior research; limited contacts with manufacturers of pollution-abatement equipment; and lack of space for installation of equipment.

A recent Japanese White Paper on Small and Medium Enterprises (1993) discusses issues of global environmental problems and of energy efficiency. Problems faced by the SMEs in introducing measures against global warming and ozone-layer-destroying materials, as well as adopting recycling of waste, receive particular attention. Despite tax privileges, the SMEs at present find it difficult to introduce appropriate measures owing to a lack of funds and of necessary information and knowledge. Carbon dioxide is the major source of global warming and 80 per cent of the carbon dioxide is created through the use of oil and coke. An increase in efficiency in the use of energy and reduction in its consumption by enterprises is therefore necessary. In Japan, since 1983, energy consumption by SMEs has increased with material-based industries (e.g. ceramics, pulp and paper, steel and chemicals) accounting for the lion's share. As shown in Figure 7.1 the energy-saving measures were adopted by both large and small enterprises, though the former were more effective in reducing energy consumption per unit of production.

Some of the specific measures adopted by the SMEs to save energy include changes in the product mix, improvements in manufacturing processes and recycling of waste. Problems encountered by the SMEs in enforcing energy-saving measures included lack of managerial and technical staff, lack of adequate knowledge about technology and processes, and difficulties in obtaining funds. Furthermore, the management attitudes of small and medium enterprises (and large ones for that matter) may be one of the reasons for their failure to prevent or control pollution. Other bottlenecks are the limited capacity to absorb and

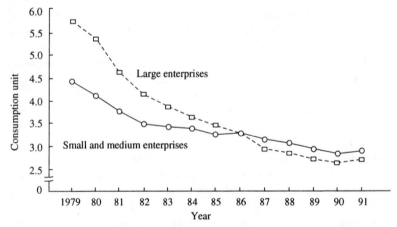

Notes: 1.   Small and medium enterprises are defined as those with 30–299 employees, whereas large enterprises employ more than 300 employees.
2.   The figure is based on the concept of energy consumption unit which is defined as: energy consumption amount/production amount x 100.
3.   The real values (yen) of energy consumption and total production are deflated with the total wholesale commodity price index.
Source: Compiled by Ministry of International Trade and Industry, *Industrial Statistics*, Bank of Japan *Annual Reports of Commodity Index*.

Figure 7.1   Changes in energy consumption by scale of industrial enterprises

assimilate cleaner technologies. The environmental regulations and standards are also more difficult to enforce among a large number of small and dispersed enterprises. Three main reasons are often given for this situation: (a) technical inefficiencies in production; (b) diseconomies of small scale in the use of technology, materials and other inputs; and (c) the non-compliance by SMEs with environmental regulations and standards, and difficulties in enforcement owing to the dispersed nature of these enterprises.

The protagonists of SMEs present a rather different picture – they argue that these enterprises may be more environment friendly because they require simpler processes and infrastructure (Carr, 1987). Certain activities in small-scale informal production, e.g. collection and recycling of such materials as paper, plastic, glass and metal, may no doubt contribute positively to the urban environment. Creation of non-farm employment releases pressures on marginal areas and scarce land. However this positive contribution needs to be considered against the negative consequences of some 'informal activities' (e.g. street vending of food) which can emit chemical and toxic substances hazardous to health, and cause overcrowding in urban areas (Sethuraman, 1992).

Can the extent of pollution in SMEs be reduced through technological solutions? Of course, there is no *a priori* reason why this should not be possible. However, there may sometimes be technical problems involved – which apply to both small and large firms – in reducing effluents and industrial discharges. For example, options for clean operations are more limited in pulping based on agricultural residues (e.g. straw, bagasse) owing to the nature of the specific properties of raw materials. On the other hand, wood pulping lends itself to cleaner operations. In China, the use of more than 60 per cent of the non-wood raw materials in pulp and paper mills makes cleaner production difficult (Kuang, 1991).

Some unanswered questions

One needs to pose the following questions in the context of the use of cleaner technologies in small and medium enterprises. First, if SMEs are more polluting, is it because of the nature of the industry, the raw material used or the lack of access of the enterprises to cleaner technologies? Beyond a certain point, technical change and new investments are required for cleaner production. The smaller enterprises, less endowed with capital and resources, will be unable to afford investing in cleaner technologies and products to prevent pollution. And such investments are unlikely to be economically viable at small scales of operation. The development of such technologies is clearly beyond the capacity of the small and medium enterprises. It requires massive public R&D which only large enterprises and governments can undertake.

Do the SMEs suffer from a lack of access to cleaner technologies? This question has to do with a lack of information and the cost of technology search which the SMEs may not be able to afford, even when cleaner technologies are available. Even large enterprises may find it difficult to assess systematically environmental prevention or control and its costs and benefits.

Thirdly, are the SMEs effective as agents of transfer of environment-friendly technologies to developing countries? A recent study of SMEs in a number of developing and developed countries points to the increasing importance of SMEs as technology suppliers. It is also claimed that 'in a number of environmental sectors (waste treatment, energy conservation systems and management, some areas of biotechnology, etc.) smaller firms are likely to be important suppliers' (IDRC, 1993). However, there is very little hard data to support this assertion. More studies are needed to document the relevant costs and benefits of SMEs as agents of transfer of cleaner technologies to developing countries.

Comparative costs of production using 'clean' and 'polluting' technologies in small and large enterprises are rarely available. But at the least we can say that the capital costs of 'clean' technologies are most likely to be higher. For example, the capital cost of clean coal technology (Fluidized-Bed Combustion) is known to be higher than the conventional systems where emission levels are not restricted. These costs are likely to be particularly high for small enterprises in developing countries. For example, for the small family-based tanning units in these countries, the cost of obtaining a special drum for hair recovery (a cleaner technology), including the necessary auxiliary equipment, can be twice as high as the conventional drum (UNIDO, 1992a). It is estimated that 'in China the budget for a pulp and paper chemical recovery system for a large capacity mill ... is $4.5 million' an amount which is clearly beyond the capacity of SMEs (UNIDO, 1992a).

IMPACT ON LABOUR

The socioeconomic impact of cleaner technologies is not easy to quantify in the absence of necessary and adequate data. Therefore, we discuss below, in rather qualitative terms, their impact on employment, on education and training, and on worker safety.

Employment

Does a shift to cleaner technologies create or destroy jobs and livelihoods? Poor factual information and data at present defies any easy answer to this question for either industrialized or developing countries. Notwithstanding this lacuna, some hypotheses can be presented.

The introduction of cleaner technologies and products will no doubt generate some additional employment through, *inter alia*, the development and maintenance of pollution abatement equipment. Some jobs can also be created by focusing specifically on labour-intensive environmental protection activities such as recycling and waste reduction and management. However, the developing countries, which do not produce pollution-control technologies, are unlikely to count on such extra employment.

At least in the short run, transition to cleaner production and technologies may entail both job gains and job losses. Loss of jobs may occur through closure of polluting firms and industries, through a ban on polluting products, and through a possible rise in product prices which may lead to a decline in demand and in output and employment.

The positive and negative impact of cleaner technology and production needs to be compared to determine the net overall effect on employment. In principle, the net effect can be positive if a very high priority is given to labour-intensive activities like waste management, recycling, and energy conservation, and if capital-intensive activities and industries (e.g. chemicals, mining and transport) are controlled and transformed. In other words, a shift in the product-mix and consumption patterns and styles is an important pre-condition for generating more employment. UNIDO (1992) has noted that the present pattern of industrialization in developing countries is not generating much additional employment and that it is rather energy intensive.

Generation of non-farm employment opportunities for marginalized populations in developing countries can have an indirect positive effect on the prevention or reduction of deforestation, desertification and depletion of top soils. We noted earlier that small enterprises, by generating non-farm employment, release pressures on land and may prevent people from resorting to overgrazing and similar other environmentally unfriendly practices. The issues of poverty, low productivity and unemployment are closely linked to resource depletion and environmental degradation which are caused, *inter alia*, by rapid population growth and the resulting pressures on natural resources in rural areas. In the least developed countries, most of which are in sub-Saharan Africa, employment generation (which is an important means of poverty alleviation) can go a long way in preserving environment. An optimal use of the abundant human resource – labour – and economical use of scarce natural resources are the most effective recipe for achieving sustainable development (see Karshenas, 1992).

Most developing countries have now introduced liberalization measures to participate more actively in the emerging global economy. This growing interdependence between developed and developing countries is reflected, *inter alia*, in trade and capital flows. Employment generation in developing countries would thus depend on whether those countries can expand their exports to developed countries when the latter have introduced stringent environmental standards. The impact of these standards on employment in developing countries can be negative and similar to the effect of protective barriers.

In industrialized countries some attempts have been made in estimating the employment effects of environmental policy (Doeleman, 1992). The estimates show wide variations across sectors and countries for several reasons. Firstly, different national estimates are based on differing definitions of environmental protective sectors and policies. Secondly, the data used are neither robust nor comparable. Thirdly, most studies deal only with industry and with direct employment effects. Indirect employment effects are almost completely ignored. Finally, technology gaps between countries may also account for variations in employment generated in different countries.

An early ILO study (Koo, 1979) examined the impact of pollution control measures in the United States on the employment and incomes of trading partners like Thailand and the Republic of Korea. Input–output tables were used to estimate the output and employment effects induced by changes in exports resulting from pollution control in the United States. These estimates are given in Table 7.2. For the Republic of Korea the negative employment effect is substantial, perhaps owing to a drastic assumption made that the Korean pollution-intensive goods would lose their entire export market in the United States (Kim, 1979).

Similar studies in other developing countries are needed before one can be certain about the magnitude and direction of the employment impact of environmental standards.

Education and training

Any technological change calls for a shift in occupational structures and skill mix. The development and promotion of cleaner technologies and the growth of environment-protection sectors will generate a demand

Table 7.2   Possible impact of United States pollution control measures on national income, employee income and employment in the Republic of Korea and Thailand

Country	National income	Employee income	Employment (thousands of jobs)
Republic of Korea (millions of *wons*)			
Increase resulting from increase in certain Korean exports	1 445		1 837
Decrease resulting from decrease in certain Korean exports	23 168		36 731
Net change	–21 723		–34 894
Thailand (millions of *bahts*)			
Increase resulting from increase in certain Thai exports	796	92	
Decrease resulting from decrease in certain Thai exports	1 068	178	
Net change	–272	–86	+5.4

Source: Kim, 1979.

for new types of skills for managerial as well as technical (scientific and engineering) professions and occupations. New types of skills are needed for environmental management, environmental administration, environmental industry and environmental education and research (ILO, 1989). One of the bottlenecks in the development of cleaner technologies, even in the developed countries of Europe, is reported to be a shortage of requisite skills and trained manpower. In Western Europe for example, in the waste management sector, shortages of environmentally qualified staff have been estimated at 77 000 managerial and professional positions, 94 000 administrative and technical positions and 141 000 skilled positions (Lewis, 1991). Similarly, trained personnel are needed for the *development* of a new generation of 'cleaner' technologies. Recognizing this, in 1985 the Commission of the European Community commissioned a number of sector and country-specific studies to assess the environmental training requirements of the member countries. In the light of this study, a Community Environmental Training Programme has been launched to overcome skill shortages (ILO, 1989).

The development of cleaner technology and products will call for senior managers with specialized knowledge of scientific and engineering disciplines. Production managers will need to be trained for the development and monitoring of cleaner technologies as well as for assessing their environmental benefits and costs. More environment-related supervisor and operator skills will also be required (North, 1992). This means that educational curricula will need to incorporate environmental considerations at different levels. It has been noted that in the United Kingdom, the university post-graduate courses in environmental management give a very high priority to the subject of environmental technologies. Seventy-five per cent of the courses offered relate to this subject (ECOTEC, 1990).

The lack of adequate skills to develop, operate and maintain cleaner technologies is particularly acute in developing countries. The stock of engineering and scientific manpower in these countries is low by comparison to that in the industrialized countries. Coupled with low R&D, and attitudinal barriers on the part of industry, the utilization and maintenance of cleaner technologies (not to speak of their production) becomes a serious problem.

The government, the educational planners and the private sector, as well as donors and international organizations, all have an important role to play in helping to overcome manpower shortages. Government-supported environmental education and training programmes will need to be expanded, especially since lead times are often long. Private firms will need to introduce on-the-job training and management courses necessary for creating awareness of the need for cleaner products and technologies as a management tool, as well as for developing specialized skills to operate and master new technologies. In this connection the transfer of cleaner technologies from the Western countries to developing countries and countries in transition in Eastern and Central Europe needs to be seen as a 'package' with adequate resources allocated also to the transfer of required skills and training. A beginning has been made in this direction with the Swedish and Finnish firms entering into joint-venture agreements with Estonian authorities to clean up the Baltic Sea as well as to prevent industrial pollution.

The need for suitable environmental training strategies cannot be underestimated. International cooperation through development aid in skill formation and technology transfer, and international networking and partnerships between training and research institutions in the North and South, would be desirable.

Worker safety

Occupational and health hazards to workers at the work place are often associated with the use of 'polluting' technologies. Noise and air pollution can cause several diseases for example. Therefore, in principle, 'cleaner' technologies, by reducing these causes of health hazards, should have beneficial effects on the workers and their working environment. But some new and adverse effects can also result from the use of new technologies to control pollution emissions or to clean up waste disposal sites.

The two main polluting industries are iron and steel, and pulp and paper. In these industries (particularly the iron and steel industry), the environment at the work place is affected by airborne dust, fumes and emissions of various hazardous gases, and workers are exposed to noise and heat. Most of the technological measures adopted towards cleaner production and greater worker safety therefore relate mainly to the control of noise and removal of dust and fumes.

Whenever cleaner technologies are introduced, their operators need prior adequate training to ensure that its start-up phase is not hazardous. It has been reported that in 'the United Kingdom, paper making accidents increased drastically during the period 1981–5 when many mills were redesigned or rebuilt and production lines altered and processes automated' (ILO, 1992a).

The safety of workers is important not only for social and humanitarian reasons; it is equally important for economic and efficiency reasons. Sickness, injuries and absence from work lead to a loss of output which can be avoided through the provision of better and cleaner environments at the work place. And healthier workers are also more productive and efficient which should contribute to economic growth. Thus cleaner technologies, by improving the working as well as the natural environment, can also contribute to economic growth.

Increasingly the working and the general (or physical) environment are more and more interrelated, since occupational hazards have effects far beyond the work place, as has indeed been demonstrated by the industrial tragedies of Bhopal and Chernobyl.

CONCLUDING REMARKS

One message that emerges from the above discussion is that information and data on cleaner technologies are lacking. Worse is the situation with regard to small-scale industry and its polluting effects, on which data are virtually non-existent. Unless such data are available, it is not possible to confirm or refute the existence of an inverse relationship between firm size and pollution. Under these circumstances, it is also difficult to venture any major conclusions regarding the prospects of cleaner technologies and production, particularly with respect to developing countries. However a few tentative conclusions can be drawn.

First, we are still in the early stages of the development of cleaner technologies and processes for many industries and activities. Cleaner technologies will need to reduce pollution and materials input per unit of output. Can time-series indicators of pollution intensity and materials intensity of production be developed so that technological change can be measured and monitored? Taking the example of the energy sector, three types of changes may be essential, namely. (a) improved energy efficiency which requires process changes; (b) product substitution, e.g. natural gas for coal; and (c) development of new products, e.g. renewable energy (see Speth, 1990). A number of factors account for a slow process of technological change in these directions, notably a lack of R&D resources, inadequate information on the part of firms (particularly small-scale firms), limited incentives and policies, and their poor enforcement.

Secondly, the access of developing countries to cleaner technologies can be improved through North–South and South–South technology cooperation and the public purchase of patents for use in developing countries. One example of North–South cooperation is the European Union–Singapore Regional Institute of Environmental Technology (UNCTAD, 1993a).

Thirdly, technological change in general is moving towards de-materialization and the use of new materials which should in principle be less polluting than the modern automated technology. For example, the microelectronics-based technology comes less into physical contact with the workers and thus may be less harmful, although certain side effects of the use of such technologies may still be unknown or unpredictable.

However, it is not clear whether the net overall impact of cleaner technologies and products is actually favourable to the natural environment even in the industrialized countries. The new polluting activities continue to grow even when less polluting ones are being promoted. Thus any improvements may continue to be offset by the expansion of polluting products for which demand may be unrestrained. This point brings out the importance of consumer behaviour and acceptance, not just that of action on the part of business and industry. Design, manufacture and marketing of new environmentally-benign products may be a major challenge for the future. Innovative marketing and advertising may be necessary here to change consumer behaviour in the desired direction. The pressure groups that are active in the industrialized countries may have an important role to play.

In developing countries such pressure groups in favour of cleaner products and technologies are few and far between. Yet there is a need for such groups to mobilize public opinion in support of action to promote cleaner production. Public pressure through green clubs may be partly responsible for better enforcement of environmental regulations and standards in the industrialized countries.

Small and medium enterprises (SMEs) will continue to escape environmental regulations as long as they are unable to afford additional costs. Therefore, public action and incentives to the SMEs in the form of tax benefits, credit on easy terms, and R&D facilities (as is in fact being done in Japan) will be necessary to encourage them to save energy and use recycled materials and raise their environment standards. Further action to reduce the pollution problems of the SMEs could be taken by providing common waste treatment facilities to industrial estates or to clusters of workshops. Effective enforcement incentives would be necessary however to encourage small firms to pay for the operating costs of such facilities.

Information on cleaner technologies can be provided to the SMEs on a collective basis through such mechanisms as trade associations and industrial banks. Sharing of these technologies through collective action by a number of SMEs can reduce the cost for each. For example, access to waste water treatment plants can be shared in order to spread the costs of environmental improvement. Sub-contracting between large and small enterprises can also enable the sharing of environmental costs of product and process improvement. At the international level a sharing of cleaner technologies between the SMEs from North and South can be encouraged through joint ventures and cooperative partnerships. Public authorities can also provide grants for acquisition of information and its processing, and facilitate access of the SMEs to venture capital. Local subsidiaries of multinational enterprises are also a useful source of information.

8 Technological Dependence*

So far we have been concerned mainly with the diffusion and impact of such new technologies as microelectronics (and, to a lesser extent, biotechnologies) and cleaner technologies in developing countries. In Chapter 5, we noted that the choice of technology framework is suitable for analysing the new technology issues, since the availability or access to new technologies essentially widens the choice. We also noted in Chapter 2 that a number of developing countries, particularly the least developed ones, may not yet be able to afford these new technologies on a massive scale, or may not have the minimum of technological capability to absorb and assimilate these technologies.

It is therefore essential to examine the levels of technological capabilities in developing countries to determine how they can face the new technological challenge. Technological dependence, the subject of this chapter, implies a low level of technological capability. The following Chapter 9 investigates the relationship between technological capability and socioeconomic development objectives in a broader context and discusses the need for suitable indicators to measure progress towards the achievement of technological capability, which we believe is a precondition for facing the technological challenge successfully.

The first section in this chapter describes the concept of technological dependence. The second section examines some cross-country data for a number of developing countries to assess the degree and nature of prevailing technological dependence. The situation of African countries is contrasted with that of NICs and near NICs. The third section outlines some of the feasible policies which help reduce such dependence and build indigenous technological capability to substitute local for imported technology, know-how and organizational structures. It also speculates on the future prospects for technological cooperation among developing countries.

*This chapter is a substantially revised and up-dated version of A.S. Bhalla, 'Technological Dependence of Africa' in ILO/ARTEP. *The Challenge of Employment and Basic Needs in Africa*, Nairobi, Oxford University Press, 1986.

THE CONCEPT

Technological dependence forms part of a broader concept of dependence which embraces the economic, cultural, and political 'subservience' of the Third World on the industrialized countries. Often the interdependence of these two groups of countries through trade, aid and technology transfer is expressed in terms of 'unequal partnership', which comes close to the concept of dependence. An UNCTAD report (1975) defines technological dependence in terms of asymmetry of relationships between advanced and developing countries (for example, asymmetry of commodity pattern, means of production, trade bondage, technical knowledge, skills, and financial flows and control).

The broader concept of dependence has found most vocal expression in Latin America where the *'dependentistas'* argued that underdevelopment was very closely related to the expansion of capitalist, industrial countries. The latter represent the 'centre' on whose growth depends the 'periphery' of most developing countries. A narrow view of dependence would confine it mainly to economic and political subservience, whereas a broader view encompasses subordination 'also in respect of social structure, ideological beliefs, and cultural elements' (Bath and James, 1976).

The centre dominates in trade and technological innovations, whereas the periphery suffers in terms of its declining terms of trade in primary commodities and heavy inflows of foreign technology (channelled by the multinational enterprises) at a very high cost to the recipients. Latin American writers like Prebisch were most vocal proponents of the terms of trade thesis and felt that gains from world trade were biased against Latin America. This led to import-substituting industrialization in the sixties and seventies. The 'dependencia school' believed that the major gains from technological change would be appropriated by the industries in the centre (for a discussion of these issues, see Cooper and Sevcovich, 1970; Street and James, 1979). The dependency of Latin America was not attributed so much to domestic policy failures as to the uncontrolled power of foreign financial centres and multinational enterprises, whose control on technical knowhow and technology transfer was assumed to retard Latin American development (see Sunkel, 1973).

In Africa, technological dependence has been explained by a low level of development, lack of industrial capabilities and slow investment in human capital formation (Lall, 1990). It has been noted that African countries invested far more in physical capital than in human resource development. Lack of adequate investments in human resources has retarded the growth of industrial and technological capabilities. Lall

(1990a) argues that inward-looking trade and industrial policies and price distortions cannot account for the low degree of industrialization in Africa as much as the lack of adequate skills (entrepreneurial and managerial capabilities), since similar policies in Asia (e.g. China and India) and some countries of Latin America contributed to the establishment of solid industrial bases.

We argue that technological dependence varies considerably with the level of development of a Third World country. Thus the nature of African dependence is not identical to that of Latin America which is at a much higher stage of development. In general, the lower the level of development, the greater is likely to be a country's dependence on industrialized countries for technology and goods. This would imply that the least developed countries (often primary producers) depend on their former colonial masters (the developed countries) for the supply of industrial goods and services. In the absence of a local technological base, with the exception of traditional technologies, skills and products, most of the technologies required are imported in the form of 'turnkey projects' with associated packaged inputs of know-how, foreign skills and maintenance staff and standards. Several authors (Yachir, 1978; Mytelka, 1993) maintain that this phenomenon reduces technology choice and variations in Africa and, by and large, keeps the level of mechanization much higher than the local factor endowments would dictate.

Put differently, at the lowest stage of development of an economy, the elements of a domestic technological capability – namely physical and human infrastructure; research and development (R&D) resources and laboratories; patent holders; scientific and engineering manpower; local consultancy firms; domestic capital goods industries, and others (discussed in Chapter 9) – are either missing or they are in a rudimentary stage. As a result, not only technology and goods have to be imported, but also the know-how, management, trained personnel, and repair and maintenance equipment services. In the least developed countries, the gap between needs and effective demand for technology is likely to be particularly wide in the rural areas. This is less likely to be true in the modern sectors of these countries, which are generally dominated by the multinationals and expatriate staff (Bhalla and Reddy, 1994).

Technological dependence is sometimes also linked to foreign investment and ownership. Foreign ownership of assets by multinational enterprises, for example, is taken as an indication of economic and technological dependence. It is for this reason that many developing countries introduced nationalization of foreign assets soon after their political independence. However, such local economic control does not necessarily reduce the technological dependence manifested in clauses in technology agreements, which provide for major decisions (in respect of investment, profits, pricing and sources of inputs, and others) to take place outside the country, at the headquarters of the multinational enterprise. As noted by Vaitsos (1971) technology contracts may also impose restrictions on exports, prices, sales volume and the sale of technology.

The nature and degree of dependence also varies between the traditional and modern sectors. In the traditional sector the technology is deeply rooted in the local traditions and relatively unaffected by the process of economic and technological modernization. In contrast, the modern sector, in developing countries, is more like enclaves of the advanced economic and technological systems imported from abroad. However, the imports of technology are not the exclusive domain of developing countries. Advanced countries are also importers of technology but they are not technologically dependent in the same way as the developing countries, partly because they are also technology exporters. One of the major differences in the situation of these two groups of countries is the difference in their bargaining power in importing technology from abroad. The terms and conditions, and the cost, of technology imports for developed countries are likely to be much more favourable to them, in view of their strong bargaining position, than those for developing countries which import but do not export technology.

Another reason for the weaker position of the developing-country technology importers is that the 'elements of technical knowledge themselves have to be transferred, but so does the capacity to use this knowledge in investment and production' (Cooper and Sercovitch, 1970). In other words, it is implied that the dependence of developing countries results partly from a lack of indigenous technological capability. The greater the local technological capability, the greater the scope for the substitution of domestic for imported technology, and the less important the consequences of technological dependence. There are some snags in this argument, however. Even where some local capacity to develop technology exists, developing countries usually have a psychological preference for imported technologies and products even if they cost more. Lack of self-confidence, limited capacity to take risks, and the inexperience of local scientists, engineers and technicians seem to explain the preference for foreign against local technology and products. This preference occurs notwithstanding the lack of relevance of imported technology to local socioeconomic conditions.

Thus it can be argued that some countries may pursue technological dependence even as a strategy which provides an alternative to building national technological capability (see Bruton, 1985). Many writers have argued (e.g. Bruton, 1985; Pack and Todaro, 1969) that a building up of the local capital goods sector within developing countries is one of the preconditions for reducing technological dependence (through learning effects and practical experience) and strengthening indigenous technological capability (see below).

Stewart (1977, 1979) analyses four interdependent factors that characterize the undesirable consequences of the technological dependence of developing countries. These are (i) the cost of technology imported; (ii) the loss of control of the recipient countries over decisions relating to technology imports and foreign investment; (iii) the unsuitable characteristics of the technology received; and (iv) the lack of effective indigenous, scientific and innovative capacity. The high cost of technology transfer to developing countries is explained by (i) the low bargaining power of developing countries; (ii) transfer pricing through over-invoicing of imports and under-invoicing of exports; (iii) the tying of purchases of imported raw materials, equipment and spare parts; and (iv) the discouragement of the use of local personnel, and others.

Having examined the broad issues of concept and analysis, we now turn to some indicators of dependence and their measurement.

INDICATORS OF TECHNOLOGICAL DEPENDENCE

A lack of adequate data makes it difficult to apply rigorously and empirically the framework of dependence reviewed above. However, some rough indication of dependence can be obtained from ratios such as scientists and technicians, and R&D scientists per 1000 population; expenditure on R&D as a percentage of GNP; patent applications and grants, and inhabitants per application. These ratios, given in Tables 8.1 and 8.2, are discussed below.

Manpower indicators of dependence

Table 8.1 presents two sets of ratios, namely, those that relate to science and technology indicators, and others which concern educational levels and the levels of industrialization measured by the share of the labour force in industry. These indicators for a number of NICs and African countries are compared. The data may not be strictly comparable, yet they show that the ratios of scientists and technicians and R&D personnel are generally much lower in African countries than those in the NICs.

Table 8.1 Technological dependence: selected manpower indicators

	Scientists & technicians per 1000 people (1) 1986–91	R&D scientists & technicians per 10 000 people (2) 1986–89	Percentage of labour force in industry (3) 1965	(3) 1990–92	Adult literacy rate (%) (4) 1970	(4) 1992	Percentage of age group in education Primary (5) 1965	Primary (5) 1990	Secondary (6) 1965	Secondary (6) 1990	Tertiary (7) 1965	Tertiary (7) 1990
Algeria	–	–	17	33	25	61	68	95	7	60	1	12
Benin	–	2.3	5	7	16	25	34	61	3	11	0	3
Botswana	1.2	–	4	11	41	75	65	110	3	46	–	3
Central African Republic	–	2.2	3	3	16	40	56	67	2	11	–	2
Côte d'Ivoire	–	–	5	8	18	56	60	–	6	20	0	–
Egypt	–	6.0	15	21	35	50	75	98	26	82	7	19
Ghana	1.5	–	15	11	31	63	69	75	13	39	1	2
Kenya	1.3	–	5	7	32	71	114	94	10	23	1	2
Mauritius	15.9	3.4	25	30	–	–	101	106	26	52	0	2
Nigeria	1.0	0.7	10	7	25	52	32	72	5	20	0	3
Rwanda	0.2	0.2	2	2	32	52	53	69	2	7	0	1
Sierra Leone	–	–	11	14	13	24	29	48	5	16	0	1
Tunisia	1.4	–	21	34	31	68	91	116	16	45	2	9
Zambia	4.4	–	8	8	52	75	53	93	7	20	–	2
Zimbabwe	–	–	8	8	55	69	110	117	6	50	0	5

Table 8.1 Continued

	Scientists & technicians per 1 000 people (1) 1986–91	R&D scientists & technicians per 10 000 people (2) 1986–89	Percentage of labour force in industry (3)		Adult literacy rate (%) (4)		Percentage of age group in education					
							Primary (5)		Secondary (6)		Tertiary (7)	
			1965	1990–92	1970	1992	1965	1990	1965	1990	1965	1990
Bangladesh	0.5	–	5	13	24	37	49	73	13	17	1	3
China	8.1	–	8	14	–	–	89	135	24	48	0	2
India	3.5	2.5	12	11	34	50	74	97	27	44	5	–
Indonesia	12.1	–	9	14	54	84	72	117	12	45	1	–
Korea, Republic of	45.9	22	15	36	88	97	101	108	35	87	6	39
Malaysia	–	4.0	13	28	60	80	90	93	28	56	2	7
Pakistan	4.0	1.5	19	20	21	36	40	37	12	22	2	3
Philippines	–	1.3	16	16	83	90	113	111	41	73	19	27
Singapore	22.9	18.7	27	35	–	–	105	110	45	69	10	8
Sri Lanka	–	2.2	14	21	77	89	93	107	35	74	2	4
Thailand	1.2	1.6	5	11	79	94	78	85	14	32	2	16
Argentina	28.4	5.4	34	34	93	96	101	111	28	74	14	–
Brazil	29.5	–	20	25	66	82	108	108	16	39	2	12
Ecuador	9.1	–	19	19	72	87	91	–	17	–	3	20
Jamaica	6.2	0.1	20	24	97	99	109	105	51	60	3	5
Mexico	–	6.1	22	29	74	89	92	112	17	53	4	14

– = not available.

Sources: Cols (1) to (4), UNDP: Human Development Report, 1994 (New York: Oxford University Press); Cols (5) to (7), World Bank, World Development Report (New York: Oxford University Press, 1992 and 1993).

Mauritius is the only exceptional case, where these ratios are higher than those in China, India, the Philippines and Thailand. The percentage of the labour force in industry, a proxy for an industrialization index, is also low, with the notable exceptions of Algeria, Egypt, Ghana, Morocco, Nigeria, and Tunisia. In many countries (notably in Africa) the share of the labour force in industry either did not increase or actually declined between 1965 and 1990–2 (the case of so-called de-industrialization).

Trends in primary and secondary education show a general improvement, but a very small percentage of the age group, particularly in Africa, are in tertiary or higher education, which is particularly important for greater technological self-reliance. The Asian and Latin American countries show a higher percentage of the population in tertiary education. One can argue that countries at low living standards but with a reasonable share of the labour force in industry, fairly high literacy rates and school enrolments, as is the case in Ghana, can nevertheless achieve technological self-reliance more rapidly than other countries where these indicators are very low.

Patent grants and applications

Patent statistics can also give some indication of the inventive activity and technological dependence. However, limitations of such an indicator should be borne in mind. Patents may not reflect innovative activity if they are not obtained for any productive use or if they require complementary know-how which is not accessible (Watanabe, 1985). The majority of these patents are not exploited. Furthermore, the bulk of patents are granted to, or are held by, foreigners. In general, in very few developing countries patent applications and grants have been made to the residents, which suggests, not surprisingly, a low level of inventive activity. The situation in the NICs and near NICs is different from that in African countries, where the number of inhabitants per application is much lower (see Table 8.2).

Recognizing the above limitations as well as those of comparability of data across countries, Table 8.2 presents information on patent grants and applications for a number of developing countries. A number of features of the Table are worth noting. First, patents granted to residents are very limited in number. Although the number of patents granted to residents increased between 1980 and 1990 in most cases, it still remains very small in countries at a low level of industrial production and development. Secondly, the number of total applications by residents is also quite small. Thirdly, the number of patents granted and patent applications seems to

Table 8.2 Patent applications and grants for selected African countries, NICs and near-NICs

Country	Patents granted				Patent applications filed				Inhabitants per application	
	Total (1)		Residents (2)		Total (3)		Residents (4)		(5)	
	1981	1990	1981	1990	1981	1990	1981	1990	1981	1990
Algeria	14	592	14	0	–	185	–	–	–	–
Botswana	–	39*	–	1*	–	68*	–	–	–	–
Egypt	257	306	8	20	797	789	59	278	728 813	187 050
Gambia	–	35*	–	–	–	62*	–	–	–	–
Ghana	19	20	–	–	19	20	–	–	–	–
Kenya	75	47*	–	1*	75	131*	–	8*	–	–
Lesotho	–	29*	–	–	–	59*	–	–	–	–
Madagascar	–	–	–	–	–	3 144	–	–	–	–
Malawi	34	35	2	–	48	3 159	7	–	885 714	–
Mauritius	–	13	–	–	–	4	–	1	–	–
Morocco	312	311	31	57	335	329	36	61	580 555	409 836
Namibia	–	139	–	3	–	163	–	5	–	400 000
Nigeria	–	170	–	10	–	258	–	12	–	9 583 333
Rwanda	7	4	–	–	7	4	–	–	–	–
Sudan	–	37*	–	–	–	3 157	–	–	–	–
Swaziland	25	28*	–	–	–	60*	–	1*	–	–
Tunisia	177	522	25	81	211	160	28	26	232 143	307 692
Uganda	55	13	–	–	55	13	–	–	–	–
Zambia	68	60	–	1	108	57	1	7	5 800 000	1 142 857
Zimbabwe	279	134	5	9	309	203	35	44	205 714	227 272

Table 8.2 Continued

Country	Patents granted				Patent applications filed				Inhabitants per application	
	Total (1)		Residents (2)		Total (3)		Residents (4)		(5)	
	1981	1990	1981	1990	1981	1990	1981	1990	1981	1990
China	–	4 122*	–	1 311*	–	11 423*	–	7 372*	–	–
India	1 289	1 572	419	306	2 901	3 820	1 067	1 147	646 860	741 063
Korea, Rep. of	1 808	7 762	232	2 554	5 303	31 387	1 319	9 083	29 492	4 734
Malaysia	–	–	–	–	–	2 427	–	106	–	169 811
Philippines	787	944*	69	45*	1 605	1 921*	91	147	545 054	418 367
Singapore	–	1 238	–	–	–	1 028	–	–	–	–
Thailand	–	141	–	7	330	1 940	26	73	1 846 154	767 123
Argentina	3 514	–	820	–	4 725	–	954	–	29 559	–
Brazil	10 292	3 355	844	453	8 284	12 434	2 171	2 430	55 504	61 728
Mexico	2 210	1 752	188	141	5 328	5 289	704	564	101 136	152 482

* = data are for 1991.

– = nil.

Sources: For columns (1) to (4) WIPO, *Industrial Property Statistics*, 1981 and 1991. For column (5), population figures in *World Bank Development Reports* are divided by figures in column (4).

increase with an increase in the level of economic and industrial development in a country. Thus, the number of patents granted in Egypt, Morocco and Zimbabwe is much higher than in the other less-developed African countries.

As the number of patent applications varies significantly depending on the size of the population, the number of inhabitants per application is also indicated in Table 8.2. The inventive activity, other things being equal, will be greater the smaller the number of inhabitants per application. Differences in inventive activity and capacity are likely to be due to differences in the level of income or industrial production and the level of education or literacy. Data in Table 8.2 therefore need to be examined together with those in Table 8.1. As is to be expected, the number of inhabitants per application is the smallest in Egypt and Zimbabwe, which are sophisticated developing economies with a solid industrial base and qualified scientific manpower. The number of inhabitants per application is the highest in Nigeria and Zambia, which are at a lower stage of industrial and economic development.

There is no clear trend in the number of inhabitants per application. While this number has increased in the case of Tunisia and Zimbabwe, it has declined in the case of Egypt, Morocco and Zambia. Among the Asian countries, the number of inhabitants per application increased in India and declined in Thailand and the Philippines. In Latin America, it increased in both Mexico and Brazil (see Table 8.2).

Other indicators

Three other indicators of technological dependence have sometimes been used – direct foreign investment, ownership and control mainly through multinational enterprises; share of capital goods imports in fixed investments; and R&D expenditure as a proportion of gross national product (GNP). We briefly discuss these below.

1. Foreign investment, ownership and control

Technological dependence is also due to the major decisions taking place outside the developing countries, particularly in the case of assets owned and controlled by the multinational enterprises (MNEs). As Stewart (1979) noted, 'restrictions on freedom of decision making tend to increase costs and reduce the firm's ability to be selective about technological choice, and to learn to generate an independent technological capacity' (p. 37). The MNEs are an agent of international technology transfers. With a growing trend in favour of economic liberalization and freer trade, their role in determining international flows of technology is becoming all the more important. However, these flows are difficult to determine and estimate since in part technology is transferred through trade in capital goods, and in part through flows of private foreign investment (UNCTC, 1991).

African experience shows that both local and foreign enterprises may be heavily dependent on foreign technology when the local technology base is poorly developed. For example, in the case of Nigeria, it is noted that in the textiles and other industries major decisions regarding choice of technology, equipment, etc. are made by foreign investors and managers who invariably choose imported technology (Ohiorhenuan and Poloamina, 1992). In the case of Tanzania, Wangwe (1992) states that 'the bulk of preinvestment activities were performed by foreign experts who also helped to mobilize foreign finance'. Even in the actual execution of projects, the participation of local personnel has been limited, thanks to the powerful alliance of foreign engineering consultants, machinery suppliers and foreign capital. Wangwe (1992) also notes that technological learning and capacity building was made secondary to the quick achievement of output targets. The use of foreign capital is seen as inhibiting local technological capability. Mytelka (1992) concludes that in Côte d'Ivoire 'expatriate managers and technology suppliers took all major investment and technological decisions and imported technology was chosen that was more suited for large-scale mass production requiring large domestic markets and sophisticated skills'.

In Table 8.3 we present data on the share of direct foreign investment in gross fixed capital formation for a number of developing countries. Caution is needed in interpreting this indicator for determining technological dependence. First, there is the inherent limitation of the data: while foreign direct investment (FDI) reflects both the acquisition of existing assets in the host country as well as newly-established investment, gross fixed capital formation refers only to the additions to the existing stock of domestic capital. Secondly, the data on FDI are expressed in both stocks and flows, gross and net flows and actual receipts and approvals, and thus they tend not to be comparable across countries. They also seem to be 'subject to error and conflict ... rather surprisingly in view of the international nature of the transactions' (Lall, 1990). Furthermore, they do not include such activities of MNEs as the supply of technological services, including management and marketing. Another limitation is that the data are heavily influenced by the policies of the host countries towards multinational and foreign investment. In some cases these

Table 8.3   Other indicators: Direct foreign investment in gross fixed capital formation, capital goods imports in gross fixed capital formation and R&D expenditures as percentage of GNP

	Share of direct foreign investment (percentages)			Share of capital goods[a] imports (percentages)		R&D as percentage of GNP
	1971–5	1976–80	1986–91	1970		
Algeria	1.9	1.4	0.05	28	20 (1991)	–
Côte d'Ivoire	5.4	2.5	5.3	43	41 (1985)	0.3 (1975)
Egypt	–	7.1	7.8	24	28 (1990)	0.2 (1982)
Gabon	10.8	3.2	7.6	26	22 (1983)	0.9 (1980)
Ghana	9.7	1.8	0.9	40	19 (1982)	0.8 (1975)
Kenya	2.9	4.4	2.1	40	45 (1988)	–
Madagascar	4.2	–0.6	4.1	–	–	0.6 (1988)
Malawi	–	–	–	60	58 (1985)	0.2 (1977)
Morocco	0.4	1.6	2.6	37	34 (1991)	0.3 (1980)
Nigeria	4.9	0.5	16.3	28	38 (1987)	0.1 (1985)
Rwanda	4.6	2.9	1.7	32	43 (1980)	0.5 (1985)
Senegal	0.02	0.02	0.0	51 (1980)	44 (1990)	1.0 (1976)
Sierra Leone	–8.0	2.6	0.9[b]	68	24 (1984)	0.2 (1980)
Togo	–5.3	11.7	1.2	37 (1980)	35 (1990)	–
Argentina	0.1	2.1	14.5[c]	11	15 (1990)	0.5 (1988)
Brazil	4.2	3.9	1.7[c]	13	8 (1991)	0.4 (1985)
Chile	–7.3	4.2	5.7	32	52 (1990)	
China	0.0	0.08	2.3	9 (1984)	26 (1991)	–
Colombia	1.7	2.2	6.1	30	27 (1991)	–
India	0.3	0.1	0.3	6	5 (1991)	0.9 (1986)
Korea (Republic of)	1.9	0.4	1.1	27	26 (1991)	2.3 (1987)
Jamaica	12.9	1.6	6.6	–	–	–
Malaysia	15.2	11.9	9.7	49	119 (1991)	–
Mexico	3.5	3.6	7.0	16	25 (1990)	0.6 (1984)
Pakistan	0.5	0.9	2.3	26	38 (1991)	–
Philippines	1.0	0.9	5.7	38	35 (1991)	0.1 (1984)
Singapore	15.0	16.6	29.4	91	183 (1991)	0.9 (1987)
Thailand	3.0	1.5	6.3	27	40 (1991)	0.2 (1987)

[a] Capital goods include machinery and transport equipment. Ratios are calculated on the basis of national and international data.
[b] 1986–9.
[c] 1986–90.
Sources: United Nations Centre on Transnational Corporations, *World Investment Report* (1993); UN (1981, 1983, 1990); IMF (1983, 1991); UNESCO, *Statistical Yearbook* (1988, 1989, 1990).

investments may be concentrated in those developing countries which are abundant in raw materials and a cheap labour supply. In other cases, low ratios may be due to rigorous policies of nationalization in the post-independence period.

In the past, nationalization and indigenization were the two means by which the developing countries attempted to exercise control and ownership of private foreign investment. Nationalization involves partial or full state participation in foreign enterprises, whereas indigenization calls for the 'statutory divestment of part or all of the equity of such enterprises to private nationals of the host country' (Hoogvelt, 1980). Indigenization or localization policies adopted by some developing countries are intended to acquire technical knowledge to strengthen technological capability. However, participation of nationals in equity and state ownership do not automatically reduce dependence. Mytelka (1992) concludes that in Côte d'Ivoire, 'although the indigenization of management became official policy, it remained divorced from the goal of technical mastery'. If the initial level of technical competence is low, the domestic producers may face a major challenge which may be met only by greater foreign technical assistance (Pack, 1987). This seems to be the case particularly in Africa, where despite the rhetoric of localization, dependence on foreign technology, finance and personnel has continued, and localization targets have often remained unattained (Wangwe, 1992a). There seems to be a vicious circle operating here. Lack of local participation occurs due to low local competence, which in turn means subsequent failure to master and adapt imported technology. Thus the low levels of manpower indicators noted in Table 8.1 above explain, *inter alia*, a failure to build technological capabilities and reduce dependence.

The greater involvement of international agencies may be essential to 'help attain the necessary economic conditions and infrastructural requirements to attract significant amounts of FDI' into Africa (UNCTC, 1992, p. 30). The low levels of FDI, particularly in the least-developed countries, seem to be due to the uncertainty about economic development rather than the 'localization or nationalization' policies mentioned above. Both these factors discourage the MNEs from making investments.

The shares of direct foreign investment in different developing countries vary a great deal, as is seen in Table 8.3. There is no clear trend towards an increase in foreign investment in a number of African countries. In many countries (e.g. Algeria, Ghana, and Madagascar) the shares have actually declined. For Africa as a whole, direct 'investment flows are rather low (7 per cent) and show no signs of significant growth' (UNCTC, 1992). This marginalization of Africa is likely to continue since these investment flows are highly concentrated in a few NICs and resource-rich countries (OECD, 1992, p. 259). A host of factors – political instability, national policies as mentioned above, stagnant economies and debts – may explain this trend. In other countries (e.g. Argentina, China, Nigeria and Pakistan) the share of foreign investment has been rising.

2. Capital goods imports

The share of capital goods imports as a proportion of fixed investment – sometimes called the import dependency ratio – can also be used as a crude indicator of technological dependence. The higher the ratio, the greater the technological dependence. Table 8.3 gives these ratios for a number of developing countries. For lack of data, it is not easy to determine a clear pattern over time. The ratios for most African countries are generally higher than those for more advanced developing countries like Argentina, Brazil and the Republic of Korea. However, the ratios for Malaysia and Singapore are also very high. One reason for their high ratios may be that they may be importing a lot of electrical components (electrical machinery is included in capital goods) as intermediate goods for reprocessing.

In absolute value, Africa witnessed a significant decline in the capital goods imports during the 1980s (from US$23.5 billion in 1980 to US$18.2 billion in 1989), while Asia and the Pacific Region showed a considerable increase (from US$56.7 billion in 1980 to US$95.8 billion in 1989) (UNCTC, 1992, p. 140).

As an index of technological dependence, capital goods imports suffer from a number of limitations. First, capacity to manufacture capital goods within a country may be necessary but not a sufficient condition for its technological independence. In many cases, for reasons of pride and prestige, many developing countries set up domestic capital-goods industries – even when they are not economically viable owing to the limited local market. In such cases, these industries are highly dependent on imports of technology and materials from abroad. In an open economy framework it may be cheaper to import capital goods than to produce them domestically, especially if the developing country concerned does not have any comparative advantage in its production. Second, some countries followed import-substitution policies whereas others followed more liberal import policies. In practice the nature of policies in different countries also influences data. This seems to account for a particularly low ratio in India and a relatively high ratio in the Republic of Korea in Table 8.3. Third, even industrialized countries with a small domestic market for capital goods may have a high technological capacity, and yet they may show high import ratios, since they export some capital goods produced with imported technology and import others in which local production may not have a comparative advantage.

So far we have considered two private channels of technology transfer, namely, flows of direct foreign investment and capital goods imports. For many developing countries, particularly in Africa, direct payments in the form of technical cooperation grants are also an important source of technology transfer. In Table 8.4, which presents data on foreign direct investment, capital goods imports and technical cooperation grants for different regions, direct foreign investment flows seem to be least important in Africa.

3. R&D expenditures

The role of formal and informal shop-floor R&D can be important in technology development and adaptation and in reducing technological dependence, but its impact is hard to quantify. Even data on formal public-funded R&D for developing countries are rare (see Table 8.3 for the limited information that is available on R&D expenditures as a proportion of GNP). Notwithstanding any lack of data, one thing is quite clear: the share of developing countries in general in R&D is extremely small, even

Table 8.4   Structure of technology flows to developing countries (1988)
($ billion, current prices)

	Foreign direct investment inflows	Capital goods imports	Technical co-operation grants
All developing countries	28.7	144	12.6[1]
Africa	2.1	17	4.9
Asia	14.9	87	2.9
Latin America and the Caribbean	11.4	36	2
cf.			
Least developed countries	0.1	4	2.6

[1] Grants not allocated in individual countries are included in total, but not in regional groups.
Source: UNCTAD, *Transfer and Development of Technology in a Changing World Environment: The Challenges of the 1990s* (TD/8/C.6/153) Table 2: updated data from UNCTAD Secretariat; International Monetary Fund balance-of-payments tape (cited in OECD, 1992).

though it has been rising. The share of Africa is almost negligible which suggests persistent and even growing technological dependence in this region. With the introduction of structural adjustment measures in many developing countries, and in the face of serious debt situations, the government expenditures on R&D, with long-term pay-off and uncertain results, are likely to be reduced even further in the future.

POLICIES TO REDUCE TECHNOLOGY DEPENDENCE

If many countries suffer from technological dependence, what can be done to reduce it? As we argued earlier, technological dependence is but one manifestation of economic dependence. Therefore, the attainment of economic-independence should in the long run reduce technological dependence. However, in the short run, a number of measures can contribute towards the building up of national technological capabilities to reduce dependence.

First, unpackaging of technology imports should in principle improve the bargaining position of recipient countries. It implies a better identification of the components of the technological package, which is a precondition for the eventual mastery of technology. However, there is a dilemma here. Unpackaging is possible only if there is a basic knowledge and some mastery of technology on the part of the recipient countries. This may or may not be available in many developing countries (particularly in Africa) where the process of indigenization has not yet achieved the desired results. Secondly, unpackaging requires diversification of the sources of imports. Tying of aid and tying of equipment procurement by donors and multinational enterprises has tended to hinder such diversification in the past. This situation may change in future with an increasing international competition among technology suppliers. This new phenomenon, particularly in the case of new technology (microelectronics) where barriers to entry have been reduced, may offer developing countries new opportunities of improved bargaining for access to this technology (see Ernst and O'Connor, 1989, p. 24).

Perhaps within the framework of such regional groupings as ASEAN, SADCC and MERCOSUR, it may in future be feasible for interested countries to agree on common innovation policies and projects. A recent OECD study (1994) strikes an optimistic note when it states that 'developing innovation-driven forms of South–South cooperation is ... more feasible in the 1990s, ... the need to pool resources has become evident to states and other social and economic actors in the South' (p. 14).

Economies of scale in production are essential for competing successfully in the international market. Increasing pressures towards regionalization and increasing competition between developing countries and the NICs will certainly provide a driving force towards technological sophistication. Furthermore, within the Third World, technological accumulation has occurred in a number of sectors. The rising costs of R&D and production in microelectronics and biotechnologies, and the need for closer linkages between suppliers and clients, point towards greater cross-border collaboration. However, whether this will lead to technological cooperation and regional projects is not certain. For example, the Asian region is increasingly dependent on Japan for technology and capital goods which may hinder the promotion of regional technological cooperation.

South–South technology transfers (for example, between African countries and the NICs) imply a complementary nature of the economies of participating countries; the existence of technology exporters among them; and the prevalence of indigenous innovations within these countries. These preconditions are not always fulfilled, with the result that the volume of technology transfers among developing countries is at present quite limited.

But potential exists for bilateral and multilateral co-operation between the African countries and the other more advanced developing countries. Some technical co-operation in small-scale industry between India and African countries such as Kenya and the United Republic of Tanzania is already taking place (see Kathuria, 1992). Joint ventures, industrial and construction consultancy services, and transfer of technical know-how, are but a few examples of the exports of technology from India to African countries. As the NICs and many African countries are at somewhat different stages of development, the economies of these two groups of countries are complementary, which should enable greater technology transfers assuming of course that political factors do not stand in the way.

With increasing economic liberalization, the focus of technology efforts is shifting from the public institutions to the private enterprises. To facilitate innovation, regional and sub-regional networking with financial participation from donors and foundations has been recommended. Mytelka (1993) has proposed 'a Fund for Innovation and Development in Africa', based on an endowment consisting of contributions from private companies and governments. One of the main purposes of such a mechanism will be to strengthen firm-level technological capabilities 'by underwriting the costs and risks of innovation'. Although similar funding mechanisms have been proposed before, the Mytelka proposal is based on the premise that partnership between the government and the private sector is a precondition for reducing technological dependence.

In the final analysis, appropriate economic incentives, institutions, infrastructure and human resources development should go a long way in reducing dependence. We now consider these ingredients in Chapter 9 in the broader context of socioeconomic development.

9 Technology Indicators, Capability and Development*

In this concluding chapter, our intention is not to summarize the findings of earlier analysis. Instead we would like to put the earlier discussion on the technological challenge faced by developing countries in a broader perspective of national technological capability and socio-economic development. Achievement of capability over time needs to be monitored regularly, a task for which suitable technological indicators would be needed. Furthermore, the development and adoption of new and conventional technologies by the developing countries should contribute to the attainment of their overall development objectives.

We start with an analysis of the relevance of technological indicators and their suitability for monitoring a country's technological capability and its contribution to national development objectives. This discussion is followed by a review of existing technological indicators. The third section argues that the indicators should give some indication of a country's technological capability and the fourth section outlines a framework for linking capability to overall development objectives.

THE RELEVANCE OF TECHNOLOGICAL INDICATORS

Because of the relative neglect of the empirical measurement of science and technology *per se*, not to speak of the measurement of its contribution to growth and development, technological change still remains something of a 'black box'. In spite of work on socioeconomic indicators for over two decades now, science and technology (S and T) indicators were either not included as *development* indicators or were treated very marginally.[1]

Indicators are variables which reflect or represent other variables. For example, school enrolment ratios are a measure of the amount of school

---

*Revised and updated version of A.S. Bhalla and A.G. Fluitman, 'Science and technology indicators and socioeconomic development', *World Development*, Feb. 1985.

enrolment, but may be used as an indicator of the educational level of a country; body temperature is an indicator of sickness; death rates may indicate the state of public health. In other words, 'indicators are not simply statistics, and statistics are not *ipso facto* indicators – unless some theory or assumption makes them so by relating the indicator variable to a phenomenon that is not what it directly and fully measures' (McGranahan, 1972, p. 91).

Although science and technology are invariably grouped together, it is useful for conceptual clarification, empirical precision and policy formulation to make a distinction between indicators of scientific knowledge such as expenditure on R&D, number of scientific journals, and stock of high-level scientists on the one hand, and indicators of technological change such as labour productivity, use of mechanical power, and use of irrigation and fertilisers, on the other (Bell, 1968). Indigenous technological capability cannot exist without a minimum threshold of scientific knowledge. However, while scientific activity requires conceptualization and analysis, technological activity – and in particular the development of new technologies – involves a synthesis of existing knowledge and experimentation.

Baster (1972) and others (e.g. Adelman and Morris, 1972) have pointed out that the systematization of indicators can be approached from two directions. Ideally, one should start from a broad concept such as development, and break it down into its component variables; if these again are not directly measurable, they would be represented by indicators; the indicators are selected on the basis of plausible assumptions about their relationship, usually one of cause and effect, with the variable they represent. Once a conceptual framework has thus been established, data will be collected to give the indicator a value. Unfortunately, such data are usually not available. Alternatively, and this is the method more frequently used, one could start from existing inter-country data that seem relevant, and use correlation techniques to establish assumptions about the relationship between variables. This approach is simpler but likely to suffer from a number of limitations, in particular the fact that a correlation coefficient itself says nothing about causation. For example, a high and significant correlation between the number of television sets and per capita paper consumption in 150 countries does not indicate any cause and effect relationship, but is determined by a third variable such as per capita income; a high correlation between the number of television sets and days with rain in August is possible but can only be explained in terms of chance.

Indicators which explain relationships between variables at a point in time, or historical trends, may be useful in determining the nature and level of resources to be allocated to scientific and technological endeavours and to sectors which support such activity. Also they may provide the necessary data for assessing past performance in the building up of technological capability and its utilization.

These indicators can thus make a contribution to the planning and evaluation of technological progress. However, such planning and evaluation have meaning only in a context of national development goals. This being the case, the formulation of indicators for given countries, or parts thereof, deserves a higher priority than of indicators which facilitate cross-country comparisons. This is simply because a review of policy and programme formulation is more meaningful and operational in terms of national action.

Indicators are no doubt more meaningful if they are related to outputs rather than inputs. Input indicators say little about the contribution of science and technology to economic aggregates like GNP and its growth over time. For example, the number of scientists and engineers involved in R&D may give some hints for the planning requirements of education, science and technology; and R&D institutions. But it does not give any qualitative or efficiency indication of how scientific manpower inputs contribute to meeting objectives such as the fulfilment of basic needs and employment generation. Likewise, the number of doctors per 1000 population tells us nothing about the geographical distribution of these doctors, their specialization, or supporting medical services. Yet, this is what would be required if we were to measure the contribution of medical personnel and services to the satisfaction of the health needs of given target groups of a population.[2]

Disaggregation of indicators is essential if one is interested in measuring the contribution of technology to the fulfilment of specific development objectives. For example, basic needs and employment objectives are more likely to be met if the bulk of R&D expenditure were allocated to specific small-scale sectors, rather than to a few large projects of a highly capital-intensive nature. Admittedly, the limited availability of data will create serious problems. Nevertheless, some bold attempts have been made to estimate R&D for appropriate technology generation in developing countries. Jéquier and Blanc (1983) have compiled data on the level and trends, size of funding and geographical distribution of appropriate technology efforts.

Indicators are also needed to measure the effect of a given technology on the welfare of specific target groups of people. One may consider a matrix approach in which alternative technologies, represented by indicators such as the capital–labour ratio, correspond to the attributes of different development strategies. Although it might thus be possible to show favourable influence – of improved traditional or appropriate technology on the welfare of low-income poverty groups, its impact would vary from one poverty group to another (see James, 1985 and 1989).

As we noted in Chapter 1, it is possible to test empirically the impact of different technologies in individual countries in an input–output or social accounting framework. Such a framework enables, at least in principle, an integration of data on production, technology and income distribution in an intersectoral manner.

EXISTING TECHNOLOGICAL INDICATORS: A BRIEF REVIEW

Most of the work undertaken so far on indicators deals with the measurement of social progress and a large degree of disaggregation has been achieved for this purpose (UN, 1978; OECD, 1978, 1982; WHO, 1981). However, there have been relatively few attempts to link science and technology explicitly to socioeconomic goals, presumably because of conceptual difficulties and inadequate statistics (Teitel, 1987; 1989).

To the extent that conceptual difficulties are associated with indicators in general, the work of the United Nations Research Institute for Social Development (UNRISD) needs to be mentioned, since it constitutes a solid stepping stone for further work on science and technology or any other type of indicator (McGranahan et al. 1979). The UNRISD Research Data Bank of 73 development indicators includes only two technology indicators, namely (a) professional, technical and related workers as a percentage of the total economically active population; and (b) scientists and engineers engaged in research and development per 10 000 population. OECD is another organization engaged in work on the measurement of scientific and technical activities which goes back to the early 1960s. In 1963, the first version of the 'Proposed Standard Practice for Surveys of Research and Experimental Development', better known as the 'Frascati Manual', was published. The manual is basically a guide for member countries in compiling and analysing statistics on inputs to R&D. That only R&D inputs are included is considered 'regrettable since we are more interested in R&D because of the new knowledge and inventions which result from it than in the activity itself ... While indicators of the output of R&D are clearly needed to complement input statistics, they are far more difficult to define and collect' (OECD, 1981, p. 17). The fourth edition of the Frascati Manual contains a short annex on the measurement of output of R&D, and refers, *inter alia*, to indicators of the number and cost of innovations, patent statistics, the technological balance of payments and productivity indices. As we noted in Chapter 8 there are limitations in using patent statistics as an indicator of national technological capability in developing countries. The OECD Science and Technology Indicators series regularly provides an analysis of structure and trends by a range of science and technology indicators, for example R&D expenditures and personnel, higher education expenditure, patent applications and technology balance of payments. In addition to the revision of these S and T indicators and the Frascati Manual, the OECD is engaged in developing a new statistical series on technology balance of payments data, innovative activity in industry and scientific and technical manpower (Annerstedt, 1994). UNESCO's work on scientific and technological indicators is based on a 'model' of relationships between socioeconomic development, technological development, scientific and technological potential, and political, economic, and socio-cultural receptivity to scientific and technological development.

A study by Teitel (1987) examined the relationship between technology indicators (e.g. scientists and engineers in a country, number of scientists and engineers in R&D, and expenditure on R&D) and explanatory variables, namely, income per capita and population. Teitel (1994, 1994a) extended this empirical work to output indicators, namely patents and scientific publications. These indicators were related to explanatory variables like stock of scientists and engineers, expenditure on R&D, income *per capita* and population. Regression analysis was used to test the hypothesis that the three technological indicators are positively correlated with *per capita* income and population, implying that the larger the country and the more developed it is, the larger would be the stock of scientists and engineers for example. The econometric results show that the technological indicators chosen, particularly the utilization of scientists and engineers in R&D, do not easily lend themselves to international comparisons due to the non-comparability of data and inadequate statistical base.

The above brief review of work on technological indicators suggests that quantitative efforts to develop these indicators (both input and output), and to link them to broader development objectives and socioeconomic indicators, have not been all that successful. Annerstedt (1994) noted that 'despite continuous efforts, neither UNESCO, nor any other international agency has yet been able to implement, through the many national statistical units, a world standard on how to collect R&D data and further specify the kinds of innovative activities that should be measured as well' (p. 104). The inadequacy of statistical data is only one part of the problem.

Some issues related to development are not easily quantifiable, which reinforces the need to supplement quantitative indicators with qualitative ones. This is what is attempted in the following sections.

LINKING TECHNOLOGICAL CAPABILITY TO DEVELOPMENT

The above technological indicators should give some indication of a country's technological capability at a given point in time. However, before one can identify suitable indicators it is essential to be clear about what technological capability means in various circumstances and at different stages of development.

Technological capability need not always match national objectives. This is shown by the story of creating an indigenous capacity to manufacture tractors and combine harvesters in India. Punjab Tractors Ltd, an enterprise specially commissioned by the State Government, was successful in designing an indigenous tractor – *Swaraj* – which now competes successfully with imported tractors. Encouraged by this success in technological self-reliance, Punjab Tractors Ltd proceeded with a crash programme to design and manufacture combine harvesters. Morehouse (1982) stated that:

> creating the capacity for generating indigenous technology, is like opening up Pandora's box. Once created, it can be used for good or for ill. What is the social merit, sceptics would ask, of using this indigenous capacity to design and build self-propelled job destroyers such as combine harvesters in the labour-surplus Indian economy? Yet that is exactly what has occurred and forms an integral part of the unfolding story of the Indian tractor industry (p. 181).

However, one can also argue that the design and manufacture of combine harvesters in Punjab was a rational economic response to acute agricultural labour shortages in the peak seasons and, thus, to real demand for this machinery.

A lot has already been written on technological capability at both the levels of firm and aggregate national economy (Dahlman and Westphal, 1982; Pack and Westphal, 1986; Fransman 1986; Teitel, 1981; Westphal, 1982; Lall, 1987, 1990, 1993; Enos, 1991; Girvan, 1979). Yet there is no clear agreement on the nature, scope and relationship of technological capability to broader development objectives. However, there is agreement on one thing, namely, the acquisition of national technological capabilities is a long-term phenomenon. The development of capabilities at a micro or firm level (capabilities in production, design, engineering, project execution, etc.) does not automatically ensure their positive overall contribution to national development objectives. Even if such capabilities are developed, the objective of sustainable development may not be achieved if the existing wasteful consumption patterns do not change.

Furthermore, different elements of technological capability may not reinforce each other, neither may they be developed at the same time. Nevertheless, from a policy and a practical point of view, it is important to know the precise interrelationships between different elements of technological capability. For example, how is the capability for production engineering related to that for project execution? Similarly, how important is local capital-goods manufacture for building up learning and adaptive capability?

On the basis of their studies on the Republic of Korea, Dahlman and Westphal (1981) come to the conclusion that 'high indigenous levels of all types of technological mastery are not necessary for the initial stages of industrial development'. This reinforces the argument in favour of a proper sequencing of different types of capability over time. In fact, Dahlman and Westphal found that by relying on foreign sources of technology it was possible to choose a technology without having first mastered its use. Such transfers *per se* need not inhibit the development of indigenous technological mastery; they might be a first step in the exploitation of available knowledge. Likewise, technologies may be effectively applied without mastering their reproduction. This is not to underemphasize the importance of innovation and formal R&D, which are required for absorbing or imitating sophisticated imported technologies (Lall, 1990).

Technological capabilities can also vary between sectors (Enos, 1991; Zahlan, 1990). In the industrial sector, the elements of technology capability – production engineering, manufacture of capital goods and research and development, etc. – are different from those essential, for example, for the services sector (Dahlman and Westphal, 1982). Technological capabilities may exist in both large and small industrial sectors. An ILO study examines technological capabilities in the small-scale informal sector of developing countries (Maldonado and Sethuraman, 1992). It is based on sample surveys undertaken in capital cities and urban towns in Asia (India, Bangladesh and Thailand), Latin America (Ecuador and Peru) and Africa (Mali and Rwanda). Contrary to expectations, it finds that even very small metalworking production units possess a capacity to adapt and modify tools and equipment. In some cases, these units demonstrate an indigenous capacity and ingenuity to manufacture simple equipment. The contributions of such innovations to development often remain unnoticed.

In examining technology policy studies for the Caribbean, Girvan (1979) devotes considerable attention to the issue of the strengthening of local technological development, which is defined in terms of six major constituents, namely: (i) the educational system; (ii) the R&D establishment; (iii) specialist workshops and facilities; (iv) engineering and consultancy; (v) information systems and mechanisms; and (vi) management, planning and financing. For an effective technological capability, it is important that 'each constituent of it must be supportive of every other, through a network of demand and supply relationships and through a pattern of pressure and response' (Girvan, 1979). We have adapted Girvan's analysis slightly to bring out the relevance and importance of indicators under each of the constituent elements enumerated above. This is done in Table 9.1. Figure 9.1 shows these relationships among different constituents of national technological capability. For example, technical training centres produce technicians who should be supplied to the specialist workshops, which in turn will be required to make an effective use of this trained manpower; engineering and consultancy institutions should make use of the work of R&D organizations, but the latter must undertake projects relevant to the needs of the former.

McGranahan (1972) points out that since indicators are meant to measure some conception, the nature and scope of the indicators, as well as the nature of the relations between them, will depend on this conception. He then reviews a number of major 'conceptual models' which are used or assumed in the definition of development. According to one of these models, development is defined as enhancing the capacity of a society to function for the well-being of its members over the long run.

[This] capacity-performance model [of development] embraces not only technological and educational capacities but also structural and institutional capacities; it suggests the importance of structural and institutional indicators and of building up 'capacity indicators' in general. At the same time, it is made quite clear that quantitative indicators have their limitations and should not be confused with development as a whole. The problem is to devise a scheme of developmental analysis that combines quantitative and non-quantitative elements (McGranahan, 1972, pp. 97–8).

Table 9.1   Indicators of technological capability at the national level

Input indicators	Output indicators	Technological functions
(1) Educational system		
(a) Number and quality of primary and secondary educational institutions.	Personnel with basic education capable of absorbing formal or on-the-job training in technologically related skills.	Provision of basic infrastructure to support functions below:
(b) Number and quality of technical vocational and industrial training institutions.	Skilled technicians, workers, craftsmen and artisans.	Absorption, modification and adaptation of techniques and process; fabrication of specialist tools, equipment and instruments.
(c) Number and quality of university and higher educational institutions	Scientists (natural, agricultural, medical, etc.), engineers, researchers, consultants, etc.	Research and Development, design, engineering, consultancy, management, absorption, adaptation, modification, and innovation of technique, processes and systems.
(2) Research and development establishment		
(a) Number of research laboratories/ stations/facilities.	Basic scientific knowledge. Applied scientific knowledge of potential practical use.	Basic research. Applied research on techniques, processes and systems.
(b) Number of pilot plants/experimental stations etc.	Economically useful knowledge.	Testing research. Applied research on techniques, processes and systems.
(3) Specialist workshops and facilities		
Number of mechanical, metalworking, repair and maintenance workshops and facilities	Tools and equipment including prototypes, components and spares.	Repair, maintenance, modification and adaptation of hardware; fabrication of components, tools, equipment and plant incorporating results of technical change from other functions.

Table 9.1 Continued

Input indicators	Output indicators	Technological functions
(4) Engineering and consultancy		
(a) Number and quality of consultant firms.	Consultancy contracts embodying knowledge and advice of a specialist or general nature.	Technology search, selection and evaluation; dissemination of technical knowledge.
(b) Number and quality of engineering (design and building) firms.	Project and plant designs.	Technology search, selection, evaluation and disaggregation; design, modification, adaptation of systems, incorporation or technical change.
(5) Information systems and mechanisms		
Research units in institutions, research institutions, survey departments, libraries, etc.	Brochures, leaflets, papers giving general and specific information.	Importation of knowledge, generation of local knowledge, dissemination of foreign and local knowledge to technology users to support (1) and (4) above.
(6) Management, planning and financing		
Science and technology plans.	Directives and guidelines for (1) to (5) and programme of activities.	Orientation of science and technology towards goals and strategies of development; rationalization, coordination and integration of technology functions and activities (1) to (5) above with development policy, planning and projects.

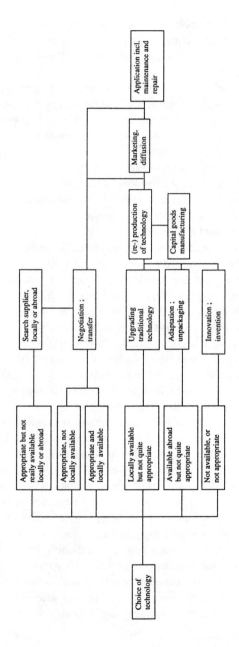

Figure 9.1   Elements of indigenous technological capability

TECHNOLOGICAL CAPABILITY AND NATIONAL OBJECTIVES

In reviewing work on technological indicators, one can conclude that the precise purpose of such indicators is not always clear. In any case, a variety of problems surround the definition and measurement of a country's technological capability – a fairly complex concept which must be disaggregated in order to be better understood. In the previous section, we referred to a number of approaches towards disaggregation. We will now suggest a somewhat different approach, which is both comprehensive and flexible. We argue that it is within such a framework that indicators of various kinds could play a useful role. A few points deserve reiteration and elaboration before presenting our approach.

The concept of technological capability is not absolute but relative; the term needs to be used in relation to specific national objectives. In other words, technological capability is a means and not an end: it is a necessary but not the only ingredient in a mix of factors giving rise to socioeconomic change. As countries have different development objectives, the nature of technological capability required to meet such objectives will vary from one country to another, and from one period of time to the next.

Whatever the nature of indicators, it is clear that the linking of technological capability to national objectives requires that micro or firm-level and sectoral capabilities (in agriculture, manufacturing and services, for example) are given a sense of direction and purpose. In this context, Enos (1991) defines technological capability in terms of three main components: (i) skilled and experienced individuals; (ii) institutions to which individuals belong and which are necessary to integrate different types of knowledge; and (iii) the common purpose or goals for which the individuals cooperate. This last element, though somewhat ambiguous, highlights our concern to link technological capability to (long-term) development goals. Institutions and individuals need a common purpose or objective to work towards, without which capabilities and their productive outcomes are unlikely to take place. A country which wishes to produce sufficient food, thereby employing as many of its citizens as possible, is likely to need and adopt technology policies which differ substantially from those of a country more interested in the conquest of space.

The fact that a certain technological capability exists does not necessarily mean that such capacity is exploited. It would appear that in many countries a certain latent capability exists which is not matched with concomitant needs and objectives. A technological capability which does not match priority objectives is not very useful from a society's point of view.

Technological capability needs to be defined in terms of its elements and, for reasons mentioned above, in terms of national objectives. Indigenous technological capability may be defined as the ability of a country to choose, to acquire, to generate and to apply technologies which are appropriate in the sense that their application contributes to meeting development objectives such as the reduction of poverty, unemployment and inequality, and sustainability. This definition implies that countries, as a matter of policy, decide, or have an influence on, what is being produced and how. Thus, a country with a basic-needs-oriented development strategy would promote the production of more food per acre with improved tools, or the use of labour-based methods in building rural feeder roads; and a country with a strategy of export-led industrialization would facilitate the importation of advanced technologies so as to be able to compete in international markets. The increasing globalization of production and worldwide competition makes it imperative that appropriate capability is developed to adapt and absorb new technologies.

Technological capability can be further disaggregated. The capability to search and select the most appropriate from a menu of alternative technologies is of course fundamental; but technologies which are known to exist need not be readily available at a reasonable price. The capability to acquire them includes the capacity to identify technology sources, the capability to negotiate reasonable conditions, and the capacity to transfer technology, as and when necessary from abroad, or within countries for example, from one sector of the economy to another.[3]

If available technologies are not considered appropriate enough, alternatives may be created – of course, after a time lag. The capability to generate technology includes the capacity to upgrade traditional indigenous technologies, and to adapt imported ones (e.g. through unpackaging), the capacity to innovate and to invent, as well as a capacity to test, to produce and to diffuse whatever has been generated. A capability to produce tools and machines, capital goods required to generate and reproduce technological alternatives, is another element to be mentioned here (see also Chapter 8). Finally, the crucial capability to apply technologies which are technically and economically viable is composed of the capability to get technologies widely adopted, properly used, maintained and repaired.

These partial capabilities are inter-dependent. For example, it is not very helpful to invest in a capacity to generate technologies if there is no capacity eventually to apply whatever technologies are developed. Bottlenecks may in fact occur throughout the system. This inter-dependence is illustrated in Figure 9.1.

Disaggregation of indigenous technological capability may clarify the concept but it does not necessarily facilitate its measurement. To this end, the factors which determine the level and nature of each and all of the elements of indigenous technological capability must be identified. In general, every partial capability is a matter of abilities and opportunities as shaped by various resources, policies, institutions, and environments. More specifically, indigenous technological capability, whether considered *in toto* or in terms of its elements, depends on the following factors (these differ slightly from those of Girvan discussed in the previous section):

(i) *Human and financial resources* where and when required; the quality of *human* resources in terms of formal knowledge and practical experience, as well as skill and attitude; the level of domestic and external *financial* resources and the conditions imposed by lenders, donors;

(ii) *useful information* e.g. on technological alternatives; on technology sources; on technology related health hazards; on research in progress.

(iii) *Technology policies, objectives and targets, directives and incentives*; their consistency, internally as well as with development objectives; distortions caused by other policies (e.g. fiscal and monetary)

(iv) *Number, quality and location of institutions for education and training*; for research and development, for engineering, design, consultancy and extension; for the collection and dissemination of useful information; for the promotion of invention and innovation outside the formal R&D framework; for screening technology imports; other infrastructure and facilities.

(v) *Natural environment*: natural resources, climate; socio-cultural environment: religion, customs, attitudes; political system.

(vi) *Other factors*: political situation; relations with other countries; impact of multinational enterprises; externalities.

A framework of analysis

As noted in the previous section, these determinants – and possibly others – are again inter-related; some of them, it might be argued, are inseparable. It should also be noted that some are more crucial than others, both in themselves and in the context of circumstances peculiar to each country. Disaggregation to this extent is nonetheless suggested because it facilitates a comprehensive analysis of technological capability.

It is now possible to develop a framework for such an analysis by constructing a matrix of objective-oriented elements of technological capability on the one hand, and the factors which shape them on the other.

For illustrative purposes, the framework may be represented by a cube, the third dimension being added to make a mixture of priority objectives explicit (see Figure 9.2).

This particular cube has (only) 125 cells; it should be evident from the above that the framework can be easily adjusted to include many more. For example, cell 3, i, I concerns the capability to generate technologies which contribute to food self-sufficiency, in terms of the resources – manpower, finance, information – required for that purpose. As objectives may be combined, the assessment could be extended to cover 3, i, I + II, which specifies the above so as to ensure that the desired increase in output is compatible with job creation.

It is suggested that in the process of making plans, whether sectoral or comprehensive, a multi-disciplinary team of experts should find answers to the following type of questions:

(i) Does a given country have the technological capability to achieve objectives X, Y and Z?
(ii) If the answer is positive, have the objectives been fulfilled in the past? If not, why were they not achieved?
(iii) If the answer is negative, which remedial measures may be taken to remove the constraints in building such capability?
(iv) If such measures cannot be taken, how should the objectives X, Y and Z be reformulated? Or should their introduction be postponed?

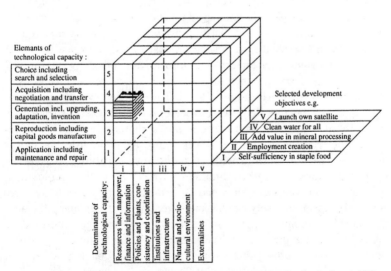

Figure 9.2 A diagrammatic exposition of assessment of technological capability

We are mainly concerned with diagnosis, that is, with the use of indicators in answering the first of these questions. But our framework has the advantage that policy prescriptions would follow rather directly from the diagnosis.

As not all cells of the cube are equally important, the idea is to identify and estimate at least the crucial ones, where possible on the basis of facts and figures, and in their absence, based on expert opinion. Taken together, such judgements may themselves be seen as a set of indicators of technological capability. Speaking of facts and figures, it appears that discussions on indicators often amount to complaints about the lack of adequate statistics and problems of quantification; as if figures were sacrosanct. Notwithstanding the usefulness of data, we argue that more stress should be placed on the significance of expert opinion or qualitative judgements.

An illustrative example

We will consider the priority objective of a country X, namely, to become self-sufficient in its staple food (maize) in five years, time and in such a way that rural underemployment is eased rather than aggravated. The policymaker would like to know whether it can be done, and what are the technological requirements of this specific objective.

The example reflects a problem which is common to many developing countries. Moreover, it is particularly interesting in the context of strengthening *indigenous* technological capabilities. Agricultural technology encompasses a biogenetic dimension; growth processes are affected by differences in soil qualities, temperatures, water availability, and a number of other environmental factors. Possibilities for importing appropriate varieties from abroad are therefore limited and local research capacity is all the more critical (Evenson, 1981). The biochemical dimension of agricultural technology (fertiliser, pesticide) is relatively less dependent on local R&D; the more important issue is that of imports vs. local production. But the mechanical dimension of agricultural technology is again primarily associated with an indigenous capability to generate (improve, adapt, invent) technologies; in view of the employment objective, improved local tools and equipment would probably be more appropriate than relatively capital-intensive, imported machinery. Finally, the capability to apply appropriate agricultural technologies must not be taken for granted: there are indeed a variety of case histories of farming practices which prove that more appropriate technologies are not automatically adopted (Griffin, 1974; Pearce, 1980; Ahmed, 1981).

In order to assist the policymaker, a multi-disciplinary team of experts is constituted. They start their work with a general assessment of the status quo. How much maize is produced today, and where, by whom and how? What role does technology play? How much should be produced for achieving self-sufficiency five years hence? To what extent are fluctuations in output explained by relative prices, and by such non-economic factors as the weather? Is any maize exported, or used for non-food purposes like starch-making? What are the post-harvest losses if any? What can be said about the level and nature of rural underemployment? And so on and so forth.

It should be possible for a team of experts to draw certain tentative conclusions from such an assessment, or rather to indicate certain critical areas. For example, it may be found that pests, or irregular supplies of fertiliser, or lack of irrigation, explain a large part of maize shortages. Or, it may be concluded that shortages can only be overcome by using high-yielding varieties.

The matrix – the front slice of the cube – may now be used to formulate additional questions, as a scanning device which should pinpoint the weak spots of the technology-development nexus. In our example, one might expect the experts to come up with pertinent questions such as:

(i)   Is sufficient information available to select more appropriate pesticides (1, i)?[4]
(ii)   Are there any policies which favour the importation of capital-intensive machines (2, ii)?
(iii) Do we have the necessary scientists to undertake bio-genetic research (3, i)?
(iv)   How much more should be spent on R&D to achieve the self-sufficiency objective (3, i)?
(v)   Is the existing maize research institute properly equipped (3, iii)?
(vi)   Can improved tools be manufactured locally (4, iii)?
(vii) Do farmers have access to credit to adopt improved technologies (5, i)?
(viii) Is fertiliser delivered on time or not (5, iii)?
(ix)   Is enough water available to grow the additional output (5, iv)?
(x)   Is average farm-size conducive to mechanical harvesting (5, v)?

In trying to answer such questions, the experts will have to rely on indicators, that is, on relevant facts and figures, but also on their expert judgement. The first question, for example, may be partly answered by searching the information bank of the maize research institute; and possibly by comparing the results to what is available in the International

Maize Research Institute. But there is judgement required in deciding what is most suitable for local conditions.

The experts would probably find it useful to answer the second question, on policies which favour the importation of capital-intensive machines, in the broader context of an enquiry into the availability of necessary capital goods for maize production. Information would be collected on various alternatives for meeting machine requirements, including data on imports and local procurement, on relative factor proportions, and relative prices, the latter possibly indicated in 'shadow' rates. Thus a variety of new and very specific indicators would be used to assess a fundamental aspect of indigenous technological capability.

Answers to the third and fourth questions, on the necessary R&D capacity, would no doubt require the use of more traditional S and T indicators, be it in disaggregated form. Pertinent input and output indicators would have to be adjusted for qualitative differences. For example, to measure the input in inventive activity, one may need

> to (i) spot individuals who, over a given period, engage in inventive activity, (ii) ascertain the hours spent on such activity, and (iii) weigh these hours by some scale of inventive ability. Multiplying the hours by the appropriate weights we could then say that so many equivalent man-hours of inventive capacity have been 'put-in' during the year (Kuznets, 1982, p. 32).

This type of approach can be extended to different categories of labour to measure their quality. For example, weights could be determined for such indicators of labour quality as primary and secondary education, on-the-job experience, health, nutrition (e.g. calories per capita), etc. (Galenson and Pyatt, 1964).

Similarly, quantitative indicators like R&D expenditure have been followed up by more efficiency-oriented ones like internal rates of return from research. Taking the specific case of food and agriculture, returns on investment in research may be measured by linking R&D expenditure with agricultural output using a production function model (Ruttan, 1982). While this cost-benefit approach is an advance over the conventional input indicators, it suffers from conceptual as well as empirical difficulties, especially in developing countries, on account of the inadequacy of the quantity and quality of data on inputs, and the yearly fluctuations in agricultural output. Their interpretation is often difficult and simplistic. For example, the state-wise estimates of rates of return on investment in Indian agriculture would suggest that Punjab underinvests in agricultural research relative to West Bengal or Assam, which is not borne out by reality (Mukhopadhyay, 1988).

A final example concerns the question about the timing of fertilizer deliveries. This may seem somewhat far-fetched in relation to technological capability, but it has in fact been noted in several countries that flaws in the distribution of fertilizer constitute a major bottleneck in augmenting agricultural output. It may be because the necessary lorries are not in running order, or petrol is hard to obtain; the organization of the effort may leave much to be desired, or perhaps the fertilizer factory cannot cope with the demand. In any event, it is of little use to blame seeds, scientists or farm machinery, if farmers find time and again that an essential component of their technology is unavailable when they need it.

The example is meant to show that the number of lorries required to deliver X tonnes of fertilizer, required to produce Y tonnes of maize, could well be one of the key indicators for experts to judge a country's ability to meet its priority objective. It is a good indicator for planners as it suggests a specific remedial measure, namely, to provide for additional lorries as and when necessary.

CONCLUDING REMARKS

We have found in this chapter that work on science and technology indicators has so far remained limited, in particular, to the collection and processing of input statistics. We have confirmed what others have also found, namely, that such indicators are of little use in measuring and monitoring progress towards building technological capability and achieving national development goals. It is not always clear what conclusions should be drawn from them.

A number of models have been presented in which science and technology are related to socioeconomic development. We have ourselves suggested that an assessment of indigenous technological capability must be related to *specific* socioeconomic objectives and explained in terms of the factors which shape the various elements of such capability. Indicators should be considered as facts, figures and opinions which help us to arrive at conclusions about the quantities which give substance to such a model.

In fact, we have suggested a framework which experts of diverse disciplines may use to assist in setting priorities and targets towards the achievements of development objectives. In answering specific questions, the experts would identify indicators as and when necessary. Expert analysis should not therefore be treated as a mechanistic procedure in which standard indicators assume significance. On the contrary, imagination and flexibility are called for to arrive at meaningful conclusions. It is hoped that such an approach to science and technology indicators will be tested in practice and assessed for further refinement.

Finally, we conclude that the developing countries face a major technological challenge at the turn of the century. They can face up to this challenge only if they develop and strengthen their macro and micro technological capabilities over time. The creation of these capabilities *per se* cannot help meet the formidable challenge. These capabilities will also need to be harnessed to achieve the long-term development goals of economic prosperity. Technology is a means to an end; a servant not a master. The end should be human development and enrichment.

Notes

1. For example, a 'special issue on development indicators' of the *Journal of Development Studies* (April 1972), reproduced as Baster (1972), did not find it possible to include a paper on indicators of technological development.
2. In general, for goals such as the reduction of poverty and the satisfaction of basic needs to show up in a measure of development, yardsticks other than output and growth are required (see, for example, Hicks and Streeten, 1979).
3. At this point a reference should be made to the significance of the word 'indigenous' (native, belonging naturally). Although 'endogenous' (growing from within) may be a better word, the term 'indigenous technological capability' would seem to be used more frequently to underline the efforts made by developing countries to reduce their technological dependence. It is widely acknowledged, however, that such efforts are not meant to rule out technology transfers among countries. As in the case of 'endogenous' and 'indigenous', it appears from the literature that the words 'capacity' and 'capability' are used interchangeably.
4. The figures in brackets refer to the cells of the matrix presented in Figure 9.2.

Bibliography

ACERO, L. (1983) *Impact of Technical Change on Skill Requirements in Traditional Industries: The Case of Textiles* (Brighton: Science Policy Research Unit (SPRU), University of Sussex) (mimeo.).

ADELMAN, I. and T. MORRIS (1972) 'The Measurement of Institutional Characteristics of Nations: Methodological Considerations', in N. Baster (ed.), *Measuring Development: The Role and Adequacy of Development Indicators* (London: Frank Cass).

AHMED, I. (1981) *Technological Change and Agrarian Structure: A Study of Bangladesh* (Geneva: ILO).

AHMED, I. (ed.) (1992) *Biotechnology – A Hope or a Threat?* (London: Macmillan Press).

AHMED, I. and V. RUTTAN (1988) *Generation and Diffusion of Agricultural Innovations: The Role of Institutional Factors* (Aldershot: Gower).

ALCORTA, L. (1992) 'The Impact of New Technologies on Scale in Manufacturing Industry: Issues and Evidence', *United Nations University (UNU) Institute for New Technologies (INTECH), Working Paper 5* (Maastricht).

ALFTHAN, T. (1985) 'Developing Skills for Technological Change: Some Policy Issues', *International Labour Review*, September–October.

ALMEIDA, CELSO (1993) 'Development and Transfer of Environmentally Sound Technologies in Manufacturing – A Survey', *UNCTAD Discussion Paper No. 58* (Geneva).

ANANDAKRISHNAN, M. et al. (1988) 'Microcomputers in Schools in Developing Countries', in A.S. Bhalla and D.D. James (eds), *New Technologies and Development* (Boulder, Colorado: Lynne Rienner Publishers).

ANDERSON, KYM, and YONG-IL PARK (1987) *China and the International Relocation of World Textile and Clothing Activity* (mimeo), October.

ANNERSTEDT, JAN (1994) 'Measuring Science, Technology and Innovation', in J.J. Salomon, et al. (eds), *The Uncertain Quest – Science, Technology and Development* (Tokyo: UNU Press).

Appropriate Technology (1983) London, Vol. 10, No. 3.

ATKINSON, A.B. and J.B. STIGLITZ (1969) A New View of Technological Change, *Economic Journal*, September.

BAARK, ERIK (1988) 'High Technology Innovation at the Chinese Academy of Sciences', *Science and Public Policy*, April.

BAARK, E. (1990) 'China's Software Industry', *Information Technology for Development*, Vol. 5, No. 2, June.

BAARK, E. (1991) 'Fragmented Innovation: China's Science and Technology Policy Reforms in Retrospect', in *China's Dilemmas in the 1990s: The Problems of Reforms, Modernization and Interdependence* (Washington, DC: US Congress, Joint Economic Committee), Vol. 2.

BAARK, E. (1993) 'China's Policy Response to the Challenge of New Technology', in Claus Brundenius and Bo Göransson (eds), *New Technologies and Global Restructuring – The Third World at a Crossroads* (London: Taylor Graham).

Bibliography

BAARK, ERIK, and YANG ANXIAN (1985) 'Sweden and China: A Comparative Study of the Conditions for Industrial Automation,' *ATAS Bulletin*, No. 2.

BABA, Y. et al. (1993) *The Evolution of the Software Industry in Japan* (Tokyo: RACE, University of Tokyo).

BAGCHI, AMIYA (1987) 'The Differential Impact of New Technologies on Developing Countries: A Framework of Analysis', *Working Paper Series WEP 2-22/WP. 176* (Geneva:ILO) June.

BAGCHI, A. (1987a) 'Review of Bessant and Cole (1985)', *International Labour Review,* January–February.

BAGCHI, AMIYA KUMAR (1995) *New Technology and the Workers' Response – Microelectronics, Labor and Society* (New Delhi: SAGE Publications).

BAGCHI, A.K and BANERJEE, D. (1986) 'The Impact of Microelectronics-based Technologies: The Case of India', *Working Paper Series, WEP 2-22/WP. 169* (Geneva: ILO) September.

BALESTRI, A. (1982) *Industrial Organisation in the Manufacture of Fashion Goods: The Textile District of Prato* (1950–1980) (M.Phil. Thesis: University of Lancaster, UK).

BAOZHEN, H. et al. (1986) 'The Development of Electronics and Employment in China', paper prepared for the *UNU New Technologies Centre Feasibility Study* (Maastricht).

BASTER, N. (ed.) (1972) *Measuring Development: The Role and Adequacy of Development Indicators* (London: Frank Cass).

BATH, C.R. and D. JAMES (1976) 'Dependency Analysis of Latin America: Some Criticisms, Some Suggestions', *Latin American Research Review*, Vol. XI, No. 3.

BAUM, RICHARD (1989) 'DOS ex machina: The Microelectronic Ghost in China's Modernisation Machine' in D.F. Simon and M. Goldman (eds). *Science and Technology in Post-Mao China* (Cambridge, Mass. Harvard University Press).

BECATTINI, G. (1990) 'Italy', in W. Sengenberger, G.W. Loveman and M.J. Piore (eds). *The Re-emergence of Small Enterprises* (Geneva: International Institute of Labour Studies).

BECKERMAN, W. (1992) 'Economic Growth and the Environment: Whose Growth? Whose Environment?', *World Development*, April.

BELL, D. (1968) 'The Measurement of Knowledge and Technology', in E. Sheldon, and W.B. Moore, *Indicators of Social Change: Concepts and Measurement* (New York: Russell Sage Foundation).

BELUSSI, F. (1987) 'Benetton: Information Technology in Production and Distribution: A Case Study of the Innovative Potential of Traditional Sectors', *Occasional Paper Series, No. 25* (Science Policy Research Unit: University of Sussex).

BENACHENOU, A. (1983) 'South–South Cooperation: The Lagos Plan of Action and Africa's Independence', *Africa Development*, Vol. 8, No. 4.

BERTRAND, W.E., A. RUBEN and A. BERTRAN (1988) 'Microcomputer Applications in the Health and Social Service Sectors of Developing Countries', in A.S. Bhalla, A.S. and D. James, , *New Technologies and Development* (Boulder: Lynne Reiner Publishers).

BESSANT, J. et al. (1981) 'Microelectronics in Manufacturing Industry', in T. Forester (ed.). *The Microelectronic Revolution – The Complete Guide to New Technology and its Impact on Society* (Cambridge: Mass. MIT Press).

BESSANT, J. and S. COLE (1985) *Stacking the Chips – Information Technology and the Distribution of Income* (London: Frances Pinter).

BHALLA, A.S. (1964) 'Investment Allocation and Technological Choice', *Economic Journal*, September.

BHALLA, A.S. (1965) 'Choosing Techniques: Handpounding vs. Rice Milling Techniques', *Oxford Economic Papers*, March.

BHALLA, A.S. (1973) 'Implications of Technological Choice in Africa', *Afrika Spectrum* (Hamburg) No. 1.

BHALLA, A.S. (1974) 'Small Industry, Technology Transfer and Labour Absorption' in OECD, *Transfer of Technology for Small Industry* (Paris: Development Centre).

BHALLA, A.S. (1974a) 'Technology Choice in Construction in Two Asian Countries', *World Development*, March.

BHALLA, A.S. (ed.) (1975, 1981, 1985) *Technology and Employment in Industry* (Geneva: ILO).

BHALLA, A.S. (1976) 'Technology and Employment: Some Conclusions', *International Labour Review*, March–April.

BHALLA, A.S. (1976a) 'Transfert de Technologies, Technologies Appropriée et l'Agriculture', *Revue Tiers-Monde*, January–March.

BHALLA, A.S. (1976b) 'Low-cost Technology, Cost of Labour Management and Industrialization', in OECD, *Appropriate Technology: Problems and Policies* (Paris: Development Centre).

BHALLA, A.S. (ed.) (1979) *Towards Global Action for Appropriate Technology* (Oxford: Pergamon Press).

BHALLA, A.S. (1984) 'Technological Transformation in China', *Economia Internazionale*, February–May.

BHALLA, A.S. (1984a) 'India's Rural Educational Television Broadcasting', in A.S. Bhalla and D.D. James (eds), *New Technologies and Development* (Boulder: Lynne Rienner).

BHALLA, A.S. (1984b) 'Third World's Technological Dilemma', *Labour and Society*, October–December.

BHALLA, A.S. (1984c) 'Internal Technology Transfers in China', in R. Lalkaka and M. Wu (eds), *Managing Science Policy and Technology Acquisition: Strategies for China and a Changing World* (Dublin: Tycooly Publishers).

BHALLA, A.S. (1986) 'Microelectronics and Small-scale Production', *Economic and Political Weekly*, 29 November.

BHALLA, A.S. (1986a) 'Technological Dependence in Africa', in ILO/JASPA, *The Challenge of Employment and Basic Needs in Africa* (Nairobi: Oxford University Press).

BHALLA, A.S. (1986b) 'New Technologies and Employment', *Agora* (Rome) No. 1.

BHALLA, A.S. (1987) 'Can High Technology Help Third World Take Off?', *Economic and Political Weekly*, 4 July.

BHALLA, A.S. (1987a) 'Assessment of the Social Impact of New Technologies', *ATAS Bulletin*, New York, United Nations, No. 5.

BHALLA, A.S. (1989) 'Innovations and Small Producers in Developing Countries', *Economic and Political Weekly*, 26 February.

BHALLA, A.S. (1990) 'Computerisation in Chinese Industry', *Science and Public Policy*, August.

BHALLA, A.S. (1991) 'New Technologies, Rural Development and Employment' in M. Singh, et al. (eds), *Proceedings of the Third Asian Conference on Technology for Rural Development* (Asia Tech' 1991) Kuala Lumpur.

BHALLA, A.S. (ed.) (1991a) *Small and Medium Enterprises: Technology Policies and Options* (Westport: Greenwood Press, and London: Intermediate Technology Publications, 1992).

BHALLA, A.S. (ed.) (1992) *Environment, Employment and Development* (Geneva: ILO).

BHALLA, A.S. (1992a) *Uneven Development in the Third World* (London: Macmillan Press).

BHALLA, A.S. (1992b) 'Classes, Technology and Access', in A.S. Bhalla, *Uneven Development in the Third World* (London: Macmillan Press).

BHALLA, A.S. (1993) 'On Technology Blending and Rural Employment', in M.S. Swaminathan and V. Hoon (eds), *Ecotechnology and Rural Employment, Proceedings No. 7*, Madras, April.

BHALLA, A.S (1994) 'Technology Choice and Development', in J.J. Salomon, F. Sagasti and C. Sachs-Jeantet (eds), *The Uncertain Quest – Science, Technology and Development* (Tokyo: United Nations University).

BHALLA, A.S. (1995) 'Cleaner Technologies with Special Reference to Small Enterprises', *Science, Technology and Development*, April.

BHALLA, A.S. and F. Stewart (1976) 'International Action for Appropriate Technology', in ILO, *World Employment Conference Background Papers, Vol. II* (Geneva).

BHALLA, A.S. and P. Kilby (1976a) 'Technological Innovation and Adaptation' (in Flemish), *Tijdschrift-voor Ontwikkelings-Samenweiking-Tewerkstelling*, No. 1, April.

BHALLA, A.S. and J. James (1983) 'An Approach Towards Integration of Traditional and Emerging Technologies' in E. von Weiszäcker, M.S. Swaminathan and A. Lemma (eds), *New Frontiers in Technology Applications* (Dublin: Tycooly Publishers).

BHALLA, A.S. and J. JAMES (1984) 'New Technology Revolution: Myth or Reality for Developing Countries?', *Greek Economic Review*, December; also reprinted in Hall, P. (ed.) (1986) *Technology, Innovation and Economic Policy* (Oxford: Philip Allan).

BHALLA, A.S. and D.D. JAMES, Y. Stevens (eds) (1984a) *Blending of New and Traditional Technologies* (Dublin: Tycooly publishers).

BHALLA, A.S. and D. JAMES (1984b) 'Towards New Technological Frontiers', *Productivity* (New Delhi) October–December.

BHALLA A.S. and A.G. FLUITMAN (1985) 'Science and Technology Indicators and Socioeconomic Development', *World Development*, February.

BHALLA, A.S. and D. JAMES (1986) 'Technological Blending: Frontier Technology in Traditional Sectors', *Journal of Economic Issues*, June.

BHALLA, A.S. and D.D. JAMES (eds), (1988) *New Technologies and Development* (Boulder: Lynne Rienner Publishers).

BHALLA, A.S. and D.D. JAMES (1991) 'Integrating New Technologies with Traditional Economic Activities in Developing Countries: An Evaluative Look at "Technology Blending" ', *Journal of Developing Areas*, July.

BHALLA, A.S. and P.P. BIFANI (1992) 'Some Global Issues', in A.S. Bhalla *Environment, Employment and Development* (Geneva: ILO).

BHALLA, A.S. and J. JAMES (1993) 'Flexible Specialization, New Technologies and the Future of Industrialization', *Futures*, July–August.

BHALLA, A.S. and A.K.N. REDDY (1994) *The Technological Transformation of Rural India* (London: Intermediate Technology (IT)).

BHATIA, R. (1988) 'Photovoltaic Street Lighting in India', in A.S. Bhalla and D. James, *New Technologies and Development* (Boulder: Lynne Rienner Publishers).

BHATIA, R. (1988a) 'Photovoltaic Lighting in Fiji', ibid.

BHATIA, R. (1988b) 'Energy Alternatives for Irrigation Pumping: An Economic Analysis for North India', in R. Bhatia and A. Pereira, *Socioeconomic Aspects of Renewable Energy Technologies* (New York: Praeger Publishers).

BIFANI, P. (1988) 'New Biotechnologies for Food Production in Developing Countries with Special Reference to Cuba and Mexico', in A.S. Bhalla and D. James, *New Technologies and Development* (Boulder: Lynne Rienner Publishers).

BIFANI, P. (1988a) 'Biotechnology: Overview and Developments in Latin America', in Inter-American Development Bank, *Economic and Social Progress in Latin America* (1988 Report), Washington D.C.

BIFANI, P. (1992) 'New Biotechnologies for Rural Development', in I. Ahmed, (ed.), *Biotechnology: A Hope or a Threat?* (London: Macmillan Press).

BINSWANGER, H. (1982) 'Agricultural Mechanization: A Comparative Historical Perspective', *Research Unit, Agriculture and Rural Development Department*, World Bank, Washington D.C.

BINSWANGER, H., P. Pingali and Y. Bigo (1987) *Agricultural Mechanization and the Evolution of Farming Systems Research in Sub-Saharan Africa* (Baltimore: Johns Hopkins University Press).

BOON, G.K. (1986) *'Computer-Based Techniques; Diffusion, Impact, Trade and Policy in Global Perspective'*, Noordwijk, Netherlands, Technology Scientific Foundation, June.

BOYER, R. and B. CORIAT (1986) *Technical Flexibility and Macro Stabilisation: Preliminary Insights*, Paper prepared for Conference on Innovation Diffusion (Venice) 17–21 March.

BRABANT, de F. (1989) 'The Prato Telematics Project' in U. Colombo and Keichi Oshima (eds), *Technology Blending: An Appropriate Response to Development* (London: Tycooly).

BROWN, L.D. (1986) *Private Voluntary Organizations and Development Partnerships*, Paper prepared for the Conference on Organizational and Behavioural Perspectives for Social Development, Indian Institute of Management, Ahmedabad, December.

BRUSCO, S. (1990) 'The Idea of the Industrial District: Its Genesis', in F. Pyke, G. Becattini and W. Sengenberger (eds), *Industrial Districts and Inter-Firm Co-operation in Italy* (Geneva: ILO, International Institute for Labour Studies).

BRUTON, H. (1985) 'On the Production of a National Technology', in J. James, S. Watanabe (eds), *Technology, Institutions and Government Policies* (London: Macmillan).

BRYSON, C. (1991) 'More Than Just a Paper Chase', *Occupational Health and Safety Canada*, May–June 1991.

CAMPBELL, D. (1993) 'The Globalizing Firm and Labour Institutions', in P. Baily, A. Parisotto and G. Renshaw (eds), *Multinationals and Employment* (Geneva: ILO).

CARNOY, MARTIN et al. (1993) 'Labour Institutions and Technological Change: A Framework of Analysis and a Review of the Literature' *International Institute of Labour Studies Discussion Paper*, No. DP/61/1993 (Geneva).

CARR, M. (1987) *Industry and Appropriate Technology: Mass Production or Production by the Masses*, Paper presented to the International Institute of Environment and Development's Conference on Sustainable Development (London) April.

CASSIOLATO, J. (1992) 'The User-Producer Connection in High Tech: A Case Study of Banking Automation in Brazil', in H. Schmitz and J. Cassiolato (eds), *High Tech for Industrial Development* (London: Routledge).

CASTELLS, M. (1988) *Information Technology, Economic Restructuring and Urban-Regional Development* (Oxford: Basil Blackwell).

CASTELLS, MANUAL (1989) 'High Technology and the New International Division of Labour, *Labour and Society*, Vol. 14.

CASTELLS, M. (1993) 'The Informational Economy and the New International Division of Labour' in Centre for Science and Environment, 1985, *The State of India's Environment*, 1984–85 (New Delhi).

CHARPOLRAK, C. (1989) 'Micro Hydro Electric Generation for the Remote Rural Village,' in U. Colombo and K. Oshima (eds), *Technology Blending: An Appropriate Response to Development* (London: Tycooly).

CHINA, STATE SCIENCE AND TECHNOLOGY COMMISSION (1992) *The Main Programmes of Science and Technology* (Beijing).

CHINA, STATE STATISTICAL BUREAU (several years), *Statistical Yearbook of China* (Beijing).

CHIVETA, C. and M.W. MHANGO (1992) 'Biotechnology and Labour Absorption in Malawi Agriculture', in I. Ahmed (ed.), *Biotechnology: A Hope or a Threat?* (London: Macmillan Press)

CHO, MYUNG-RAE (1992) 'Weaving Flexibility: Large-Small Firm Relations, Flexibility and Regional Clusters in South Korea', paper prepared for EADI Industrialization Strategies Working Group Workshop on New Approaches to Industrialization: Flexible Production and Innovation Networks in the South, Lund, Research Policy Institute, 26–27 June.

COLE, S. (1986) 'The Global Impact of Information Technology', *World Development*, October–November.

COLOMBO, U. (1989) 'Technology Blending as an Instrument in the Rejuvenation of Traditional Sectors: The Italian Experience and its Relevance to the Third World in U. Colombo and Keichi Oshima (eds) (1989) *Technology Blending: An Appropriate Response to Development* (London: Tycooly).

COLOMBO, U. (1991) *Diffusing High Technology in Traditional Sectors: The Experience of ENEA*, Lecture delivered at the International Centre for Science and High Technology Course on Research and Innovation Management (Venice) September 20.

COLOMBO, U., D. MAZZONIS and G. LANZAVECCHIA (1983) 'Cooperative Organisation and Constant Modernisation of the Textile Industry at Prato, Italy', in E.U. Weizsäcker, M.S. Swaminathan, and A. Lemma (eds), *New Frontiers in Technology Application – Integration of Emerging and Traditional Technologies* (Dublin: Tycooly).

COLOMBO, U. and D. MAZZONIS (1984) 'Integration of Old and New Technologies in the Italian (Prato) Textile Industry', in Bhalla, et al. (1984). *Blending of New and Traditional Technologies* (Dublin: Tycooly)

COLOMBO, U. and K. OSHIMA (eds) (1989) *Technology Blending – An Appropriate Response to Development* (London: Tycooly-Cassell).

CONROY, R. (1984) 'Technological Change and Industrial Development', in G. Young (ed.), *China's Modernisation: The Latest Phase* (London: Croom Helm).

CONROY, R. (1992) *Technological Change in China* (Paris: Development Centre, OECD).

COOPER, C. (1991) 'Are Innovation Studies on Industrialized Economies Relevant to Technology Policy in Developing Countries?' *UNU/INTECH Working Paper No. 3,* June.

COOPER, C. and F. Sercovich (1970) *The Channels and Mechanisms for the Transfer of Technology from Developed and Developing Economies* (UNCTAD, TD/D/AC.11/5).

COOPER, C.M. and J.M. CLARK (1982) *Employment, Economics and Technology: The Impact of Technical Change on the Labour Market* (Brighton: Wheatsheaf).

CROTT, R. (1986) 'The Impact of Isoglucose in the International Sugar market', in S. Jacobsson, et al. (eds), *The Biotechnological Challenge* (London: Cambridge University Press).

DAHLMAN C. and L. WESTPHAL (1981) 'The Meaning of Technological Mastery in Relation to Transfer of Technology', *The Annals of the American Academy of Political and Social Science*, Vol. 458, November.

DAHLMAN, C. and L. WESTPHAL (1982) 'Technological Effort in Industrial Development – An Interpretative Survey of Recent Research', in F. Stewart and J. James (eds), *The Economics of New Technology in Developing Countries* (London: Frances Pinter).

DAHLMAN, C., B. ROSS-LARSON and L. WESTPHAL (1987) 'Managing Technological Development, Lessons from the Newly Industrialising Countries', *World Development*, Vol. 15, No. 6.

DEDRICK, J. and K.L. KRAEMER (1993) 'Information Technology in India: The Quest for Self-Reliance', *Asian Survey*, May.

DEFOURNY, J. and E. THORBECKE (1984) 'Structural Path Analysis and Multiplier Decomposition within a Social Accounting Framework', *Economic Journal*, March.

DENISON, E.F. (1962) *The Sources of Economic Growth in the United States and the Alternative Before Us*, Supplementary Paper No. 13, New York, Committee for Economic Development (Washington, DC: The Brookings Institution).

DOBB, M.H. (1956) 'Second Thoughts on Capital Intensity of Investment', *Review of Economic Studies*, Vol. XXIV, No. 1.

DODGSON, M. (1985) *Advanced Manufacturing Technology in the Small Firm* (London: Technical Change Centre).

DOELEMAN, J.A. (1992) 'Employment Concerns and Environmental Policy', in Bhalla, A.S. (ed.), *Environment, Employment and Development* (Geneva: ILO).

DOMINQUEZ-VILLALOBOS, L. (1987) 'Microelectronics-based Innovations and Employment in Mexican Industries', *World Employment Programme Research Working Paper Series WEP 2-22/WP.183* (Geneva: International Labour Office).

DOMINQUEZ-VILLALOBOS, L. and F.B. GROSSMAN (1992) 'Employment and Income Effects of Structural and Technological Changes in Footwear Manufacturing in Mexico', *World Employment Programme Research Working Paper Series No. WEP 2-22/WP.224* (Geneva: ILO).

DOSI, G., C. FREEMAN, R. NELSON, G. SILVERBERG and L. SOETE (eds) (1988) *Technical Change and Economic Theory* (London: Pinter Publishers).

DRUCKER, P.F. (1986) 'The Changed World Economy', *Foreign Affairs*, Spring.

EASTMOND, A. and M.L. ROBERT (1992) 'Advanced Plant Biotechnology in Mexico: A Hope for the Neglected?' in I. Ahmed (ed.), *Biotechnology, A Hope or a Threat?* (London: Macmillan Press)

ECKAUS, R.S. (1955) 'The Factor Proportion Problem in Underdeveloped Areas', *American Economic Review*, Vol. 45.

ECOTEC (1990) *The Impact of Environmental Management on Skills and Jobs in Birmingham*, Research and Consultancy Ltd.

EDQUIST, C. and S. JACOBSSON (1988) *Flexible Automation: The Global Diffusion of New Technology in the Engineering Industry* (Oxford: Basil Blackwell).

ELKINGTON, J. (1984) 'Cloning of Palm Oil Trees in Malaysia' in A.S. Bhalla et al., *Blending of New and Traditional Technologies* (Dublin: Tycooly).

ENOS, J. (1962) 'Invention and Innovation in the Petroleum Refining Industry', in National Bureau of Economic Research (NBER), *The Rate and Direction of Inventive Activity – Economic and Social Factors* (New Jersey: Princeton University Press).

ENOS, J. (1985) 'A Game Theoretic Approach to Choice of Technology in Developing Countries', in J. James and S. Watanabe (eds), *Technology, Institutions and Government Policies* (London: Macmillan Press).

ENOS, J. (1989) 'Transfer of Technology', *Asian-Pacific Economic Literature*, Vol. 3, No. 1, March.

ENOS, J.L. (1991) *The Creation of Technology Capability in Developing Countries* (London: Pinter Publishers).

ERNST, D. (1994) 'Network Transactions, Market Structure and Technology Diffusion – Implications for South–South Cooperation', in L. Mytelka (ed.), *South–South Cooperation in a Global Perspective* (Paris: OECD Development Centre).

ERNST, D. and D. O'CONNOR (1989) *Technology and Global Competition – The Challenge for Newly Industrializing Economies* (Paris: OECD).

EVANS, PETER B. (1992) 'Indian Informatics in the 1980s: The Changing Character of State Involvement', *World Development*, Vol. 20, No. 1.

EVENSON, R.E. (1981) 'Benefits and Obstacles to Appropriate Agricultural Technology', *The Annals of the American Academy of Political and Social Science*, November.

FEDER, G., R. JUST and D. ZILBERMAN (1985) 'Adoption of Agricultural Innovations in Developing Countries: A Survey', *Economic Development and Cultural Change*, January.

FEI, J., G. RANIS and F. STEWART (1985) *Towards Viable Balanced Growth: A Locational Perspective* (Vienna: UNIDO).

FLEURY, A. (1988) 'The Impacts of Microelectronics on Employment and Income in the Brazilian Metal-Engineering Industry', *World Employment Programme Research Working Paper Series WEP 2-22/WP. 188* (Geneva: ILO) February.

FONG, CHAN ONN (1993) 'Malaysia and Singapore', in S. Watanabe (ed.), *Microelectronics and Third-World Industries* (London, Macmillan Press).

FRANSMAN, M. (1986) *A New Approach to the Study of Technological Capability in Less Developed Countries, WEP Research Working Paper Series No. WEP 2-22/WP.166* (Geneva: ILO).

FRANSMAN, M. (1991) 'Biotechnology: Generation, Diffusion and Policy', *UNU/INTECH Working Paper No. 1* (Maastricht) June.

FRANSMAN, M. and K. KING (1984) *Technological Capability in the Third World* (London: Macmillan Press).

FREEMAN, C. (1970) *The Measurement of Output of Research and Experimental Development* (Paris: UNESCO) STC/16.

FREEMAN, C. (1984) 'Prometheus Unbound', *Futures*, No. 15.

FREEMAN, C. (1987) 'Information Technology and Change in Techno-Economic Paradigm', in C. Freeman and L. Soete (eds), *Technical Change and Full Employment* (Oxford: Basil Blackwell).

FREEMAN C. and L. SOETE (eds) (1987) *Technical Change and Full Employment* (Oxford: Basil Blackwell).

FREEMAN, C. (1993) 'Technical Change and Future Trends in the World Economy', *Futures*, July–August.

FREEMAN, C. (1994) The Economics of Technical Change, *Cambridge Journal of Economics*, October.

FREEMAN, C., C. J. CLARK and L. SOETE (1982) *Unemployment and Technical Innovation – A Study of Long Waves and Economic Development* (London: Frances Pinter).

FREEMAN, C. and L. SOETE (1985) *Information Technology and Employment: An Assessment* (Brussels: IBM).

FREEMAN, C. and L. SOETE (1993) *Information Technology and Employment*, paper prepared for IBM, Europe, December.

GAGLIARDI, R. and T. ALFTHAN (1993) *Environmental Training: Policies and Practice for Sustainable Development* (Geneva: ILO) June (mimeo).

GAIO, F. (1992) 'Software Strategies for Developing Countries: Lessons from the International and Brazilian Experience', in H. Schmitz and J. Cassiolato (eds), *High Tech for Industrial Development* (Routledge: London).

GALAL, E. (1988) 'Applications of Microcomputers in Primary Health Delivery Services in Egypt', in A. Bhalla and D. James (eds), *New Technologies and Development* (Boulder: Lynne Rienner Publishers).

GALENSON, W. and H. LEIBENSTEIN (1955) 'Investment Criteria, Productivity and Economic Development', *Quarterly Journal of Economics*, August.

GALENSON, W. and G. PYATT (1964) *The Quality of Labour and Economic Development in Certain Countries – A Preliminary Study* (Geneva: ILO).

GALHARDI, R. (1993) *Employment and Income Effects of Biotechnology in Latin America: A Speculative Assessment* (Geneva: ILO).

GALTUNG, JOHAN (1980) 'The North/South Debate: Technology, Basic Human Needs and the New International Economic Order', *World Order Models Project, Working Paper No. 12*.

GATT (1984) *Textiles and Clothing in the World Economy*, Appendices I to IV (Geneva) July.

GAUDE, J. (1975) 'A Planning Model Incorporating Technological Choices and Non-Homogeneous Supplies of Labour', *World Employment Programme Research Working Paper Series WEP 2-22/WP.17* (Geneva: ILO) June.

GERMIDIS, D. (1977) *Transfer of Technology by Multinational Corporations*, 2 vols. Paris, OECD Development Centre.

GERWIN, D. and T.K. LEUNG (1980) 'The Organisational Impacts of FMS: Some Initial Findings', *Discussion Paper, Institute of Social Research in Industry*, Trondheim, Norway.

GILLILAND, M.W. (1988) 'A Study of Nitrogen Fixing Biotechnologies for Corn in Mexico', *Environment*, Vol. 30, No. 3, April.

GIRVAN, N. (1979) 'The Approach to Technology Policy Studies', *Social and Economic Studies*, March.

GOVERNMENT OF JAPAN (1989) *Survey on Technology Development by Small and Medium Enterprises*, Tokyo, December.

GOVERNMENT OF KENYA, Ministry of National Development and Planning (1990) *Report on the National Seminar on Technological Issues in Small-scale and Jua Kali Enterprises in Kenya* (Nairobi) 5–9 February.

GRIECO, J.M. (1984) *Between Dependency and Autonomy: India's Experience with the International Computer Industry* (Berkeley: University of California Press).

GRIFFIN, K. (1974) *The Political Economy of Agrarian Change* (London: Macmillan Press).

GRIFFIN, K. and A.R. KHAN (1992) *Globalization and the Developing World* (Geneva: UNRISD).

HACKING, A.J. (1986) *Economic Aspects of Biotechnology* (Cambridge: Cambridge University Press).

HAGGBLADE, STEVEN and PETER HAZELL (1989) 'Agricultural Technology and Farm – Non-farm Growth Linkages', *Agricultural Economics*, 3.

HAMILL, J. (1993) 'Cross-border Mergers, Acquisitions and Strategic Alliances', in ILO *Multinationals and Employment* (Geneva).

HARRIS, R.G. (1993) 'Globalization, Trade and Income' *Canadian Journal of Economics*, Nov.

HAWTHORNE, E.P. (ed.) (1971) *The Transfer of Technology* (Paris: OECD).

HÉDEN, C.G. (1979) 'Microbiological Science for Development: A Global Technological Opportunity', in J. Ramesh and C. Weiss, Jr. (eds), *Mobilising Technology for World Development* (New York: Praeger).

HEWITT, T. (1992) 'Employment and Skills in the Brazilian Electronics Industry', in H. Schmitz and J. Cassiolato (eds), *High Tech for Industrial Development* (London: Routledge).

HICKS, N. and P. STREETEN (1979) 'Indicators of Development: The Search for a Basic Needs Yardstick', *World Development*, Vol. 7.

HIRSCHHORN, J. (1990) *The Technological Potential: Pollution Prevention*, a background paper prepared for a Symposium *Towards 2000: Environment, Technology and the New Century*, Washington D.C., World Resources Institute, 13–15 June.

HO, S.K.M. (1988) *Information Technology Development for Small and Medium Enterprises in Asian NICs and Japan* (Tokyo: Asian Productivity Organization).

HOBBELINK, H. (1987) 'New Hope or False Promise: Biotechnology and the Third World Agriculture', in *International Coalition for Development Action* (Brussels) March.

HOBBELINK, H. (1991) *Biotechnology and the Future of World Agriculture* (London: Zed Books).

HOBDAY, M. (1994) 'Technological Learning in Singapore: A Test Case for Leapfrogging', *Journal of Development Studies*, July.

HOFFMAN, K. (1989) 'Technological Advance and Organizational Innovation in the Engineering Industry', *Industry and Energy Department Working Paper, Industry Series Paper No. 4*, The World Bank, Washington D.C.

HOFFMAN, K., H. RUSH (1982) 'Microelectronics and the Garments Industry: Not Yet a Perfect Fit', Institute of Development Studies (IDS) *Bulletin.*

HOFFMAN, K. and H. RUSH (1988) *Microelectronics and Clothing* (New York: Praeger Publishers).

HOOGVELT, A. (1979) 'Indigenisation and Foreign Capital: Industrialization in Nigeria', *Review of African Political Economy*, January–April.

HOOGVELT, A. (1980) 'Indigenisation and Technological Dependency', *Development and Change*, Vol. 11, No. 2.

HOPPER, R.S.S. and K.N.S. NAIR (1993) 'Biovillages – A New Approach to Sustainable Development' in M.S. Swaminathan and V. Hoon (eds), *Eco-technology and Rural Employment*, Proceedings No. 7 (Madras) April.

HUANG, J. (1986) *Research Report*, Beijing.

INTERNATIONAL DEVELOPMENT RESEARCH CENTRE (IDRC). (1993) *Green Technologies for Development* (Ottawa) p. 31.

ILO (1970) *Towards Full Employment – A Programme for Colombia* (Geneva).

ILO/Jobs and Skills Programme for Africa (JASPA) (1977) *Narrowing the Gaps – Planning for Basic Needs and Productive Employment in Zambia* (Addis Ababa).

ILO (1980) *Report of the Second Tripartite Meeting for the Clothing Industry* (Geneva).

ILO/JASPA (1986) *The Challenge of Employment and Basic Needs in Africa* (Nairobi: Oxford University Press).

ILO (1985) *Socioeconomic Effects of New Technologies*, Report II, ILO Advisory Committee on Technology, First Session (Geneva).

ILO (1988) *Technological Change, Work Organization and Pay: Lessons for Asia*, ILO Labour-Management Relations Series No. 68 (Geneva).

ILO (1989) *Employment and Training Implications of Environmental Policies in Europe*, paper for the Tripartite Meeting of Experts on Employment and Training Implications of Environmental Policies in Europe (29 November to 5 December 1989) (Geneva).

ILO (1991) *The Application of Modern Agricultural Technology*, Report VI for the International Labour Conference, 78th Session (Geneva).

ILO (1992) *Social and Labour Issues in the Pulp and Paper Industry*, Tripartite Meeting (Geneva).

ILO (1992a) *Recent Developments in the Iron and Steel Industry*, Report I, Iron and Steel Committee, Twelfth Session (Geneva).

ILO (1992b) *Employment and Working Conditions and Competitiveness in the Leather and Footwear Industry* (Geneva).

ILO (1993) *Multinationals and Employment – The Global Economy of the 1990s*, edited by Paul Bailey, Aurelio Parisotto and Geoffrey Renshaw (Geneva).

ILO (1994) *Recent Developments in the Metal Trades,* Report I, Metal Trades Committee, 13th Session (Geneva).

INTERNATIONAL TEXTILE MANUFACTURERS' FEDERATION (1985) *International Textile Machinery Shipments Statistics* (Zurich).

JAMES, JEFFREY (1976) 'Products, Processes and Incomes: Cotton Clothing in India', *World Development*, February.

JAMES, JEFFREY (1985) *The Employment and Income Distributional Impact of Microelectronics: A Prospective Analysis for the Third World*, WEP Research Working Paper Series, WEP 2-22/WP. 153 (Geneva: ILO) September.

JAMES, JEFFREY (1985a) 'The Role of Appropriate Technology in a Redistributive Strategy', in J. James and S. Watanabe (eds), *Technology, Institutions and Government Policies* (London: Macmillan Press).

JAMES, J. (1985b) 'Bureaucratic, Engineering and Economic Men: Decision Making for Technology in Tanzania's State-Owned Enterprises', in S. Lall and F. Stewart (eds), *Theory and Reality in Development* (London: Macmillan Press).

JAMES, J. (1989) *Improving Traditional Rural Technologies* (London: Macmillan Press).

JAMES, J. (1991) 'Microelectronics and the Third World – An Integrative Survey of Literature', *UNU/INTECH Working Paper No. 2* (Maastricht) June.

JAMES, J. (1993) 'New Technologies, Employment and Labour Markets in Developing Countries', *Development and Change*, July.

JAMES, JEFFREY and FRANCES STEWART (1981) 'New Products: A Discussion of the Welfare Effects of the Introduction of New Products in Developing Countries', *Oxford Economic Papers*, March.

JAMES, J. and S. WATANABE (eds) (1985) *Technology, Institutions and Government Policies* (London: Macmillan).

JAPAN EXTERNAL TRADE ORGANIZATION (JETRO) (1992) *Smaller Enterprises in the Era of Change and Diversity* – a summary of 1972 White Paper on Small and Medium Enterprises in Japan, June.

JAPAN INFORMATION SERVICE INDUSTRY ASSOCIATION (1988) *Joho Service Sangyo Hakusho* (White Paper of Information Service Industry) (Tokyo).

JAPAN, SMALL AND MEDIUM ENTERPRISE AGENCY, Ministry of International Trade and Industry (MITI) (1981) *Survey on Technology Development by Small and Medium Enterprises* (Tokyo) December.

JAPAN, SMALL AND MEDIUM ENTERPRISE AGENCY, Ministry of International Trade and Industry (MITI) 1993, *Small Business in Japan* – White Paper on Small and Medium Enterprises, Tokyo.

JÉQUIER, N. (1979) 'Appropriate Technology: Some Criteria', in A.S.Bhalla (ed.), *Towards Global Action for Appropriate Technology* (Oxford: Pergamon Press).

JÉQUIER, N. and G. Blanc (1983) *The World of Appropriate Technology: A Quantitative Analysis* (Paris: OECD).

JOHNS, B.L. (1976) 'The Transfer of Foreign Technology to Australia and Japan' (Canberra: Australian National University) *Pacific Economic Paper No. 36*, February.

JOHNSTON, B. and W. CLARK (1982) *Redesigning Rural Development: A Strategic Perspective* (Baltimore: Johns Hopkins University Press).

JONISH, J. (1988) 'Laser Technology for Land Levelling in Egypt', in A.S. Bhalla and D. James (eds), *New Technologies and Development* (Boulder: Lynne Rienner Publishers)

KAPLINSKY, RAPHAEL (1982) 'Is There a Skill Constraint in the Diffusion of Microelectronics?', *IDS Bulletin*, Vol. 13, No. 2, March.

KAPLINSKY, RAPHAEL (1983) 'Compute-Aided Design – Electronics and the Technological Gap Between DCs and LDCs', in S. Jacobsson and J. Sigurdson (eds), *Technological Trends and Challenges in Electronics*, Lund, Research Policy Institute, University of Lund.

KAPLINSKY, RAPHAEL (1984) 'The International Context for Industrialization in the Third World', *Journal of Development Studies*, Vol. 21, No. 1.

KAPLINSKY, RAPHAEL (1987) *Microelectronics and Employment Revisited – A Review* (Geneva: ILO).

KAPLINSKY, RAPHAEL (1988) *Industrial Restructuring in LDCs: The Role of Information Technology*, paper prepared for Conference of Technology Policy in the Americas (Stanford University) 1–3 December.

KAPLINSKY, RAPHAEL (1989) Book Review of A. Bhalla and D. James (1988), *Journal of International Development*, April.

KAPLINSKY, RAPHAEL (1990) *The Economies of Small: Appropriate Technology in a Changing World* (London: I.T. Publications).

KAPLINSKY, RAPHAEL (1991) *From Mass Production to Flexible Specialization: Micro-Level Restructuring in a British Engineering Firm*, IDS, Sussex (mimeo).

KAPLINSKY, RAPHAEL (1991a) 'Direct Foreign Investment in Third World Manufacturing: Is the Future an Extension of the Past?', *IDS Bulletin*, Vol. 22, No. 2.

KARSHENAS, M. (1992) 'Environment, Development and Employment: Some Conceptual Issues', in A.S. Bhalla (ed.), *Environment, Employment and Development* (Geneva: ILO).

KATHURIA, S. (1992) 'Transfer of Small-Scale Industrial Technology from India to Africa and other Less Developed Regions', in R. Islam (ed.), *Transfer, Adoption and Diffusion of Technology for Small and Cottage Industries* (New Delhi: ILO, ARTEP).

KATZ, J. (1987) *Technology Generation in Latin American Manufacturing Industries* (London: Macmillan Press).

KATZ, J. (1987a) 'Domestic Technology Generation in LDCs: A Review of Research Findings', in Katz, J., ibid.

KEHOE, LOUISE (1992) 'China Sets Sights on Electronics', London, *Financial Times*, 24 November.

KENT, L. (1991) *Relationship between Small Enterprises and Environmental Degradation in the Developing World*, Bethesda, Maryland, Development Alternatives, Inc., September.

KENYA, MINISTRY OF NATIONAL DEVELOPMENT AND PLANNING (1990) *Report on the National Seminar on Technological Issues in Small-Scale and Juakali Enterprises in Kenya*, February.

KHAN, A.R. and M. MUQTADA (1994) 'Introduction' to A.R. Khan and M. Muqtada (eds), *Employment Expansion and Macroeconomic Stability* (Geneva: ILO) forthcoming.

KHAN, HAIDER ALI (1985) 'Technology Choice in the Energy and Textile Sectors in the Republic of Korea', in A.S. Bhalla (ed.), *Technology and Employment in Industry* (Geneva: ILO)

KHAN, HAIDER ALI, and ERIK THORBECKE (1988) *Macroeconomic Effects and Diffusion of Alternative Technologies with a Social Accounting Matrix Framework* (Aldershot: Gower, on behalf of the ILO).

KHAN, M.U. (1987) 'Impacts of Microelectronics in India', *Science and Public Policy*, August.

KHANNA, ANUPAM (1986) 'Issues in the Technological Development of China's Electronic Sector', *World Bank Staff Working Papers No. 762* (Washington DC).

KIM K.S. and J.K. PARK (1985) *Economic Growth in Korea, 1943–1982* (Seoul: Korean Development Institute).

KIM, L. (1986) *New Technologies and their Economic Effects: A Study of Korea* – Paper prepared for United Nations University New Technology Centre Feasibility Study (Maastricht: Netherlands) November.

KIM, S.Y. (1979) 'The Effect on Selected Developing Countries', in Koo, Anthony, *Environmental Repercussions on Trade and Investment* (East Lansing: Michigan State University, on behalf of the ILO).

KING, K. (1974) 'Kenya's Informal Machine Makers – A Study of Small-scale Industry in Kenya's Emergent Artisan Society', *World Development*, April–May.

KING, KENNETH and MARTIN FRANSMAN (eds) (1984) *Technological Capability in the Thirld World* (London: Macmillan Press).

KOJIMA, K. (1977) 'Transfer of Technology to Developing Countries – Japanese Type versus American Type', *Hitotsubashi Journal of Economics*, February.

KOO, ANTHONY (1979) *Environmental Repercussions on Trade and Investment* (East Lansing: Michigan State University on behalf of the ILO).

KOSHIRO, K. (1990) 'Japan', in W. Sengenberger, et al. (eds), *The Re-emergence of Small Enterprises – Industrial Restructuring in Industrialised Countries* (Geneva: International Institute of Labour Studies).

KUANG, S. (1991) *Environmental Aspects of China's Pulp and Paper Industry*, Thirty-Second Session of the FAO Advisory Committee on Pulp and Paper (Rome) 20–22 May.

KUZNETS, S. (1982) 'Inventive Activity: Problems of Definition and Measurement' in National Bureau of Economic Research (NBER), *The Rate of Direction of Inventive Activity: Economic and Social Factors* (Princeton: Princeton University Press).

LALL, S. (1987) *Learning to Industrialise: The Acquisition of Technological Capability in India* (London: Macmillan Press).

LALL, S. (1990) *Building Industrial Competitiveness in Developing Countries* (Paris: OECD).

LALL, S. (1990a) 'Human Resources Development and Industrialization with Special Reference to Sub-Saharan Africa', in K. Griffin and J. Knight (eds), *Human Development and the International Development Strategy for the 1990s* (London: Macmillan Press).

LALL, S. (1993) 'Understanding Technology Development', *Development and Change*, October.

LEE, LOKE-CHONG (1986) 'Singapore', in Asian Productivity Organisation (APO), *Technology Assimilation and Adaptation – Survey and Symposium Report* (Tokyo).

LEIBENSTEIN, H. (1966) 'Allocative Efficiency vs. X-efficiency', *American Economic Review*, June.

LEITE, E. M. (1985) *Novas Tecnologias, Emprego e Qualificacaona Industria Mecanica: Resumo* (São Paulo: Servicio Nacional de Aprendizagem Industrial, Departamento Regional de Sao Paulo) June.

LELE, U. (1981) 'Cooperatives and the Poor: A Comparative Perspective', *World Development*, April–May.

LEONTIEF, W.W. and F. DUCHIN (1986) *The Impact of Automation on Workers* (Oxford: Oxford University Press).

LEWIS, K. (1991) *Employment and Training Implications of the Waste Management Industry* (Geneva) (mimeographed).

LIN, Y.C. (1987) 'Computer Development in Mainland China', *Issues and Studies*, October.

LIPSEY, R.G. (1992) 'Global Change and Economic Policy', in N. Stehr, R. Ericson (eds), *The Culture and Power of Knowledge* (New York: Water de Cruyta).

LIPTON, M. (1981) 'Agricultural Finance and Rural Credit in Poor Countries' in Streeten, P. and R. Jolly (eds), *Recent Issues in World Development* (Oxford: Pergamon Press).

LIPTON, M. with R. LONGHURST (1989) *New Seeds and Poor People* (London: Unwin Hyman).

LIVINGSTONE, I. (1991) 'A Reassessment of Kenya's Rural and Urban Informal Sector', *World Development*, Vol. 19, No. 6, June.

LORENZONI, G. (1989) 'From Vertical Integration to Vertical Disintegration', in Colombo and Keichi Oshima (eds), *Technology Blending: An Appropriate Response to Development* (London: Tycooly).

LUCAS, B.A. and S. FREEDMEN (eds) (1983) *Technology Choice and Change in Developing Countries: Internal and External Constraints* (Dublin: Tycooly).

LUND, R.T. (1982) *Microprocessor Applications and Industrial Development*, UNIDO, ID/WG.372/14, 9 August.

MALDONADO, C. and S. SETHURAMAN (eds) (1992) *Building Technological Capability in the Informal Sector – Metal Manufacturing in Developing Countries* (Geneva: ILO).

MARSDEN, D. (1990) 'United Kingdom', in W. Sengenberger, et al. (eds), *The Re-Emergence of Small Enterprises-Industrial Restructuring in Industrialised Countries* (Geneva: International Institute of Labour Studies).

MASON, R.H. (1970) 'Some Aspects of Technology Transfer: A Case Study comparing United States Subsidiaries and Local Counterparts in the Philippines', *Philippines Economic Journal*, Vol. 9, No. 1.

MASON, R.H. (1971) *The Transfer of Technology and Factor Proportions Problem: The Philippines and Mexico* (New York: UNITAR Report No. 10).

MAZZONIS, D. (1989) 'A Project for Innovation in Prato', in Umberto Colombo and Keichi Oshima (eds), *Technology Blending: An Appropriate Response to Development* (London: Tycooly)

MAZZONIS, D. and M. PIANTA (1991) 'A New Approach to Innovation in Traditional Industries: The Italian Experience', in A.S. Bhalla (ed.), *Small and Medium Enterprises: Technology Policies and Options* (Westport: Greenwood Press).

McCULLOCK, R. (1989) 'China Steel Looks to Offshore Expansion', *Metal Bulletin Monthly*, May.

McGRANAHAN, D. (1972) 'Development Indicators and Development Models', in N. Baster (ed.), *Measuring Development: The Role and Adequacy of Development Indicators* (London: Frank Cass).

McGRANAHAN, D., C. PIZZARO. and C. RICHARD (1979) *Methodological Problems in Selection and Analysis of Socioeconomic Development Indicators* (Geneva: United Nations Research Institute for Social Development) (UNRISD).

MKANDAWIRE, T. (1981) 'Capital Goods and Technological Change: Some Theoretical and Practical Issues from Africa', *WEP Research Working Paper Series, WEP 2-22, WP.82* (Geneva: ILO).

MODY, ASHOKA (1985) 'Policy for Electronics Industry: The Options', *Economic and Political Weekly*, 23 March.

MODY, ASHOKA (1990) *Learning Through Alliances*, Washington, DC., World Bank (mimeo).

MODY, A. and D. WHEELER (1990) *Automation and World Competition* (London: Macmillan Press).

MODY, A. and C. DAHLMAN(1992) 'Performance and Potential of Information Technology: An International Perspective', *World Development*, December.

MODY, A. and C. DAHLMAN (1992a) 'Diffusion of Information Technology: Opportunities and Constraints', *World Development*, December, Vol. 20, No. 12.

MODY, A., R. SURI and J. SANDERS (1992b) 'Keeping Pace with Change: Organizational and Technological Imperatives', *World Development*, December.

MORAWETZ, D. (1974) 'Employment Implications of Industrialisation in Developing Countries – A Survey', *Economic Journal*, Vol. 84.

MOREHOUSE, W. (1982) 'Opening Pandora's Box: Technology and Social Performance in the Indian Tractor Industry', in F. Stewart and J. James (eds), *The Economics of New Technologies in Developing Countries* (London: Frances Pinter)

MOUSSA, A., R. SCHWARE (1992) 'Informatics in Africa: Lessons from World Bank Experience', *World Development*, December.

MUKHOPADHYAY, S.K. (1988) 'Factors Affecting Agricultural Research and Technology: A Case Study of India', in I. Ahmed and V. Ruttan (eds), *Generation and Diffusion of Agricultural Innovations: The Role of Institutional Factors* (Aldershot: Gower).

MUQTADA, M. and P. BASU (1994) *Macroeconomic Policies, Growth and Employment Expansion: The Experience of South Asia* (Geneva: ILO) (mimeo).

MUREITHI, L.P. and B.F. Makau (1992) 'Biotechnology and Farm Siże in Kenya', in Ahmed, I. (ed.), *Biotechnology: A Hope or a Threat*? (London: Macmillan Press).

MYTELKA, L. (1981) 'Direct Foreign Investment and Technological Choice in the Ivorian Textile and Wool Industries', *Vierteljahresberichte*, No. 83.

MYTELKA, L. (1985) 'Stimulating Effective Technology Transfer: The Case of Textiles in Africa', in N. Rosenberg and C. Frischtak (eds), *International Technology Transfer: Concepts, Measures and Comparisons* (New York: Praeger Publishers).

MYTELKA, L. (1989) *NICs and Would-be NICs in the Global Textile and Clothing Industries* (mimeo).

MYTELKA, L. (1992) 'Ivorian Industry at the Cross-roads', in F. Stewart, S. Lall, and S. Wangwe (eds), *Alternative Development Strategies in Sub-Saharan Africa* (London: Macmillan Press).

MYTELKA, L. (1993) 'Rethinking Development: A Role for Innovation Networking in the "Other Two-Thirds" ', *Futures*, July–August.

MYTELKA, L. (ed.) (1994) *South–South Cooperation in a Global Perspective* (Paris: OECD, Development Centre).

NADVI, A. (1992) 'Flexible Specialisation, Industrial Districts and Employment in Pakistan', *World Employment Programme Research Working Paper Series, WEP 2-22/ WP.232* (Geneva ILO) June.

NADVI, A. (1992a) *Industrial District Experiences in Developing Countries* – background paper for the UNCTAD/GTZ Symposium on the Role of Industrial Districts in the Application, Adaptation and Diffusion of Technology (Geneva) 16–17 November.

NORTH, KLAUS (1992) *Environmental Business Management, An Introduction* (Geneva: ILO).

NORTHCOTT, J. (1986) *Microelectronics in Industry: Promise and Performance* (London: Policy Studies Institute).

NORTHCOTT, J. and P. ROGERS (1982) *Microelectronics in Industry: What is Happening to Britain?* (London: Policy Studies Institute).

NORTHCOTT, J. and P. ROGERS (1984) *Microelectronics in British Industry: The Patterns of Change* (London: Policy Studies Institute).

NORTHCOTT, J. and P. ROGERS (1985) *Microelectronics in Industry: An International Comparison: Britain, Germany, France* (London: Policy Studies Institute).

NORTHCOTT, J. and A. WALLING (1988) *The Impact of Microelectronics – Diffusion, Benefits and Problems in British Industry* (London: Policy Studies Institute).

NUGENT, J. (1985) 'The Potential for South–South Trade in Capital Goods Industries', Vienna, *Industry and Development*, No. 14.

NYATI, K.P. (1988) *Problems of Pollution and its Control in Small-scale Industries* (New Delhi: F. Ebert Foundation).

O'CONNER, D. (1984) 'Policy Issues relevant to the International Transfer of Semi-conductor Technology to China', in R. Lalkaka and W. Mingyu (eds), *Managing Science Policy and Technology Acquisition: Strategies for China and a Changing World* (Dublin: Tycooly).

OECD (1978) *Urban Environmental Indicators* (Paris).

OECD (1981) *The Measurement of Scientific and Technical Activities – Frascati Manual, 1980*, Fourth Edition (Paris).

OECD (1982) *The OECD List of Social Indicators* (Paris).

OECD (1984) *OECD Science and Technology Indicators – Resources Devoted to R and D* (Paris).

OECD (1988) *Industrial Revival Through Technology* (Paris).

OECD (1988a) *New Technologies in the 1990s – A Socioeconomic Strategy* (Paris).

OECD (1990) *Current Problems Relating to Science, Technology and Industry Indicators* (Paris).

OECD (1991) *The State of the Environment* (Paris).

OECD (1992) *Technology and the Economy – The Key Relationships* (Paris).

OECD (1992a) *Trade Issues in the Transfer of Clean Technologies* (Paris).

OHIORHENUAN, J.F.E. and I.D. POLOAMINA (1992) 'Building Indigenous Technological Capacity in African Industry: The Nigerian Case', in F. Stewart et al. (eds), *Alternative Development Strategies in Sub-Saharan Africa* (London: Macmillan).

OLSON, M. (1965) *The Logic of Collective Action* (Cambridge, Mass: Harvard University Press).

OMAN, C. (1994) *Globalization and Regionalization: The Challenge of Developing Countries* (Paris: OECD Development Centre).

OTERO, G. (1992) 'The Differential Impact of Biotechnology: The Mexico-United States Contrast' in I. Ahmed (ed.), *Biotechnology: A Hope or a Threat?* (London: Macmillan Press).

PACK, H. (1982) 'Aggregate Implications of Factor Substitution in Industrial Processes', *Journal of Development Economics*, Vol. 11.

PACK, H. (1987) *Productivity, Technology and Industrial Development: A Case Study in Textiles* (New York: Oxford University Press).

PACK, H. and M.P. TODARO (1969) 'Technical Transfer, Labour Absorption and Economic Development', *Oxford Economic Papers*, November.

PACK, H. and L.E. WESTPHAL (1986) 'Industrial Strategy and Technological Change: Theory versus Reality', *Journal of Development Economics*.

PANAYOTOU, T. (1993) 'Empirical Tests and Policy Analysis of Environmental Degradation at Different Stages of Economic Development', *World Employment Programme Research Working Paper Series*, No. WEP 2-22/WP.238 (Geneva: ILO).

PANAYOTOU, T. (1994) *Innovative Strategies for Expanding Technology Financing for Sustainable Development*, paper commissioned by the UNDP for the Commission on Sustainable Development Intersessional Working Group on Technology Transfer (22–5 February 1994) (New York) January.

PARISOTTO, A. (1993) 'Direct Employment in Multinational Enterprises in Industrialized and Developing Countries', in *ILO, Multinationals and Employment – The Global Economy of the 1990s* (Geneva).

PATEL, S. (1973) 'The Cost of Technological Dependence', *Ceres*, Rome, March–April.

PATEL, S. (1974) 'The Technological Dependence of Developing Countries', *Journal of Modern African Studies*, Vol. 12, No. 1.

PEARCE, A. (1980) *Seeds of Plenty, Seeds of Want: Social and Economic Implications of the Green Revolution* (Oxford: Clarendon Press).

PEREIRA, ARMAND (1991) 'Technology Policy for Environmental Sustainability and for Employment and Income Generation: Conceptual and Methodological Issues', *World Employment Programme Research Working Paper Series WEP 2-22/WP.215* (Geneva: ILO).

PEREZ, C. (1985) 'Microelectronics, Long Waves and Structural Change: New Perspectives for Developing Countries', *World Development*, Vol. 13, No. 3.

PEREZ, C. (1994) 'Technical Change and the New Context for Development' in Mytelka, L. (ed.), *South–South Cooperation in Global Perspective* (Paris: OECD Development Centre).

PEREZ, C. and L. SOETE (1988) 'Catching up in Technology: Entry Barriers and Windows of Opportunity', in G. Dosi, et al. (eds), *Technical Change and Economic Theory* (London: Pinter Publishers).

PERRINGS, C. (1994) 'Sustainable Livelihoods and Environmentally Sound Technologies, *International Labour Review*, Vol. 133. No. 3.

PETTILOT, FLORENCE (1986) 'The Policies and Methods Established for Promoting the Development of Clean Technologies in French Industry', *Industry and Environment*, October–December.

PICKETT, JAMES (1977) 'The Choice of Technology in Developing Countries', *World Development*, Vol. 5, Nos. 9–16, Sept.–Oct.

PINGXIN, GUO (1984) 'Developing New Technologies and Investing in High Risk Project', in R. Lalkaka and W. Mingyu (eds), *Managing Science Policy and Technology Acquisition: Strategies for China and a Changing World* (Dublin: Tycooly).

PIORE, M. (1985) 'Outline for a Research Agenda for "The New Industrial Organization"', Memorandum prepared for the Director of the Institute of Labour Studies of the ILO (Geneva) (mimeo).

PIORE, M. and C.F. SABEL (1984) *The Second Industrial Divide: Possibility for Prosperity* (New York: Basic Books).

PROCHNIK, V. (1992) 'Spurious Flexibility: Technical Modernization and Social Inequalities in the Brazilian Footwear Industry', *World Employment Programme Research Working Paper Series WEP 2-22/WP.222* (Geneva: ILO) January.

PURKAYASTHA, P. (1994) 'New Technologies and Emerging Structures of Global Dominance', *Economic and Political Weekly*, August 27.

PYO, K. (1986) 'The Impact of Microelectronics on Employment and Indigenous Technological Capacity in the Republic of Korea', *World Employment Programme Research Working Paper Series WEP 2-22/ WP. 172* (Geneva: ILO).

RADA, J. (1980) *The Impact of Microelectronics* (Geneva: ILO).

RADNOR, M. (1982) *Prospects of Microelectronics Application in Process and Product Development in Developing Countries* UNIDO/ECLA Expert Group Meeting on Implications of Microelectronics for the ECLA Region (Mexico City, 7–11 June, ID/WG.372/1).

RADNOR, M. and A. Wad (1981) *A Programme for Microprocessor Capability Development for African Nations – A Proposed Outline* (Illinois: Northwestern University).

RANIS, G. (1981) 'Technology Choice and the Distribution of Income', *Annals of the American Academy of Political and Social Science*, November.

RANIS, G. (1990) 'Rural Linkages and Choice of Technology', in F. Stewart, H. Thomas and T. de Wilde, *The Other Policy – The Influence of Policies on Technology Choice and Small Enterprise Development* (London: Intermediate Technology (IT) Publications).

RANIS, G. and F. STEWART (1993) 'Rural Non-agricultural Activities in Development: Theory and Application', *Journal of Development Economics*, February (London: Oxford University Press).

RAO, D.C. (1974) 'Urban Target Groups', in Chenery, H., et al., *Redistribution with Growth* (London: Oxford University Press).

RASMUSSEN, J. (1992) 'The Small Enterprise Environment in Zimbabwe: Growing in the Shadow of Large Enterprises', *IDS Bulletin*, Vol. 23, No. 3, July.

RASSMUSSEN, J. and A. SVERRISSON (1994) 'Flexible Specialization, Technology and Employment' in *World Employment Programme Research Working Paper Series No. WEP 2-22/WP.241* (Geneva: ILO) March.

RAWSKI, G. THOMAS (1984) 'Productivity, Incentive and Reform in China's Industrial sector' – paper delivered at the 36th annual meeting of the Association for Asian Studies (Washington DC) 23–5 March.

REDDY, A.K.N. (1979) 'Some Thoughts on Traditional Technologies' – paper presented at a United Nations University Conference on Sharing of Traditional Technologies, Yogyakarta, Indonesia, 15–22 April.

RENNER, M. (1991) 'Jobs in a Sustainable Economy', *Worldwatch Paper No. 104* (Washington DC: Worldwatch Institute).

ROLDAN, M. (1991) *JIT (Just in Time) Technological Innovations, Industrial Restructuring and Gender Relations*, International Workshop on Women Organizing in the Process of Industrialization, Institute of Social Studies, The Hague, April.

ROSENBERG, N. (1988) 'New Technologies and Old Debates', in A.S.Bhall, and D. James (eds), *New Technologies and Development* (Boulder: Lynne Rienner Publishers).

ROSENBERG, N. and C. FRISCHTAK (eds) (1985) *International Technology Transfer: Concepts, Measures and Comparisons* (New York: Praeger Publications).

RUAS, R.L. et al. (1994) 'Inter-Firm Relations, Collective Efficiency and Employment in Two Brazilian Clusters', *World Employment Programme Research Working Paper Series No. WEP 2-22/WP.242* (Geneva: ILO) March.

RUSH, H. and J. C. FERREZ (1993) 'Employment and Skills in Brazil: The Implications of New Technologies and Organizational Techniques', *International Labour Review*, Vol. 132, No. 1.

RUTTAN, V. (1982) *Agricultural Research Policy* (Minneapolis: University of Minnesota Press).

SABEL, C. (1982) 'Italy's High Technology Cottage Industry', *Transatlantic Perspectives*, No. 7, December.

SABEL, C. (1986) 'Changing Models of Economic Efficiency and their Implications for Industrialization in the Third World', in A. Foxley, M. McPherson and G. O'Donnell (eds), *Development, Democracy and the Art of Trespassing* (Notre Dame, Indiana: University of Notre Dame Press).

SALOMON, J.J. et al. (1994) (eds), *The Uncertain Quest – Science, Technology and Development* (Tokyo: UNU Press).

SALTER, W. (1960) *Productivity and Technical Change* (Cambridge: Cambridge University Press).

SANTIAGO, C.E. and E. THORBECKE (1984) 'Regional and Technological Dualism: A Dual–Dual Development Framework applied to Puerto Rico', *Journal of Development Studies*, July.

SAYER, A. (1989) 'Post-Fordism in Question', *International Journal of Urban and Regional Research*, Vol. 13, No. 4.

SCHMIDHEINY, S. (1992) *Changing Course – A Global Business Perspective on Development and the Environment* (Cambridge: MIT Press).

SCHMITZ, H. (1989) 'Flexible Specialisation: A New Paradigm of Small-Scale Industrialisation', *IDS Discussion Paper No. 261*, May.

SCHMITZ, H. (1990) *Flexible Specialization in Third World Industry: Prospects and Research Requirements*, Industrialization Seminar, Institute of Social Studies, The Hague, 20 April.

SCHIMTZ, H. (1990a) 'Small Firms and Flexible Specialisation in Developing Countries', *Labour and Society*, Vol. 15, No. 3.

SCHIMTZ, H. and J. CASSIOLATO: (1992) *High-Tech for Industrial Development* (London: Routledge).

SCHIMTZ, H. and T. HEWITT (1992) 'An Assessment of the Market Reserve for the Brazilian Computer Industry', in Schmitz and Cassiolato, ibid.

SCHUMACHER, E. F. (1973) *Small is Beautiful* (London: Sphere).

SCHWARE, R. and A. TREMBOUR (1985) 'Rethinking Microcomputer Technology Transfer to Third World Countries', *Science and Public Policy*, Vol. 2 No. 1.

SCHWARTZ, H. HUGH (1987) 'Perception, Judgement and Motivation in Manufacturing Enterprises: Findings and Preliminary Hypotheses in In-Depth Interviews', *Journal of Economic Behaviour and Organisation*, December.

SELG, H. and J. CARLSSON (1980) *Trends in the Development of Numerically Controlled Machine Tools and Industrial Robots in Sweden*, Computers and Electronics Commission, Department of Industry, Stockholm.

SEN, AMARTYA (1957) 'Some Notes on the Choice of Capital Intensity in Development Planning', *Quarterly Journal of Economics*, November.

SEN, AMARTYA (1960) *Choice of Techniques* (Oxford: Clarendon Press).

SEN, AMARTYA (1975) *Employment, Technology and Development* (Oxford: Clarendon Press on behalf of the ILO).

SETHURAMAN, S.V. (1992) 'Urbanisation, Employment and the Environment', in A. S. Bhalla (ed.), *Environment, Employment and Development* (Geneva: ILO).

SHELDON, E. and W.B. MOORE (eds) (1968) *Indicators of Social Change: Concepts and Measurement* (New York: Russell Sage Foundation).

SHI, GUANG-CHANG (1983) 'Chinese Experiences with Applying New Technologies to Traditional Sectors', in von E.U. Weiszäcker, M.S. Swaminathan, and A. Lemma (eds), *New Frontiers in Technology Application – Integration of Emerging and Traditional Technologies* (Dublin: Tycooly).

SHINOHARA, M. and D. FISHER (1968) *The Role of Small Industry in the Process of Economic Growth*, The Hague, Mouton & Co.

SIGURDSON, JOHN and PRADEEP BHARGAVA (1983) 'The Challenges of the Electronics Industry in China and India', in S. Jacobsson and J. Sigurdson (eds), *Technological Trends and Challenges in Electronics* (Lund: Research Policy Institute University of Lund).

SIMON, DENIS, F. (1987) 'Managing Technology in China – Is the Development and Application of Computers the Answer?', in M. Warner (ed.), *Management Reforms in China* (London: Frances Pinter).

SIMON, DENIS, F. (1989) 'Technology Transfer and China's Emerging Role in the World Economy', in D.F. Simon and M. Goldman (eds), *Science and Technology in Post-Mao China* (Cambridge Mass.: Harvard University Press).

SIMON, H. (1959) 'Theories of Decision Making in Economics and Behaviourial Sciences', *American Economic Review*, June.

SMYTH, I. (1992) 'Collective Efficiency and Selective Benefits: the Growth of the Ruttan Industry of Tegalwangi (Indonesia)', *IDS Bulletin*, Vol. 23, No. 3, July.

SMYTH, I. et al. (1994) 'Flexible Specialization and Small-Scale Industries, An Indonesian Case Study', *World Employment Research Programme Working Paper Series, No. WEP 2-22/WP.245* (Geneva: ILO) March.

SOETE, L. (1981) 'Technical Change, Catching Up and the Productivity Slowdown', in O. Grandstrand and J. Sigurdson (eds), *Technological and Industrial Policy in China and Europe* (Lund: Research Policy Institute).

SOETE, LUC (1985) 'International Diffusion of Technology, Industrial Development and Technological Leapfrogging', *World Development*, Vol. 13, No. 3.

SOETE, LUC (1986) 'The Social and Economic Implications of Microelectronics on the Economies of Industrialised Countries: A Survey' – paper prepared for the United Nations University (UNU) New Technology Centre Feasibility Study (Maastricht: Netherlands) November.

SOETE, L. (1990) 'Opportunities for and Limitations to Technological Leapfrogging', in UNCTAD, *Technology, Trade Policy and the Uruguay Round* (Geneva) (UNCTAD/ITP/23).

'Special Issue on High Tech and Labour in Asia' (1989) *Labour and Society*, Vol. 14.

SPETH, J.G. (1990) *Needed: An Environment Revolution in Technology* – background paper prepared for a Symposium, *Towards 2000: Environment, Technology and the New Century* (Washington DC: World Resources Institute) (13–15 June).

STATE SCIENCE AND TECHNOLOGY COMMISSION, PEOPLE'S REPUBLIC OF CHINA (1988) *TORCH Program: a Program for China's High Technology Industries* (Beijing) November.

STEWART, FRANCES (1977) *Technology and Underdevelopment* (London: Macmillan).

STEWART, F. (1979) 'International Technology Transfer: Issues and Policy Options', *World Bank Staff Working Paper No. 344*, July.

STEWART, F. (1981) 'International Technology Transfer: Issues and Policy Options' in P. Streeten and R. Jolly (eds), *Recent Issues in World Development* (Oxford: Pergamon Press).

STEWART, FRANCES (1987) (ed.), *Macro-Policies for Appropriate Technology in Developing Countries* (Boulder: Westview Press).

STEWART, FRANCES and JAMES, JEFFREY (eds) (1982) *The Economics of New Technologies in Developing Countries* (London: Frances Pinter).

STEWART, F. and G. RANIS (1990) 'Macro-Policies for Appropriate Technology: A Synthesis of Findings', in F. Stewart, H. Thomas and T. de Wilde (eds) 1990, *The Other Policy: The Influence of Policies on Technology Choice and Small Enterprise Development* (London: IT Publications).

STEWART, F., S. LALL and S. WANGWE (eds) (1992) *Alternative Development Strategies in Sub-Saharan Africa* (London: Macmillan).

STRASSMANN, W. (1959) 'Creative Destruction and Partial Obsolescence in American Economic Development', *Journal of Economic History*, September.

STREET, JAMES and D. JAMES (1979) *Technological Progress in Latin America: The Prospects for Overcoming Defendency* (Boulder: Westview Press).

SU, JING (1990) *The Role of Technology Transfer in Fostering Internal Technological Capacity: A Case Study of China's Computer Industry* – MS Economics Thesis, University of Texas at El Paso

SUNKEL, O. (1973) 'The Pattern of Latin American Dependence', in V. Urquidi and R. Thorp (eds), *Latin America in the International Economy* (London: Macmillan Press).

SUTTMEIER, R.P. (1990) 'Science and Technology and Reform in the Giants' in R. Feinberg, et al. (eds), *Economic Reform in Three Giants* (Washington DC: Overseas Development Council and Transaction Books, New Brunswick).

SVEJNAR, J. and E. THORBECKE (1983) 'Determinants and Effects of Technological Choice', in B. Lucas and S. Freedman (ed.), *Technology Choice and Change in Developing Countries: Internal and External Constraints* (Dublin: Tycooly).

SWAMINATHAN, M.S. (1983) 'Utilisation of Rice Biomass: An Opportunity for Income Generation and Training By Doing', in E. von Weiszäcker, et al. op. cit.

SWAMINATHAN, M.S. (ed.) (1993) *Information Technology – A Dialogue* (Madras: Macmillan India).

SWAMINATHAN, M.S. (ed.) (1993a) *Biotechnology in Agriculture – A Dialogue* (Madras: Macmillan India, Ltd).

SWAMINATHAN, M.S. and V. HOON (eds) (1993b) *Ecotechnology and Rural Employment*, Background Papers, Draf-Proceedings (of an Interdisciplinary Dialogue) No. 7 (Madras) April.

SWAMINATHAN (M.S.) Research Foundation (1992, 1993) *Second Annual Report, 1991–92; and Third Annual Report*, 1992–93 (Madras).

TAUILE, J.R. (1987) 'Microelectronics and the Internationalization of the Brazilian Automobile Industry', in S. Watanabe (ed.), *Microelectronics, Automation and Employment in the Automobile Industry* (Chichester: John Wiley & Sons).

TAYLOR, D.F. (1984) 'Now Small Can Be Effective as well as Beautiful', in *Computers in the World of Textiles*, papers presented at The Textile Institute (Manchester) Annual World Conference, Hong Kong, 26–9 September.

TEITEL, Simón (1978) 'On the Concept of Appropriate Technology for Less Industrialised Countries', in *Technological Forecasting and Social Change* (New York Elsevier, North-Holland) Vol. 11.

TEITEL, Simón (1981) 'Towards an Understanding of Technical Change in Semi-Industrialised Countries', *Research Policy*, No. 10.

TEITEL, Simón (1987) 'Science and Technical Indicators, Country Size and Economic Development: An International Comparison', *World Development* Vol. 15, No. 9.

TEITEL, Simón (1994) Scientific Publications, R&D Expenditures, Country Size, and Per Capita Income: A Cross-Section Analysis, *Technological Forecasting and Social Change*, Vol. 46.

TEITEL, Simón (1994a) Patents, R & D Expenditures, Country size, and Per Capita Income: An International Comparison, *Scientonatives*, 317 Vol. 29, No. 1.

THUROW, L. (1992) *Head to Head: The Coming Economic Battle among Japan, Europe and America* (New York: William Morrow & Co).

TIDRICK, GENE (1986) 'Productivity Growth and Technological Change in Chinese Industry', *World Bank Staff Working Papers No. 761* (Washington DC) February.

TIGRE, P. (1983) *Technology and Competition in the Brazilian Computer Industry* (London: Frances Pinter).

TIMMER, C. PETER et al. (1975) *The Choice of Technology in Developing Countries: Some Cautionary Tales*, Harvard Studies in International Affairs, No. 32 (Cambridge Mass: Harvard University Press).

TOKMAN, VICTOR E. (1974) 'Distribution of Income, Technology and Employment: An Analysis of the Industrial Sector of Ecuador, Peru and Venezuela', *World Development*, Vol. 2, Nos. 10–12, Oct.–Dec.

TULPULE, B. and R.C. DATTA (1990) New Technology in Indian Manufacturing – An Evaluation of Introduction of CNC Machines, *Economic and Political Weekly*, July 28.

TULSI, B. (1985) *The Blending of Emerging and Traditional Garment Technologies: An Examination of the Swedish Experience and General Implications for the Third World Industry* – paper prepared for a Meeting of the UNCSTD/UNACSTD on the Blending of Emerging and Traditional Technologies (San Miniato, Italy) 28–30 November.

UNITED NATIONS (UN) (1978) *Social Indicators: Preliminary Guidelines and Illustrative Series*, ST/ES/STAT/SER.M/63 (New York).

UNITED NATIONS (UN) (1985) *Production and Use of Industrial Robots*, ECE/ENG (New York) August.

UNITED NATIONS (1990) *Industrial Statistics Yearbook*, Vol. I.

UNITED NATIONS (several years), *African Statistical Yearbook* (New York).

UNITED NATIONS (several years), *Yearbook of International Trade Statistics* (New York).

UNITED NATIONS (several years), *Yearbook of National Accounts Statistics* (New York).

UNITED NATIONS CENTRE FOR TRANSNATIONAL CORPORATIONS (UNCTC) (1983) *Salient Features and Trends in Foreign Direct Investment* (New York).

UNCTC (1988) *Transnational Corporations in the International Computer Services Sector – Technical Report,* July.

UNCTC (1991) *World Investment Report: The Triad in Foreign Direct Investment* (New York).

UNCTC (1992) *World Investment Report: Transnational Corporations as Engines of Growth* (New York).

UNCTC (1993) *World Investment Report: Transnational Corporations and Integrated International Production* (New York).

United Nations Conference on Trade and Development (UNCTAD) (1975) *Technological Dependence, its Nature, Consequences and Policy Implications* (Geneva) 31 December.

UNCTAD (1991) *Report of Ad Hoc Expert Group on Technology Policies in Open Developing Country Economies* (Geneva) 5–6 December.

UNCTAD (1993) *Report of the Workshop on the Transfer and Development of Environmentally Sound Technologies (ESTs),* organized by UNCTAD and the Government of Norway, Oslo, 13–15 October 1993, UNCTAD/ITD/TEC/13 (Geneva).

UNCTAD (1993a) *Report of the Ad Hoc Working Group on Interrelationship Between Investment and Technology Transfer* (Geneva) 25 to 29 Jan.

UNCTAD (1993b) *Trends in the field of Trade and Environment in the Framework of International Cooperation* – report by the UNCTAD Secretariat, TD/B/40 (1)/6 (Geneva) August.

UNCTAD (1994) *Technological Dynamism in Industrial Districts: An Alternative Approach to Industrialization in Developing Countries?* (New York and Geneva).

UNITED NATIONS DEVELOPMENT PROGRAMME (UNDP) (1990, 1991, 1992), *Human Development Reports* (Oxford University Press).

UNITED NATIONS ECONOMIC COMMISSION FOR EUROPE (UNECE) (1985) *Production and Use of Industrial Robots,* ECE/ENG (New York) August 15.

UNITED NATIONS EDUCATIONAL, SCIENTIFIC AND CULTURAL ORGANIZATION (UNESCO) (1974) *Study on the Planning and Measurement of Scientific and Technological Development* – meeting on Indicators of Scientific and Technological Development, Paris, 24–6 September (mimeo.).

UNESCO (1983) *Intrinsic Indicators of Technological Development – Preliminary Outline of the Issues Involved* (by Bocher, J.C.) Paris (mimeo.).

UNESCO (1990) *Statistical Digest – 1990: A Statistical Summary of Data on Education, Science and Technology, Culture and Communication, by Country* (Paris).

UNITED NATIONS INDUSTRIAL DEVELOPMENT ORGANIZATION (UNIDO) (1978), *The Effectiveness of Industrial Estates in Developing Countries,* New York.

UNIDO (1982) *Microelectronics Monitor,* No. 3 (Vienna).

UNIDO Industrial Development Review Series (1985) *The People's Republic of China,* study prepared by the Division for Industrial Studies (Vienna) UNIDO/IS 582, 2 December.

UNIDO (1986) *Industry and Development – Global Report* (Vienna).

UNIDO (1992) 'The Road to Ecologically Sustainable Industrial Development' – in *Proceedings of the Conference on Ecologically Sustainable Industrial Development*, Copenhagen, 14–18 October 1991 (Vienna).

UNIDO (1992a) *Barriers Facing the Achievement of Ecologically Sound Industrial Development*, in Proceedings of the Conference on Ecologically Sustainable Industrial Development, Copenhagen, 14–18 October 1991 (Vienna).

UNITED NATIONS RESEARCH INSTITUTE FOR SOCIAL DEVELOPMENT (UNRISD) (1976, 1977) *Research Data Bank of Development Indicators*, 4 Vols (Geneva).

UNITED STATES NATIONAL SCIENCE FOUNDATION (several years) *Science Indicators* (Washington DC)

VAITSOS, C.V. (1971) *The Process of Commercialization of Technology in the Andean Pact* (Washington DC: Organization of American States).

VAN GINNEKEN, W. and C. BARON (1984) *Appropriate Products, Employment and Technology* (London: Macmillan Press).

WAD, A. (1982) 'Microelectronics: Implications and Strategies for the Third World', *Third World Quarterly*, Vol. 4, No. 4. (London).

WAD, A. (1984) 'Science, Technology and Industrialization in Africa', *Third World Quarterly*, Vol. 6, No. 2 (London) April.

WALDER, ANDREW G. (1984) 'China's Industry in Transition: to What?', *The Annals of the American Academy of Political and Social Science*, Special Issue on 'China in Transition', edited by Marvin E. Wolfgang, November.

WANGWE, S. (1992) 'Building Indigenous Technological Capacity: A Study of Selected Industries in Tanzania', in F. Stewart et al. (eds), *Alternative Development Strategies in Sub-Saharan Africa* (London: Macmillan).

WANGWE, S. (1992a) 'Building Indigenous Technological Capacity in African Industry: An Overview', in F. Stewart, et al. (eds), *Alternative Development Strategies in Sub-Saharan Africa* (London: Macmillan).

WATANABE, SUSUMU (ed.) (1983) *Technology, Marketing and Industrialisation* (New Delhi: Macmillan on behalf of the ILO).

WATANABE, SUSUMU (1983a) 'Market Structure, Industrial Organization and Technological Development: The Case of the Japanese Electronics-based NIC-Machine Tool Industry', *World Employment Programme Research Working Papers Series, No. WEP 2-22/WP 111* (Geneva: ILO) February.

WATANABE, SUSUMU (1985) 'Japan: Numerically Controlled Machines in Small Enterprises', *ATAS Bulletin*, No. 2 (UN New York) November.

WATANABE, SUSUMU (1985a) 'The Patent System and Indigenous Technology Development in the Third World', in J. James and S. Watanabe (eds), *Technology, Institutions and Government Policies* (London: Macmillan).

WATANABE, SUSUMU (1987) 'Microelectronic Information Technology: Differential Implications for Third World Countries', *Development for South–South Cooperation*, Vol. 3, No. 5.

WATANABE, SUSUMU (ed.) (1987a) *Microelectronics, Automation and Employment in the Automobile Industry* (Chichester: John Wiley & Sons).

WATANABE, SUSUMU (1989) 'International Division of Labour in the Software Industry: Employment and Income Potential for the Third World', *World Employment Programme Research Working Paper Series WEP 2-22/WP.201* (Geneva: ILO) April.

WATANABE, SUSUMU (ed.) (1993) *Microelectronics and Third-World Industries* (London: Macmillan Press).

WEISZÄCKER, VON E. U., M. S. SWAMINATHAN and A. LEMMA (eds) (1983) *New Frontiers in Technology Application: Integration of Emerging and Traditional Technologies* (Dublin: Tycooly International Publishers).

WESTPHAL, L.E. (1982) 'Fostering Technological Mastery by Means of Selective Infant Industry Protection', in M. Syrquin and S. Teitel (eds), *Trade, Stability, Technology and Equity in Latin America* (New York: Academic Press).

WHITBY, G. (1984) 'Electronic Load-controlled Mini-Hydroelectric Projects: Experiences from Colombia, Sri Lanka and Thailand', in A.S. Bhalla, et al. (ed.), *Blending of New and Traditional Technologies* (Dublin: Tycooly).

WHITE, LAWRENCE, J. (1978) 'The Evidence on Appropriate Factor Proportions for Manufacturing in Less Developed Countries: A Survey', *Economic Development and Cultural Change*, October.

WITZELL, OTTO, W., J. K. LEE SMITH (1989) *Closing the Gap: Computer Development in the People's Republic of China* (Boulder: Westview Press).

WOOD, A. (1994) *North–South Trade, Employment and Inequality* (Oxford: Clarendon Press).

WORLD BANK, INDUSTRY AND FINANCE DIVISION (1991) *Staff Appraisal Report: INDIA Industrial Control Pollution Project* (Washington DC) May.

WORLD BANK (1993) *The East Asian Miracle – Economic Growth and Public Policy* (Washington DC).

WORLD HEALTH ORGANIZATION (WHO) (1981) *Development of Indicators for Monitoring Progress Towards Health for All by the Year 2000* (Geneva).

WORLD INTELLECTUAL PROPERTY ORGANIZATION (WIPO) (several years) *Industrial Property Statistics* (Geneva).

YACHIR, F. (ed.) (1978) *Technology and Industrialisation in Africa* (Dakar: CODESRIA Book Series).

YACHIR, F. (1978a) 'Industrialisation et Dependence Technologique en Afrique' in Yachir, ibid.

YACHIR, F. (1988) 'Importation de Technologie et Développement des Capacite Techniques dans l'Industrie Algerienne', *World Employment Programme Research Working Paper Series, WEP 2-22/WP. No. 186* (Geneva: ILO) January.

YEN, CHE-LIN (1987) 'Computer Development in Mainland China', *Issues and Studies*, October.

YUANLIANG, M. (1989) *Modern Plant Biotechnology and Structure of Rural Employment in China* – paper prepared for the ILO Technology and Employment Branch (Geneva).

ZAHLAN, A.B. (1990) *Acquiring Technological Capacity: A Study of Arab Contracting and Consulting Firms* (London: Macmillan Press on behalf of the ILO).

ZANFEI, A. (1989) 'Learning from New Information Technologies: Applications in Italian Textile and Clothing Firms', in U. Colombo, and Keichi Oshima (eds), *Technology Blending: An Appropriate Response to Development* (London: Tycooly).

ZHANG, XIAOBIN (1985) 'Microelectronics Policy in China', *ATAS Bulletin*, No. 2, November.

ZHANG, YUNGCHUN (1985) 'China's Textile Industry and Open Door Policy', in *World Textiles: Investment, Innovation, Invention* – papers presented at the Annual World Conference, London, 9–14 May (Manchester: Textiles Institute).

Index

302543472U